Blur:
3862 Days

Blur:
3862 Days

The Official History

Stuart Maconie

First published in Great Britain in 1999 by
Virgin Books
an imprint of Virgin Publishing
Thames Wharf Studios
Rainville Road
London W6 9HA

Copyright © Blur and Stuart Maconie 1999

Reprinted 1999

All illustrations by Mike Smith.

A catalogue record for this book is available from the British Library.

ISBN 0 7535 0287 9

Typeset by SetSystems Ltd, Saffron Walden, Essex
Printed in Great Britain by CPD, Wales

Acknowledgements

'Rock journalism,' said Frank Zappa, 'is people who can't write interviewing people who can't talk for the benefit of people who can't read.' By and large, he was probably right. But go back a couple of centuries to another old grouch by the name of Jonathan Swift and there's another little maxim I'm reminded of. 'I heartily loathe and detest mankind but I deeply love Peter and John and so on.' Put the two together and you have a fair summary of my feelings about rock writing. In general, it's a pretty dishonourable profession, rather like selling dodgy time shares in Gran Canaria or astrology, and I'm faintly embarrassed about having earned portions of my crust from it for, crikey, ten years now.

But I don't think Frank Zappa meant me or any of the bands I know and like, or discerning, erudite readers like your good self. Nonetheless, suspicion that writing about pop groups was not a respectable job for a grown man had always kept me from 'doing a book' until now, despite the blandishments of a few publishers. Given that *Revolution in the Head* by Ian McDonald and Ian Hunter's *Diary of a Rock And Roll Star* (the best books on rock music ever) have already been written, I saw little point in adding to the groaning shelves promising the 'behind-the-scenes story of Ugly Kid Joe' or 'Tasmin Archer as you've never seen her before'.

What changed my mind was the opportunity to write about Blur, the most interesting English pop group of their generation. (I say English advisedly; their only rivals in fascination, the Manic Street Preachers, are Welsh.) I shan't bang on about why: that's all in the next couple of hundred pages. Suffice to say here that I believe their story says something illuminating about the times we've all grown up in. Originally I had very high-minded notions for the book and could hear the ringing phrases from the entirely imaginary reviews: 'More than simply a pop biography: a kind of parable of this turbulent decade . . .', 'brilliantly elucidates the nexus between pop and society. I was gripped' etc. etc. Blah and indeed blah. It's nothing of the sort of course. Just the story of a pop group told as well as I could. But it is the story of a pop group who genuinely shaped aspects of British life in the 90s, and their story is, by definition, a reflection of the story of a country and its culture.

Another compelling reason for a half-decent Blur biography was the poor standard of the existing literature. There is but one honourable exception to this: *Blur the Whole Story* by Martin Roache, who at least bothered to do extensive research. Blur fans should take a look at this and avoid all others (except this of course) like the proverbial plague.

This is an authorised biography, done with the blessing and involvement of the group; the excellent title, for instance – the timespan between their first ever band meeting and the publication of this book – was their suggestion. Authorised biography often suffers from being mere hagiography or an extended ego massage. I've striven to keep this memoir honest and candid. The group deserve no less. That said, it's the group's involvement that, I believe, gives this the edge on anything written about them thus far. Though Karen Johnson at EMI provided me with every cutting about the group that has ever reached a news-stand, this is not essentially a cuttings-based biography or a 'scissors-and-paste job', as they are unkindly known. Each group member was interviewed individually and at length, as the teetering pile of cassettes by the computer testified. This depth and range of access led me to use, where relevant, the technique of attributed parenthetical quotation (the indented bits with name tags) pilfered unashamedly from Barry Miles' excellent Paul McCartney biography, *Many Years from Now*. If you've got it, flaunt it, I say. And I had about 26 C90s of the stuff, not just from the group but from many key associates. These form the spine of the book.

The group themselves then – Damon Albarn, Graham Coxon, Alex James and Dave Rowntree as they stack alphabetically – must be first on any list of acknowledgements. They gave unstintingly of their time even while recording and preparing for the release of the *13* album. The book's merits are theirs; its faults are mine.

I am also indebted to Andy Ross, David Balfe, Nigel Hildreth, Mike Smith, Chris Morrison, Stephen Street and many more for providing hours of taped interviews. I should like to add to this

Karen Johnson, who not only shared her memories but physically delivered all kinds of invaluable research materials in black cabs across London. Simon Blackmore at Parlophone did some sterling donkey work on this score too. Niamh at CMO was unfailingly generous, accommodating and courteous at a time when the last thing she needed was a pestering hack. Likewise Selena from the same organisation and Justine Andrew. Stanway School, Colchester, and Goldsmiths College, London, were tremendously helpful, as were Martin and all at Blur FC, a fan club that puts most others to shame.

Certain colleagues in music journalism were great boons in different ways. John Aizlewood and Andrew Collins adjusted their social calendars and offered the camaraderie of the deadline-haunted author. Danny Eccleston allowed me to cherry-pick from unpublished transcripts of his Blur interviews for *Q* magazine in early 99. Dave Cavanagh co-wrote with me an exhaustive multi-part critical discography of the group for *Select* magazine in the mid-90s. I have unashamedly borrowed from this and may well have borrowed phrases of 'the Cav's', since at this remove I can't remember who wrote what. Andy Fyfe took time from his own busy schedule to hunt down these pieces and provide me with them. David Quantick put me onto some priceless archive material. My editor, Ian Gittins, was sweet reason itself, for which I'm grateful.

From the Blur entourage I should thank good friends down the years: Biffo, Smoggy, Dave Byers – Ifan, wherever he is – and the rest. Also, heartfelt thanks to flying instructor Tony for a memorable day. On a personal note, for all kinds of support I should mention the long-suffering Treatmenters, Ali, all at 62 and 31, and my friends in the North, particularly Colin, my own person from Porlock.

If you have been overlooked, it's due to failing faculties rather than any intended slight. Apologies nonetheless. I think book dedications have a whiff of the deluded ponce about them and so I won't bother but I will say that Leo Finlay will be sorely missed at the launch party. There *is* going to be a launch party, isn't there . . .?

Contents

1 Camulodunum

HE CITY, LIKE LOVE and the summer and the road, is a core concept of the pop imagination. The myth of the city – wasteland, pleasure zone, concrete jungle, human zoo – resonates in the music of Bruce Springsteen, The Clash, John Coltrane, The Supremes, Hank Williams, Kraftwerk, Iggy Pop and a thousand others. Stevie Wonder lived for it, Marshall Hain danced in it. It's the city of dreams, the city of lights, the sin city, the naked city. Starship, in their 80s poodle-rock incarnation, may have shrilled that 'we built this city on rock and roll', but really we built rock and roll on this city.

Or that's the myth at least. The truth is a little less romantic. Richey Edwards of the Manic Street Preachers once claimed, with some authority, that 'all rock and roll is homosexual'. There may just be an equally strong case for saying that all rock and roll is suburban. For the city that lies where all roads meet at the heart of pop is not an actual city of NCP car parks, Body Shops, congested ring roads, *Big Issue* vendors and bored students handing out leaflets proclaiming opening week discounts at Mobile Phone Republic (formerly Video Game World and Taco Shed). It's not the prosaic, pedestrianised, CCTV-surveyed city we know and work and shop in. It's a construct of myth, where neon lights shimmer on streets slick with rain and tramps like us are born to run through subways ringing with sirens and doo-wop and the snapping of fingers. Pop music is built on adolescent dreams of escape nurtured in the suburbs and the dormitory towns; the desire to go where no one knows your name and where no lace curtains twitch.

Nowadays Essex exemplifies contemporary suburbia. This is where Basildon Man, the rock on which first Thatcherism and then the New Labour hegemony were built, waxes his Mondeo and nods off in front of SkySports. It's a buffer zone of footballer and porn magnate mansions and ultra-violent nitespots that stops London spreading to the North Sea. A millennium or three ago, though, it was all very different: a flat coastal plain of marshes ringing with the call of seabirds and dotted with Britain's earliest settlements. In fact, its very earliest settlement and first capital – Colchester.

People lived in Colchester an astonishing seven centuries before the birth of Christ. By the first century BC it had established itself as capital of one of the sundry kingdoms of which pre-Roman, ancient Britain was composed. It was Camulodunum, seat of the warrior king Cunobelinus, lying on a ridge just north-west of where the Colne river meets the sea. Its attractive position made it an obvious target for the invading Romans who overran it in 43 AD, and made it the administrative hub of that corner of Britain and a colony for retired legionnaires. Razed to the ground during the rising of that prototype Riot Girl, Boudicca, it nevertheless grew again to become the chief town of Roman Britain.

When the Romans left, the Saxons took over, and by the ninth century AD Colchester was hotly contested between them and the new marauders, the Danes. By the time of the Domesday Book it was Colcestra, a borough of size and significance with many churches, a mint, a court and 450 households. Its subsequent history is one of expansion. The Normans brought further civic developments. It crept to the sea and grew a harbour. Industries developed and by 1300, it was making shoes and cloth and had become a major port, importing wine and trading in maize and oysters. Nearer our own time, its surrounding landscapes were immortalised by Constable. It became a centre for printing and petro-chemicals and the manufacture of electrical equipment. In 1961, the University of Essex was opened there. By 1980, it had grown to a city of well over a million when, in the town's most significant development of the modern era, Damon Albarn made fun of Graham Coxon's shoes behind the music block of Stanway Comprehensive School one sadly undated lunchtime during the spring term of that academic year.

Damon Albarn was born on 23 March 1968 in the Whitechapel Hospital, Leytonstone, to Keith and Hazel Albarn, who took their new baby home to their little terraced house in Leytonstone, east London. Esther and Abi Ofarim's bizarre 'Cinderella Rockerfella' was Number 1, though it is unlikely that it was played much on the family Dansette. The Albarns were very much creatures of their time – artistic, progressive, cultivated – and much more likely to be interested in The Beatles' new single, 'Lady Madonna', the departure of the increasingly erratic Syd Barrett from Pink Floyd or possibly Terry Riley's 'A Rainbow In Curved Air' or Peter Maxwell Davies' 'Eight Songs For A Mad King'. Or maybe the assassination of Martin Luther King or the Vietcong's Tet Offensive or the other noteworthy events of early spring 1968.

Keith Albarn's family were Quakers from Nottinghamshire. True to their beliefs, they were pacifists, and Keith's own father had been a registered conscientious objector during the Second World War. Damon's mother came from Lincolnshire, but the young couple moved to London, where they threw themselves with gusto into the capital's heady counter-cultural scene. Hazel Albarn worked in the theatre and as a stage designer at the Theatre Royal Stratford East, where Joan Littlewood was producing ground-breaking leftist dramas such as *Oh What a Lovely War* and *Sparrows Can't Sing*. She was working on *Mrs Wilson's Diary* when she was pregnant with Damon. Their second child, Jessica was born in 1971.

Damon's father was also involved in the world of contemporary arts. He studied Islamic design and later produced *The Language of Patterns*, a well-regarded academic study of Islamic art. He became involved in TV arts programming and was one of the contributors to *Late Night Line Up*, a trendy, highbrow arts review that was in some ways a precursor of *The Late Review* and *The South Bank Show*. 'It was quite strange seeing him on TV,' said Damon many years later. 'It was this weird, surreal, "Daddy's not here but he's there" thing,'

Keith Albarn also ran a gallery in Kingly Street in London's West End, putting on events and designing and making furniture and prefabricated fun palaces, artefacts from which adorned their Victorian terraced house in east London. 'The living room was painted silver and my dad's fibreglass sculptures were everywhere. We had this 30 foot red pea pod made out of fibreglass which was my little bicycle and spacecraft thing.'

In 1966, Keith Albarn also visited the first London exhibition of the work of Japanese performance artist Yoko Ono, who conducted experiments with the audience in telepathy. It was after one such exhibition that she met John Lennon. At the time of Damon's birth, Albarn was running a precarious venture that specialised in 'environmental happenings': fashionable multi-media *mélanges* of theatre, music and art. Through this his company became involved with and eventually manager of the experimental jazz-rock group Soft Machine.

Soft Machine formed in 1966, taking their name, like many other bands, from the works of William Burroughs. By the time Keith Albarn and his business partner Ian Knight became their managers, the line-up had settled around Kevin Ayers, Robert Wyatt and Mike Ratledge and they were critically feted for their adventurous, sometimes whimsical art rock. In late '68, Ayers left for a solo career and the music evolved into dense, demanding jazz-rock offset by Wyatt's laconic, very English singing style as exemplified on arguably their best work *Third*. Keith Albarn was partly responsible for the band's conceptual stage designs and their live shows were highlights of the period. On one notorious occasion, the band and Albarn mounted an elaborate 'happening' called the Discotheque Interplay on a beach in Saint Aygulf, southern France, in 1967. The local mayor accused Albarn and band of making his coastline 'look like a pig sty' and banned the event. When it was pointed out that France did not allow theatre censorship, he replied, undaunted, 'Very well. I shall ban it on grounds of safety.'

Damon spent his first ten years in this relaxed, hippyish household, festooned with books and Eastern *objets d'art* and the venue for parties where hip adults, long of sideburn, would congregate, puff on exotic cigarettes and actually talk to small children like Damon and Jessica. Damon was attending the George Thomlinson Primary School in Leytonstone and was, by his own diagnosis, a relatively normal young boy of the period, keen on 'football, fossils and girls'.

At ten, though, came a major upheaval. Keith Albarn was offered a significant career advance – a new post as head of North Essex School of Art, based in Colchester. Damon spent three months in Turkey with family friends while the practicalities of the move were organised. When he returned, the Albarns were ensconced in Essex.

DAMON ALBARN: There was a massive influx into Essex in the late 70s because of Thatcherism, I suppose. There were new estates and cheap houses and Thatcher was encouraging you to buy your own house. They'd bought a very nice, old house, four bedrooms, built in 1470; not in great condition but it only cost £10,000. So we ended up in this area on the edge of the countryside and they did it for us really, Jessica and me, to give us an extra perspective and a bit of space. We were very different from the conventional Essex family. We didn't have money. I remember our cars: an old Ford Cortina and an Austin Maxi and in-between this old Lada. But in Essex, there was this great emphasis on fitting in, in not going against the grain. On being average, really. And we weren't average.

The unfortunate consequence of this for the young Damon was that, with his cool self-possession and unconventional background, he quickly became the butt of jokes from more troglodytic classmates. 'I was the weirdo,' he later remembered. 'Posh stroke gay. "Oi, gay boy!" I was always getting called gay.' At that time, he was pretty, vaguely if unconventionally bourgeois, read Karl Marx, played the violin, was keen on drama and wore an ear-ring and glass beads that his mother had made him. On reflection, it's a testament to the tolerance of the Stanway Comprehensive School that he didn't spend his entire school-days with his head down the toilets.

But he didn't. Conversely, he became one of the school's high-profile 'stars' thanks to his proficiency in drama and music. Nigel Hildreth is a professional musician – he conducted his latest symphony at a festival in Sweden recently – as well as head of music at Colchester Sixth Form College. In 1978, he had just landed his first head of department job at Stanway Comprehensive.

NIGEL HILDRETH: I moved to Stanway School in January 1979. It was a pretty conventional comprehensive school on the outskirts of Colchester and had quite a rural intake. Lots of the kids came from the surrounding villages. I felt very positive about the school's musical culture in that a lot of kids were learning instruments but were of a fairly mediocre standard. I set about putting on productions, the first being a rock opera I'd written based on the Faust legend.

Admirably unperturbed by the dreaded term 'rock opera', *Fist* was Damon Albarn's stage debut proper and Hildreth recalls that even though only a member of the chorus, 'He had a presence. A magnetic personality. Your eye was drawn to him.' Over the next seven years, Hildreth put on nine productions, most of which the teenage Albarn was involved in to increasing degrees. Even when he wasn't in the cast, he would usually wangle a backstage production role. Sadly for pictorial archivists, he took no on-stage role in Stanway's production of *Joseph*, but helped with make-up and costumes instead. He played his first lead as Bobby in Sandy Wilson's *The Boyfriend*, in which he sang and danced the Charleston. He played Jupiter in *Orpheus in the Underworld* and Nathan Detroit in *Guys and Dolls*.

NIGEL HILDRETH: He played the violin and piano and was second violin in the Colne Valley School Orchestra as well as Stanway's own orchestra but acting was his main interest. He had a great flair for improvising and for developing his own ideas yet he couldn't play in time rhythmically and technically his piano playing was not very well developed. His violin technique was fairly weak too. But he was very creative and had very strong ideas. At GCE O level, he did composition and I encouraged that in everyone.

Indeed, one of Damon's compositions won a heat in the nationwide Young Composer of the Year competition. At this time, his mentors and gurus in the field of classical music were Satie and Vaughan Williams. Both great but very different composers, they share an unmistakable melodic gift and power to move. Erik Satie (1866–1925) was an eccentric Frenchman best known for the haunting series of 'Gymnopédies'. He was feted by Debussy and French salon society and his considerable reputation rests mainly on his piano works, which could be witty and brittle or mysterious and austere. Ralph Vaughan Williams (1872–1958) is, alongside Tippett and Walton, the major English symphonist of our century, though perhaps best known for smaller works: 'Fantasia On Greensleeves', his grave and melancholy 'Fantasia On A Theme of Tallis' and his beautiful 'The Lark Ascending' are all pieces which draw on a deep passion for English folk melodies. English twentieth-century orchestral music formed a major part of the music course at Stanway and Vaughan Williams' works, such as 'The Lark Ascending' and 'Serenade To Music', were great favourites of Albarn. So too were the musical collaborations of Bertolt Brecht and Kurt Weill, such as *The Threepenny Opera*, which he found in his parents' record collection alongside Pink Floyd, The Beatles, The Faces and the ubiquitous Soft Machine. Brecht and Weill's music, he later claimed, had a more profound and far-reaching effect on his own musical development than any pop song writers. Though Satie, Vaughan Williams and Kurt Weill were not composers from the era of periwigs and frockcoats, Damon Albarn in his mid-teens might well have concurred with Frank Zappa's maxim that 'all the good music has already been written by guys in wigs and stuff'.

On the subject of the young Damon Albarn's immersion or otherwise in pop and rock, Graham Coxon remembers that, 'Round his house I wouldn't see any records. There'd be a stuffed fox and

Osmonds in Berlin. There's a photo of me with a plastic trumpet and brown paisley pyjama bottoms and this peculiar Osmonds hat. I had a fife when I was about six. But mostly I was just tossing about on my go-cart. I would listen to Rubber Soul and mess around with the balance. Listening to the speakers in turn . . . the ones with just guitars and drums and then all the harmonies. They had this real 'stereophonic geography', as I call it. I couldn't read so I'd go through the piles of singles looking for visual clues. There was Bobby Vee and Roy Orbison and Johnny Cash – I was very confused by 'A Boy Named Sue' – and I'd look for the apple, the white side of the apple, because that was a good one, and the record I was looking for was Revolution. I still think it's the heaviest, most incredible 45. And my dad's copy was even better because it was so worn down and had white noise on it. It was worn out from him having Beatles evenings with his mates. I used to get very frustrated because not being able to read I would often get 'Turn Turn Turn' by Mary Hopkin instead, which was on Apple too. I couldn't understand why, when I wanted that DER-DER-DER guitar riff, I got this hippy shit instead.

Though he'd taken preliminary steps on the fife, drums and saxophone (which he continued to study classically to Grade Five level) while still at primary school, Graham was twelve when he was given his first guitar. He began to play it 'out of boredom' and initially had no burning ambition to become a master of his instrument. 'I just wanted to get a few chords, C F G D E A or something, so I could play 'Aunties And Uncles' by The Jam. But then I couldn't stop and I had to learn everything – all the inversions, the augmenteds and the minor sevenths. I began to play the guitar every day and I've played it every day since. I just became lured into this whole other world, like some kids become immersed in Dungeons and Dragons or something.'

As the 70s drew to a close, Graham's father left the Army and became a conductor for the Essex Constabulary Police Band. The Coxons moved to Colchester and Bob became a visiting teacher at Stanway School, a post he still holds. He chose it as the new school for his son.

GRAHAM COXON: Stanway was a decent enough school. Of course, you were scared stiff of going because you'd been wound up by the bigger boys who'd tell you that in the first year at Stanway you'd get your head flushed down the loos continually. There were lots of skins around then in the third and fourth years. Whether they were hard or not, they certainly looked it. There were these two brothers who were legendary. Glyn and Gary Urine. That was their name, honestly. Seriously hard; crombies, boots. The first time I ever saw a CND badge was on Glyn Urine's crombie. They would have play fights and break each other's collarbone. They were mythical. So you walked around at break for an hour avoiding them and skulking behind the music block.

This, of course, became the site of the first fabled exchange between Coxon and Albarn. Though this was the first time they had spoken to each other, it was not, unsurprisingly, the first time Graham had noticed his soon-to-be inseparable friend. He had noted with awe Damon's confident rendition of 'Gee Officer Krupke' from the school production of *West Side Story*, a performance sure to impress the rather gauche, shy, young Coxon.

NIGEL HILDRETH: Graham was much the quieter type and much more insecure about his abilities. Damon was a lot more self-confident and socially totally at ease with dealing with people, especially adults, which charmed some but really got up some people's noses. I attended a Stanway staff reunion recently and a lot of people were still very antagonistic towards him. He could be very frustrating to deal with because of his lack of concentration. I shouted at him something rotten but he was nearly always sweet and smart enough to come back and say, 'Sorry, you were right, Mr Hildreth.'

Though Hildreth is at pains to point out that neither student was a teenage prodigy – 'above average but not exceptional by any means' – both had clear if undisciplined musical talent. Damon had a creative and improvisational bent while Graham, remembers Hildreth, gave many accomplished saxophone recitals. 'I distinctly remember a jazz piece called "Hawk Plays Bird" that he performed beautifully from memory.' An interesting detail in view of Graham's mid-90s 'discovery' of modern jazz.

Music, though, was the real genesis of their relationship. Damon had been writing non-classical compositions alongside his more academic ones for some time, and these were occasionally performed in Stanway's many revues and shows. For *A Summer Extravaganza* he wrote a piece which was sung by their mutual friend James Hibbins, while he played piano. Graham, albeit in a more minor way than Damon, had also become a fixture in school productions, and these were the first occasions when the two shared a stage. Graham played

Styx in *Orpheus in the Underworld* and had a supporting role in *Oh What A Lovely War*. He also sang alongside Jessica Albarn in the chorus of Smetana's *Bartered Bride*, performed 8–11 June 1986 at Colchester's Mercury Theatre in conjunction with the Royal Opera. Both appeared when this was featured on BBC TV's *Blue Peter*. The *Essex County Standard*, dated 10 May 1985, carries a warm notice for a piece of Damon's entitled 'From A Basement Window', performed by Graham and Damon on saxophone and piano respectively. 'Worth noting,' it records, 'that Mr Albarn was the only performer to acknowledge his applause by taking a bow.'

By now Damon Albarn had stockpiled several pop songs, usually on the theme of 'people I didn't like. The first one I wrote was about my girlfriend's brother John who was a car mechanic.' Damon amassed several such songs, which Graham remembers as being 'pretty good'. 'They could get in the charts now if the charts were any good,' he adds. One of these, 'Beautiful Lady', gained both Nigel Hildreth and Hayley Coxon's seal of approval. 'He had an obvious natural gift,' says Graham, adding, 'I don't know where he gets it from.'

Coxon was not just the only boy in school who could play the saxophone, he was the only boy in school *with* a saxophone. 'Schools couldn't afford them, so if you wanted one you had to buy it. You start on a ruler, actually. Then if you're lucky, you get a cheap plastic clarinet. That's another reason I could never be a music teacher. Listening to 30 kids honking and squeaking like geese with salmonella would drive me round the bend.' School music rooms ring cacophonously to the sounds of recorders, chime bars, tubas and the like but a saxophone is something else. A saxophone is cool, it speaks of French Quarter decadence, of smoke-filled night-clubs, of Bowie, of Coltrane and Bird. Less glamorously, Damon Albarn probably had in mind the horribly slushy sax solos of the period like Gerry Rafferty's 'Baker Street' and Hazel O'Connor's 'Will You?' when he included a saxophone break in 'Beautiful Lady'.

Classmate Michael Morris owned a small four-track recorder which Coxon and Albarn, with some justification, found 'incredibly suave'. They wangled a session round at his house and the resulting recording, now lost to posterity, sadly, was 'really sweet', in Graham's recollection. 'It was just us and this little drum box and this dodgy Casio piano sound but it had something. Hayley loved it. She said it could get in the charts, which made us really chuffed.'

After this inauspicious start, a close and mutually nourishing friendship soon grew up between the two boys, despite the fact that Damon was a school year above Graham. Trivial now, of course, but not so in the distorted social hothouse of the secondary school. Each found something new and stimulating in their two very different though equally happy backgrounds; the one military, the other bohemian.

GRAHAM COXON: He didn't really have any friends. He had it hard because of his name, too, which people would make jokes about. 'All Bran' and stupid kids' stuff. And stuff about Damien in *The Omen*. The skins would kick him about in the toilets and hold him down and write '666' on his forehead. That's probably why he's so scarred and such an emotional wreck. I thought he was a really great bloke. I'd never known anyone like him.

DAMON ALBARN: Stanway School had a very good ethos of art and music and these kinds of activities were encouraged. I've sometimes wondered what I'd have been like if we'd stayed in London. I suppose I would have stood out far less and that would have dulled my ambition. I was very aware of being different, not viewing the world like the others did in that area. The downside was that I felt very alone and alienated and that encouraged certain . . . eccentricities at an early age that didn't make life easy and didn't make it easy for me to get on with people, but as I matured I became more comfortable with it. I sort of grew into my eccentricity.

GRAHAM COXON: His family were very arty and theatrical. Quite intellectual in those fields. It must have upset my mum and dad in some ways, the way I went overboard on them. Every Friday I'd go round and have something to eat. His mum would cook something I'd never heard of and then talk to you about stuff mums didn't talk about. It wasn't intimidating, though. It was stimulating. I was always nervous in a kind of nice way. They would talk to you like grown-ups. And there was a lot of laughter in a very subtle way. Damon's dad was and is quite a heavy bloke mentally. He's written books I wouldn't even attempt to read. It was all very exotic and weird for me, who'd had a typically, well, if not working-class, then solidly lower-middle-class background.

DAMON ALBARN: I think we both found the other interesting because of our backgrounds. He spent a lot of time at my house. My mum and dad were very artistic and encouraged that in him and he had things I didn't have. He taped everything. He had tapes of all these fantastic things like The Beatles and Mike Leigh. So we traded off each other. We both learned a lot from the other.

The agenda of their friendship was soon set. Lunchtimes would be spent at Graham's house, which abutted the school playing fields. Here, in Graham's cramped bedroom (a situation not helped by his drum kit), they would drink tea and eat Hobnobs while they watched, in what would now be called 'heavy rotation', selected and cherished videos. Favourites were *Mean Time* by the grimly comic Mike Leigh and the late 70s mod revival movie *Quadrophenia*, starring one Phil Daniels. Otherwise, they would commandeer time and space in the music block and work on material of Damon's: he now had an impressive back catalogue, including an ambitious piece about diamond smuggling between Johannesburg and Amsterdam, of which he knew nothing apart from what he had gleaned from a TV documentary. On Fridays, they would sojourn at Damon's house, where Graham would be introduced to strange new cuisines and given artistic advice from Damon's parents.

The Smiths loomed large in their adolescent world. This was no surprise. The Manchester group, then at the height of their powers, had cast their spell over most of young Britain. Their music – literate, bewitching, melancholic – was without doubt the most significant achievement in the formless British pop milieu of the middle 80s. 'The best band in the world. We all wanted to dress like Morrissey,' remembers Damon. In a celebrated incident when the pair were watching a special edition of *The South Bank Show* devoted to The Smiths, a typically provocative remark of Morrissey's to the effect that pop music was dead antagonised Damon. 'I remember thinking, No one is going to tell me pop music is finished.'

GRAHAM COXON: We spent the whole time tinkering on his little keyboard and my saxophone. Sometimes, our friend James Hibbins would come round. He'd won a competition to get a custom-made guitar from the same bloke who used to make Nik Kershaw's guitars so this was really cool. He was a tall gangly bloke in the same year as Damon; another music block drop-out. All our lunchtimes were spent hunting in tiny cupboards, trying to find a guitar with six strings. I was trying to learn finger-pickings. James Hibbins turned me on to things like *In The Court of the Crimson King* and Fripp and Eno. He was very into all that. I was more into chaos. He played me '21st Century

Schizoid Man' and made me a tape of that album and I took it home and thought the whole album was pretty awesome. Then he got into Marillion and I have to say I thought that was bollocks.

Coxon and Albarn moved through various ad hoc musical group-ings, not always meriting the status of fully fledged bands but each with a particular identity. Along with Michael Morris (he of the four-track), James Hibbins, guitarist Paul Stevens and a drummer named Kevin Ling, they rehearsed regularly and even played in public once or twice. Then came The Aftermath, by which time they had slimmed to a quartet of Damon, Graham, Hibbins and Stevens. A evanescent collective, this, remembered only for a performance of The Jimi Hendrix Experience's 'Hey Joe', played at a school assembly.

GRAHAM COXON: We were a sort of band. Me, James and Damon. We had these songs that Damon had written and some of James's. There was one of James's I quite liked about chess. They were just the sort of thing a fifteen-year-old boy listening to too much King Crimson and Marillion would produce. Once or twice we practised in my mum and dad's dining room but mainly we used to rehearse at James's. I bought my first electric guitar from him, a Kaye Les Paul that I eventually trashed, it was so frustratingly awful. Then I got another one off this beardy doctor my sister knew. I had a little Kaye practice amp. I played it flat out till it couldn't take it. When I got home from school, in the hour and a half or two hours before my mum and dad got home, I'd play along with The Who as loud as the stereo would go, with my amp as loud as it could go. I'd go up to my bedroom and go fucking berserk, acting like a little pop star. A little Peter Townsend. Before I got a guitar I used to pose with this lovely little snooker cue from my snooker table which was normally used for opening the loft. I'd pose with that in my mum and dad's full-length mirror. Me standing in the hall outside my bedroom listening to *Revolver*.

James Hibbins left the fold for reasons that are not clear but could well have been due to his burgeoning interest in Marillion. After his departure, The Aftermath evolved into Real Lives with the addition of Alistair Havers. Getting a clear notion of what kind of band Real Lives were at this point is not easy.

DAMON ALBARN: I haven't heard those tapes in a long time, though I'm sure Graham's got a few somewhere. I'm not too sure what that early music was all about but I think it was in the vein of Simple Minds and U2. We made a video that was our attempt at 'New Year's Day' filmed in black and white on a winter's day, a snow scene centred around the river Colne. We thought it was really dramatic even though the Colne never gets wider than your average living room all the way down to the Estuary.

Real Lives was a much more tangible, functioning unit than The Aftermath. For one thing it actually gigged, making its debut to students at Stanway at Christmas 1985 and appearing several times in local pubs and clubs. As part of a school project and at the instigation of classmate Lucy Stimson, the band played a much larger set of originals at Stanway on 21 April 1986. The surviving programme, complete with cover designed by G. Coxon, offers some typically and fairly wearyingly 'wacky' sixth-form insights into the nature of the group in the manner of callow pen portraits. Graham Coxon (drums, saxophone) is, we learn, the inventor of his own language called Keng and plays the drums 'like a manic fart'. Damon (vocals, piano) is 'a complete and utter idiot . . . a ladies' man to the bone . . . and a big mouth'. We also learn that former cohort James Hibbins was apparently sacked ('Ha!') after a 'jazz trip', the nature of which is not recorded.

As Damon and Graham's musical horizons expanded, so too did their emotional and social ones. Damon remembers the early part of his time at Stanway as a country adolescence. Indeed, some of their antics – dozing off side by side as the wine bottles dangled in slow-moving rivers – could come straight from Thomas Hardy or A. E. Housman. 'An innocent country life,' concurs Graham. There was also a holiday in Romania with Graham's parents. It wasn't long, however, before they fell into the usual sixth-form round of house parties, ill-informed politics, snogging, vomiting and merry-making. They experimented with Hamlet cigars, Pernod, Concorde wine and girls, Lucy Stimson later recalling that Damon was initially more successful with 'the ladies', though most felt Graham was 'sweet'. Somewhere along the line, virginities were lost. Damon later referred to this in coolly dispassionate tones ('We lay down on a very clean bed, did the business and then I went home and had a nice cup of tea and a bun'), which in turn found the young lady concerned fulminating in the *Daily Mail*, the rightful home of all good British fulmination.

Damon's opinionated and vocal personality would often get them into trouble with local youths and squaddies (Colchester maintains a significant army garrison, a fact later 'celebrated' in 'Essex Dogs'). They had several haunts, including the archetypal 80s niterie Brites, a 'fun pub', as they were misleadingly named. 'We would go down there,' Graham recalled, 'and drink three or four Holsten Pils and then be completely legless. Damon was always staring people out. Once this bloke came over and there was a bit of to-ing and fro-ing and he said to Damon, "I'm going to kick your bloody head in in a minute." Damon applauded this slowly and said very sarcastically, "Oh, you're so hard." So this bloke just went Bam! and knocked him over these tables. But it was always happening . . . I had to give up going into town to the pub with him because it would always end in trouble.'

Back within the walls of Stanway, academic trouble loomed. The relationship between Damon and Nigel Hildreth, always volatile, was growing more combustible as Damon began to lose interest in music and devote more energy to drama and the theatre.

NIGEL HILDRETH: We were both very strong personalities and towards the end of his schooldays Damon was cultivating an air of rebellion and we had a few clashes. He said to me quite bluntly that he wanted nothing more to do with music to the extent that he didn't even bother bringing the right scores to his final exam. I discussed it with his mother and she was adamant that music was never going to be the important part of his life. I wasn't so sure and I felt that even if it wasn't crucial, he could still make better use of the talents he had.

Damon failed his music A level and his Grade 8 music theory exams, squeezing home in English and history with grades of D and E respectively. Meanwhile, Graham's final report in the fifth form had read – he can still quote it verbatim – 'Graham is a gregarious extrovert who would do well to channel his energies wisely'.

GRAHAM COXON: That's very concise. Probably true. I'd scraped four O levels: human biology, music, English and art. You don't need anything else, I think. I could put a plug on a kettle. I wasn't a bad kid. I was very polite and nice, a bit clowny maybe, a bit silly. So I went into sixth form for a year and did German, which I could kind of speak anyway.

Despite remembering most (if not all) of his teachers with affection, by the end of the lower sixth Graham's appetite for standard academia had waned considerably. He'd never had the patience for the theoretical side of music and eventually abandoned his sixth-form studies entirely. With the encouragement of Damon's father Keith, he instead enrolled on a two-year foundation course in General Art and Design at the North Essex School of Art.

GRAHAM COXON: I went off to be an art student at the college that Damon's dad ran, though I don't think there was anything nepotistic about it. I think I got there on merit. Damon's dad was a great help though in how I came to understand art. He would sit and chat to me after tea about why Picasso would do two eyes on one side of the face. So I got quite a decent little folder together and I was off.

An era, if that's not too grand a way of putting it, was coming to an end. Damon was also moving on: good as his word to Nigel Hildreth, he had decided that his future lay in strutting and fretting upon the stage. He was off to take up a place at the East 15 Drama School in Debden, many a mile down the A13 or the bright red Central Line towards the beating heart of London. Music, he knew, was merely a diversion, and furthermore he was desperate to leave this town where, as he was to put it over a decade later, the English army grind their teeth to glass and cellular phones are hot with teens in the terminal pubs, where the night turns the colour of orangeade over plains of cement.

Lyrics like those from 'Essex Dogs', with their bleak portrayal of urban Colchester and its people – dehumanised, violent, vacuous – plus a few disparaging remarks about the town reported harumphingly by the local gazette, mean that the three members of Blur who grew up in the town are unlikely ever to see a rash of blue plaques in their honour. Colchester reserves such civic commemoration for men like William Gilbert. Born in Colchester in 1604, thanks to his pioneering work into magnetism and electrical studies he rose to become arguably the most distinguished man of science during Elizabeth I's reign. The good burghers of Colchester perhaps thought he might be an inspiration to the town's youth when they named a local grammar school in his honour. William Gilbert would no doubt have been delighted to know that, on the verge of the 21st century, one of his school's old boys is a prime mover behind Britain's first Mars probe. But we are getting ahead of ourselves, and there is much to transpire in the life of David 'Shady Dave' Rowntree before he becomes such an upstanding patron of science.

Dave Rowntree was born in Colchester on 8 May 1964. His father worked as a sound engineer at Broadcasting House, Portland Place, London, home of BBC radio. His mother had been an orchestral viola player before becoming disillusioned with the lot of the professional classical musician. None the less, it was a very musical household and Dave was given a set of bagpipes along with his Janet and John books, surely the act of parents whose love of music and desire to instil the same in their son could brook any agonies. The bagpipes were, frankly, too taxing for Rowntree *fils*, requiring the lung power of a grown man who thinks nothing of inflating a hot water bottle and the technical dexterity of a milkmaid who can do it standing up. A musical child, though, Dave quickly settled upon the instrument that was to prove the making of him.

> **DAVE ROWNTREE:** I was a pretty musical kid. I could read music and stuff and after a couple of false starts me and the drums just clicked. I immediately understood the mechanics of it and how it relates to your body. I was taught by this old military drummer who taped a sixpence to the middle of the skin and if you didn't hit it bang on, he would hit you over the head. That's the way they teach you in the army. Assault-course style. It put the fear of God in you. I don't think it would work with an adult but it was bloody effective on a child.

Immediately, Dave was working with other musicians. Buddy Hassler, an American boy with a fabulous name for a jazz great of the 40s, lived round the corner – his family had come over with the US air force but stayed on as civilians. Buddy was taking piano lessons so it seemed only logical that the two should form a curious piano/drums duo, augmented by Dave's sister Sara (five years his senior) on tambourine, for a performance of 'Yellow Submarine', his public debut, at a street party to celebrate the Queen's Silver Jubilee of 1977.

Dave was catholic, promiscuous even, in the musical company he kept. His father enrolled him in Saturday morning jazz classes at

Landermere music school. He played in wind bands, which forged a formidable technique. He played in brass bands, a style of music often scorned in England for its associations with pigeons, flat caps and the northern working-class, but for which he still has enormous affection. 'In some ways it dominated my life till going to polytechnic. Two rehearsals a week every week. There's nothing like brass band music; it can still make me want to cry. The way the instruments are related to each other, the ratios and shapes, create these perfect over-tones and harmonies like a choir. The drum music for brass bands is bollocks but to sit there in the middle is an amazing feeling.'

As anyone from a provincial town who has ever tried to start a teenage rock group will know, drummers are the most frustratingly elusive piece of the jigsaw. The rock axiom that declares all drum-mers are nutters is a gross slur but carries some weight. The gear is unwieldy and expensive, it's a lot more difficult than it looks, quiet solo practice is murder, and the pouting kid spouting bad poetry stands directly between you and the nice girls. For these reasons and others, good drummers are thin on the ground, as Dave Rowntree was finding out.

DAVE ROWNTREE: Drummers are always in short supply. You'll never go hungry like violinists do. Especially if word gets round you can actually play. So I was always getting asked to be in bands. One of the first was the Strategic Arms Quartet. It was the cold war, you see, and there was three of us. That was the hilarious joke. It was all very avant-garde for twelve year olds. We were young kids but we could really play. The keyboard player was called Andrew Butler. Very talented. God knows why he hasn't gone on to anything. The local paper said we were the thinking man's Barron Knights.

Next came Idle Vice, a mostly instrumental jazz-punk combo formed in the last few months before Dave left Colchester. It was at this time that he came across the teenage Graham Coxon. 'Actually we ran across each other through a shared love of drinking really rather than bands. But the band scene was very fertile. There were loads of places to play – the Oliver Twist, the Hole In The Hall – and when you got past the pub phase you could get supports at the uni.'

It was an incestuous scene where competition and cohabitation was fervid. Idle Vice guitarist Robin Anderson also played in Hazel Dean And The Carp Enters From Hell (be lenient – they were young), in which Graham was playing sax. Idle Vice were looking to augment a brass section and thus Dave and Graham played together for the first time. 'Within a couple of weeks, we were mates,' remembers Dave.

Before long, though, Dave left Colchester for Thames Polytechnic and an HND in computer science. Maths, science and computing had been among the few academic subjects Dave had taken any real interest in. The complex but scrupulously logical world of program-ming held no fears for him. Indeed, he showed a natural aptitude for it.

DAVE ROWNTREE: It was something that came very easily to me. I first got interested in computers when I was a kid and the first personal computers were emerging. My dad took me to an electronic show and I wrote a little program on a machine called a PET and I was hooked immediately. I taught myself until I was about twenty. Robin Anderson from the band was also into it. We'd lock ourselves away with the school computer which no teachers understood and hang around there till seven or eight at night. So by twenty, I knew enough to get through the poly course without doing any work. It was fantastic – two years of easy living, just going in enough to get your ticks in the register and having a nice time living in Woolwich.

Dave's facility with sub-routines, bugs and bytes meant that there was plenty of room left in life for music. He set up the music society, which exists to this day, and became its first president. Like-minded musicians would pair or form quartets or do whatever trios do and experiment with all manner of musical forms. Once a year, a gala concert was staged. Add a lake of subsidised beer, and soon Col-chester was all but forgotten for a congenial two years. Then, like many a student before him, Dave found himself clutching a qualifi-cation and abruptly and unwillingly thrust into a cold and forbid-ding job market presided over by the ice maiden herself, Mrs Thatcher. Nine to five held little allure, so together with Robin Anderson and a bassist, Dave relocated to a squat in King's Cross and tried to find regular gigs. 'We were good for a bunch of funny people from Colchester,' he states, 'but we couldn't get gigs and I desperately wanted to be a musician because I thought it wasn't like working. How wrong I was!'

It was a shabby bohemian existence which entailed moving from squat to squat. The best of these was a palatial affair in Crouch End, once used by Eddie Grant, complete with a rehearsal suite, male and female toilets and a floor for each of the three of them. Here, Dave – who had acquired the pseudonym Shady Dave – would lock himself away and hone his game-programming skills in isolation, working on his own version of 80s arcade fave, Asteroids. 'I had this blinding flash of realisation that these skills that came easy to me, drumming and computing, didn't come easy to others, and I could get paid for them. These things I almost dismissed as valueless, people were willing to pay sometimes extraordinary amounts of money for.'

Life was enlivened by the recruitment of a singer named, remarkably, Charles Windsor. 'Extrovert, drama-school type, a complete knob . . . everything you want in a front man.' Though the odd pub and college gig were forthcoming, the outlook was generally bleak. Drumming up an audience via leafleting on the street was much harder on the hard, anonymous streets of London than it was in Colchester. Eviction from the squat was forthcoming. Then the guitarist got arrested by the drug squad in a bungled surveillance operation. The judge later dismissed him with a twenty quid fine but his arrest did lead to the excellent local paper headline – SORRY! THE GIG'S CANCELLED. THE BAND'S DOING THE JAILHOUSE ROCK! They were cold, skint and underemployed when inspiration struck.

DAVE ROWNTREE: We'd go abroad, that was it! So we bought a van and went and it was fantastic. It was just as we'd fantasised. Baguettes and cheap wine and local cheese and turning up in little tourist villages and plugging our extension cable into the bar and playing. It's extraordinary how cheaply you can live if you exist on bread, cheese and wine. We lived on a couple of quid a day. We bought a manual for the van and we all became mechanical engineers overnight, which was great too. We'd earn enough to keep us and pay for the trip to the next town, sometimes sleeping in tents and the van and sometimes having the luxury of a hotel. It was impoverished but fun. But it got to November and it just started to get too bloody cold. We thought about renting and setting up base there but it seemed more attractive to come home and sign on for winter and have a bath.

Nevertheless, the band returned and spent most of the following year in France. They were particularly warmly welcomed in the northern coastal town of Berck-sur-Mer, where the mayor would throw open his windows to hear them during council meetings as the band played by the fountain in the town square. 'If things went wrong elsewhere we knew we could always come home there.' But things didn't often go wrong any more. They now had a sophisticated system of backing tapes and were existing well above the baguette line. A crucial decision loomed. 'We thought hard about settling in France. It was a real toughie. But in the end we looked at the cost of renting and stuff, realised it was a serious decision and I suppose bottled it.' So Dave returned to Colchester complete with lustrous Mohican and vague dreams of making it as a musician. The latter were short-lived.

> **DAVE ROWNTREE:** I pretty soon realised that my chances of making it as a working musician in England in the same way I'd done in France were virtually nil. On top of that, the dole were starting to get strict. They were starting to demand you attended interviews and took jobs. This didn't square with my Marxist principles at all. So I went along to the job centre and literally took the first job I could find with computers in the title. It was working for Colchester Council as a computer programmer. The level of the work meant that there was an utter lack of challenge but it was a steady job and quite good money. It was like they were paying me to breathe.

Curiously, then, late 1987 finds the three protagonists we have so far met moving in very different orbits around the ancient town of Camulodunum. One is flushed with the new-found joys of being an art student and all that that entails. One is knuckling down to life as a besuited council employee tapping at computer keyboards under the strip lighting of the town hall, perhaps daydreaming fondly of his two summers of Brie and Beaujolais and jazz and the gypsy life of the itinerant musician. The third, as we shall see soon, is making a reluctant sojourn back on to his old worn patch after a false start that has left him burning with ambition but clinging to the strands of an unravelling life.

But now our gaze must turn elsewhere. For all this time, something has been stirring on Dorset's sleepy coastline and, like that rough beast in W. B. Yeats's 'Second Coming', this rather suaver creature is now slouching towards if not Bethlehem then certainly Soho, his time having very definitely come.

2 Ars Gratia Artis

ALEX JAMES, ONE MIGHT say, grew up in a town where people go to die. He wouldn't say it ... and indeed it would be a cheap and slighting thing to say of the Dorset seaside resort of Bournemouth. But, there, we've said it now. And there's a tiny kernel of truth in there. Being an island, Britain has a wealth of coastline and every inlet, promontory and headland has its own identity, a fact later to be celebrated in Blur's psychedelic paean to the British coast, 'This Is A Low'. Thus, Blackpool is brazen, vulgar and fun, Skegness bracing, Brighton shabby genteel; there are gritty working ports such as Hull and Grimsby, Swansea and Aberdeen and the mysterious, forgotten Silloths, Zennors and Flamborough Heads.

In this way, we might characterise Bournemouth as presentable, attractive and well mannered but with, who knows, hidden depths – a sort of Carol Vorderman of the seaside. It's a relatively young town, evolving from a summer residence constructed by affluent Dorset squire Lewis Tregonwell in 1810. In 1841, there were still only 26 buildings in the town but thereafter, with the arrival of the railway in 1870, Bournemouth expanded rapidly. The sandy heaths and pinewoods that spread behind the Poole cliffs filled with homes and the town proper grew up around the river mouth where the Bourne empties into the sea.

The balmy summers and mild winters of the south coast and the town's pleasant setting meant that it developed as a resort. That same hospitable climate has meant that Bournemouth has become a Mecca for the retired. It's cruel to say that they go there to die but certainly they go to doze out their days in a very English haze of flower gardens, promenades and crazy golf. But it was also, according to Alex James, 'A great place to grow up.'

He was born in the now demolished Boscombe Hospital on 21

November 1968 as students and Soviet troops fought on the streets of Prague. Bournemouth was considerably quieter. He had a sister Deborah two years his junior – all of Blur, amateur psychologists should note, have one sister – and the family lived in Stroudon Park on the outskirts of the town, a mixture of middle-class prosperity and sprawling council estate. His class origins, he feels, were similarly mixed. 'My grandparents were pretty working-class but my dad caught trains and would be classified as middle-class.' Alex, though, describes his upbringing as 'extremely suburban – nice residential area, golf course'. Dad had been in the navy but was now employed as a sales rep selling forklift trucks for a company based in Coventry, where he was often taken on business. 'Coventry Climax, they were called. Bit saucy. But then it was the 70s.'

Later, Alex's father was to start his own rubbish compacting company but in the meantime Alex's grandfather died, leaving them an imposing guest house in the town centre, into which they moved with their menagerie of pets, including guinea pigs, tortoises and Sparky the dog. 'When my dad said we had to move, none of us wanted to. All my mates were round the corner but in the end it was the best thing we ever did. It was a big fuck-off house in the middle of town with a huge basement where we practised later when I was in bands. Absolutely great. My mum and dad did try to run it as a guest house but that nearly ended in divorce so we just lived there.'

By all accounts, Alex was a gregarious, popular youth. He was good at sport, particularly football, and, at least in secondary school, academically excellent, gaining thirteen O levels. 'I did find it easy really but all I was concerned about was being good at football. I didn't study art or music – that was what you did if you couldn't do physics and chemistry.' Outside of school, Alex remembers Bournemouth, with its long beaches stretching from Sandbanks to Hengistbury Head, as a fine place to drift through teenage life.

ALEX JAMES: The pier was the major hang. In summer it's packed but in winter, there's no one there and it's just as nice. Our guest house was near the sea so I walked down there most nights being windswept and romantic. And I soon discovered that if you took a girl down to the sea with a bottle of wine, it was very atmospheric and you could snog them. So growing up by the sea was a brilliant thing. But as a place it's stifling; there's no ambition there. I went to the grammar school where you were encouraged to believe that you were nothing special and would have to work very hard to get anywhere in life, which is a really bad message to send to kids. Most Bournemouth folk think they're going to have to spend their lives doing something shit because there are no opportunities there but then you move to London and you realise you can do what the fuck you like in life.

Contrary to most reports, Alex's academic career didn't run as smoothly as some have suggested. His studies were going, in his own words, 'catastrophically'. 'I'd gone a bit wayward, discovered booze and girls, that sort of stuff.' Though he'd been accepted by Goldsmiths College in London, he took a year off during which he amused himself in various ways. He worked on the cheese counter of Safeway and as a labourer on a building site during the construction of Winfrith nuclear power plant. 'I dropped acid on my first day there,' he recalls, rather chillingly for environmentalists. He now describes this as 'a year spent half asleep': falling in love with Justine Andrew – whom he still lives with – and moving into a house with her and his friend Charlie Bloor in nearby Charminster where Charlie and Alex would while away the hours playing guitar and dreaming of going to London and being pop stars.

Alex had never studied music at school because, as we've learnt, it seemed academically lightweight and, as he later explained, 'Because the music teacher was a buttock fondler.' His path into music was a roundabout one.

ALEX JAMES: At junior school a note came round saying your child can have violin lessons and my mum said, 'Oh, you've got to learn to play the violin. Learning an instrument would be marvellous.' So I did it because she wanted me to even though I was only interested in football and the violin is the stupidest instrument to give a child since it's very difficult to play. It sounds wank and you need twenty to make a decent noise. Then there was the recorder which is a godawful thing and you only ever play 'Pease Pudding Hot' and 'The Old Grey Goose Is Dead' so I was bounced out of recorder class for not being interested. But then the turning point came when my old man bought this 100 quid piano when I was twelve and put it in the spare room. One day, he sat down at it and raised an eyebrow and started to play twelve-bar blues and 'Blue Moon', which I had no idea he could do, and I demanded to be shown how to do that. I got the bug and after that I spent loads of time sitting at it trying to play Human League songs and 'Are Friends Electric'.

Alex's first band, The Age Of Consent, was less a group than a
prankish bit of Situationist subterfuge. In fellow conspirator Jay
Birtsmail's bedroom, they spliced an intro of their own devising on
to Fleetwood Mac's AOR classic 'The Chain', famously the theme
from BBC's Grand Prix coverage and doubtless a firm favourite *chez*
Clarkson. The resulting Frankensteinish demo they would hawk
round to parties, hoping to impress girls, until one night they fell
foul of someone who was familiar with the original, a humiliation
surely not a long time coming in the suburban Bournemouth of the
late 70s. At sixteen, Alex was desperate to be in a real band – largely
as a means of meeting girls – and was eager to extend his rudimentary keyboard abilities. 'But keyboards were 600 quid and bass
guitars were 50 and Mum and Dad didn't think I was going to take
it very seriously so for my sixteenth birthday I got a Columbus
Fender precision copy from South Bournemouth Exchange and
Mart, which is still there now. I had to wait till Christmas to get the
amp, though.'

His 'virtual' band with Jay Birtsmail and others gradually became
a reality as slowly all the people who didn't have instruments were
thrown out. A drummer who could manage 'Whole Lotta Love' was
recruited and via him Don White, the class hippy, who brought
along his decrepit Vox amp to the James basement where rehearsals
– 'fucking about, really' – took place. As soon as the venerable
antique amplifier was switched on, however, the new recruit 'got the
full 240 volts right up his arm and he was screaming "Fuck!" and
then my mother appeared at the top of the stairs screaming, "I will
not have swearing in my house." So that was my introduction to the
world of real rock and roll; swearing and screaming and loud music
and smoke everywhere.'

(Note: Alex's mother, like his band mates, would have known
him as Steven at this time. It was not until he ventured to London
that he switched to his middle name Alex. 'Like Bunbury in *The
Importance of Being Earnest*,' jokes Dave Rowntree today. 'Alex in
town and Steven in Bournemouth.')

The remainder of Alex's time on the south coast is a pageant of
variously competent bands. One foundered in fisticuffs and acri-
mony after he was caught *in flagrante delicto* with the drummer's
girlfriend. There was school band The Rising who were 'dreadful
. . . but being in a band means you're the coolest people in the
school and that's what we were interested in'. Later came Mr Pang's

Big Bangs, named after their Charminster landlord who had once achieved minor fame with appearances for Southampton Reserves football team. 'We had this song called "The Neighbours Are Coming Around", which started really quietly and then got louder until the neighbours came round. It was all cheeky experimental bollocks.' Alex also played guitar and bass in The Victorians, who were 'quite good – Gemma from that band works with The Propellerheads now'. But by now, Alex's genial, dilatory year off was coming to a close. Armed with physics, French and chemistry A levels, the bright lights and golden pavements of London beckoned. Curiously, given his aptitude for sciences, he had chosen to do a BA in French, and so it was time to bid the Dorset coast *au revoir*.

Damon Albarn's foray into the capital, begun in similar optimism, had come unglued sadly. He had commenced his course at East 15, the well-known drama college, in September 1986. The college was the Alma Mater of Alison Steadman and many other of the actors that Damon and Graham had come to admire through their work in Mike Leigh's semi-improvised darkly satirical examinations of British mores.

The school set great store by the Method system of acting espoused by the Russian dramatic teacher Konstantin Stanislavsky in works such as *An Actor Prepares*. Within 'the method', actors are encouraged to draw on their own emotional memory and fully immerse themselves in their role. Even if your role is a chambermaid, says Stanislavsky, whose part merely consists of walking on stage to answer a telephone and then leaving to get the master of the house, remember that the girl has a history – a past comprised of loves and disappointments like our own.

Method acting in its purest form has often been mocked for its excesses: when Method devotee Dustin Hoffman told *Marathon Man* co-star Laurence Olivier he was thinking of having his teeth drilled to understand the trauma of the famous dentist's chair scene, Larry replied, 'Ever tried acting, Dusty?' But there's no doubt that the principles as applied at Lee Strasberg's Actors Studio in 50s New York brought much that was good to the world stage, not least the young Marlon Brando.

For the young Damon Albarn, dramatic techniques meant an uncomfortable term of 'experiments', such as spending two months as a tramp – never difficult for a student – and impersonating a

London tart or the Ayatollah Khomeini. Classmates such as Eddie Deedigan, three years older than Damon but also a first year and soon to become a musical accomplice, are on record as saying that Albarn shone and talk of 'an immense personality' and 'an amazing aura'. They recall well-received pieces involving dramatic roles as American Indians and medieval gypsies. Damon's own memories of the period are of a less than fulfilling time, however.

> **DAMON ALBARN:** Going to London and East 15 was supposed to be a real adventure and it kind of went sour. At that point Graham was much more into the whole student thing than I was and having a much better time of it. He was really relishing being an art student at the place that my dad ran and loving the art student life and had really thrown himself into it. But I felt . . . hopeless . . . really unhappy and dissatisfied with what I was doing. I was very geeky at the time and felt very frustrated. I was unfocused, not sure what I was doing most of the time. I was very opinionated, I had ideas and theories, but I didn't move very well at all. So I was in the doldrums most of the time. I didn't feel any connection with the school.

On a brighter note, as Damon's enthusiasm for drama waned, so his appetite and propensity for music blossomed. During that year at East 15 came two happy brushes with Teutonic musical legends. First, Eddie Deedigan's woefully named band The Alternative Car Park was contracted to support legendary icy chanteuse and former Velvet Underground member Nico, now fallen from favour and promoting to little avail her *Camera Obscura* album. Though Damon was unsure who Nico was, he was convinced by a listen to some of Velvet Underground's music to help out on keyboards. At this gig at Golddiggers, a club in Chippenham, Damon premiered a composition called 'The Rain', which was well received by the mainly student audience.

Damon was also fortunate enough to play piano with the esteemed Berliner Ensemble in a performance of *The Threepenny Opera* (*Die Dreigroschenoper*) at a Brecht/Weill Festival in Ilford. Weill's music was a growing enthusiasm of Damon's – 'overwhelmingly articulate music . . . more profound an influence on me than any pop record,' he later stated – and he enjoyed the evening immensely. 'It gave me a real taste for the idea of performing good music well.' Brecht and Weill's music has exerted a considerable influence on rock performers: 'Alabama Song', 'Mack The Knife' and others have been performed by David Bowie, Jim Morrison and Ian McCulloch, with varying degrees of sympathy and success. More enjoyably, the *Mahagonny* opera has clearly left indelible marks on the music of the San Franciscan experimentalists The Residents. In Damon's future compositions, the influence of Kurt Weill was to surface not in such obvious manifestations but in the broken waltz tempos and Germanic cadences of instrumentals such as 'The Debt Collector' and 'Intermission', which his girlfriend Justine Frischmann was to loathe for their Nazi-ish connotations. Of course, the music has no such associations: both Weill and his librettist Brecht were committed left-wingers. Nigel Hildreth and his wife were in the audience for that Ilford performance and afterwards stood their former pupil a curry.

NIGEL HILDRETH: After the final conversations we'd had at Stanway and how adamant he was that music was going to play no part in his life, I was surprised to see him sitting behind the piano. But delighted in a way. He played very well and he seemed to have really enjoyed the experience. I probably knew then that there were clearly still musical ambitions burning there somewhere.

By now, musical ambitions were in fact the only ones Damon retained. He had become progressively disenchanted with the regime at East 15, which he describes as 'totally up its own arse', and the prospect of a dramatic career in general. Having come to the conclusion that he was 'the worst actor in the world', he decided to cut his losses and leave at the end of the first year, as did Deedigan. Though sure that a new direction was needed, late 1987 found him in poor spirits.

DAMON ALBARN: I left after a year feeling very disillusioned with everything and went back home for a while. That was a bad time really. I was very low, very depressed. I felt utterly unsure about everything. In a way, it made matters worse that Graham and my sister were both at art college and having a brilliant time. I mean, I was glad for them, I suppose, but it made me feel worse. I used to feel extremely uneasy about socialising with them. Somehow it made me feel dull or worthless. It sounds ridiculous now but I would invent things to say about myself in a desperate attempt to make myself more interesting. And any ray of hope of something coming up, any glimmer of anything happening, would be magnified and embellished and augmented. It was a very frustrating, upsetting time for me.

In contrast Graham had enjoyed his time at North Essex College of Art, particularly as it had left him plenty of free time to develop musically, flitting between various groups such as the aforementioned Hazel Dean And The Carp Enters From Hell, The Curious Band and others. To finance his lively social round – during which he had met Dave Rowntree – he did various odd jobs, such as shelf stacking, peapicking and the like. On leaving college, he applied to be admitted to a degree course in fine art at the prestigious Goldsmiths College in London

GRAHAM COXON: I wanted to go to Goldsmiths because at the time I badly needed to get to London: that's where Damon was, living right out in the East End and going to drama school. I wanted to get there so we could work together musically because I guess it had become quite a big deal and we knew we connected well. And a friend of mine, Adam Peacock, had gone to Goldsmiths so that would be good. Amazingly, I got in: no one thought I would. Even Tim the sculpture tutor, who was my guru, didn't think I'd get in. I think they had faith but they weren't going to let me think I'd make it. It's a tough college and I think they wanted me to understand that.

Ironically, then, as it turned out, it was Damon who was to enrol on a part-time music course at Goldsmiths to be nearer Graham, who seemed to be on a more direct and fruitful track at this juncture. Damon, conversely, was toying with being an Essex soul boy and flirting with the music of Marvin Gaye, Anita Baker and Mica Paris, as well as taking various casual jobs in order to support his musical aspirations. He worked as a barman in London's Portobello Hotel, a favourite haunt of visiting rock stars, and found himself handing bowls of peanuts to Tina Turner and making slammers for Ian McCulloch. Bono was once very rude to him – 'something I've never really forgiven him for' – although he remembers The Edge as more civilised. Later, he was to work at the Le Croissant fast-food counter at Euston Station. Amidst these stints were various periods on the dole, some mild toying with drugs – 'I did my first acid in a little tiny flat in Lewisham' – and fairly sustained spells of boozing. 'When I was twenty I went through a period of getting locked up because I used to get drunk. That's when I started to mutate slowly into whatever I am today.'

In what was to prove a significant move, an inheritance of £3,000 from his grandfather and the cashing in of some premium bonds were put towards equipment and the recording of a demo tape. Damon took this to the Beat Factory studios at Christopher Place, Euston. He told owners Graham Holdaway and Maryke Bergkamp that he chose their studio because of its excellent reputation. In fact, he had picked it from the Yellow Pages because it was near to Le Croissant, his place of work. Bergkamp and Holdaway were impressed and organised an ad hoc deal with Damon. They would manage him in a capacity that remains slightly unfathomable to outsiders and give him the run of the studio, chiefly late at night when it was unused. In return, he worked as a tea boy at the Beat Factory, as well as flogging Emmental feuilletes to commuters on Euston concourse.

DAMON ALBARN: When Graham went to Goldsmiths, that was brilliant; an amazing amount of energy seemed to be unlocked. I enrolled on a part-time music course at Goldsmiths so I'd feel a little less uncomfortable hanging out with them all. I had a lot of pride. There was so much more going on in his life. He was all wrapped up in this bohemian thing and I was the one who came from that background, art schools and stuff, and now I was on the outside. Weird but fun too. Then I started working in the Beat Factory studio and got various bands together who were just awful. Graham was playing a bit of sax with me. I had the keys to a studio run by Graham Holdaway and Maryke Bergkamp. I had an arrangement with them, a kind of weird relationship. They were managing me in a way. I was allowed to use the studio and I'd spend hours playing piano, laying on a bit of reverb, singing. It wasn't focused at all and I wrote a lot of really rubbish music before I started getting good stuff. It was a hell of a lot of hard work. It gave me such focus because I made every mistake. I find music so easy now, so much more connected with my voice and my piano playing; these are things I really enjoy now. But I never understood it then – why I wanted to sing. I just knew I wanted to do it. I certainly hadn't found my voice back then at the Beat Factory. So I did lots of embarrassing things. My enthusiasm or desire were so much stronger than my ability to articulate things so I just did all this rubbish.

Perhaps not surprisingly, given the unformed nature of Damon's compositions at this point, Graham Holdaway and partner Maryke, convinced of Damon's potential, steered him into an odd partnership called Two's A Crowd. This synth-pop pairing of Albarn with another Beat Factory client, Sam Vamplew, is the oddest phase of Albarn's development and the one he is least enamoured of. Suffice to say that a whole batch of songs – 'Reck Me', 'Let's Get Together', 'Big Religion', 'Can't Live Without You', 'Since You've Been Gone' and 'Running' – was worked on before Damon withdrew from the project. 'I was very driven and prepared to do virtually anything to succeed,' he later told Adrian Deevoy of *Q*. 'Not turn into Boyzone or anything like that – no disrespect to them – but I did go in for a few rather alarming manifestations.'

Two's A Crowd faded into memory mercifully soon and Damon pressed on with his musical efforts. He became one of London's great reservoir of 'dodgy demo musicians'. Excruciatingly for him, he mimed to his work in the office of EMI's Dave Ambrose, the man who had signed The Sex Pistols and Duran Duran. 'He mumbled something about David Bowie and that was the last I heard. Then I saw some bloke who listened to my tape for a moment, then put on the House Of Love album and told me, "This is what you should be doing."'

Undeterred, Damon began work on what was to prove a short-lived but crucial project in the evolution of the fledgling Blur. Circus was a band formed initially with Chippenham-based college friend Tom Aitkenhead and then Eddie Deedigan, who preferred the more direct guitar-rooted band sound over the strange cabaret stylings of Two's A Crowd. Several other members were accrued: Dave Brolan was a Dixons colleague of Eddie's, while Darren Filkins was once of the Alternative Car Park, his departure opening up the vacancy on the Nico support which Damon had filled. Though this new venture did not at this point include Graham, the pair were still in close contact.

GRAHAM COXON: I'd found out that he had a deal there – some contract with Graham Holdaway and Maryke, who was Dutch but you wouldn't have known. He'd do his songs there and he had this great song called 'The Red Club'. 'I'm in the red club,' it went, meaning you're broke, I suppose. When I lived in Colchester, aged eighteen, just prior to starting Goldsmiths, I used to go down to London to see him. I did a bit of sax on some of his stuff. I'd developed stomach ulcers and pretty serious anaemia. My haemoglobin count was very

low and I was always passing out. I was frightened of London too, and
the Tube, but I still came down. I remember Graham Holdaway saying
I looked very ill. I was transparent I was so anaemic. I ended up in this
old mental hospital in Colchester with all these old blokes like Old
Stan, who used to sneak my Superkings in.

Just prior to the advent of Circus proper, Damon, in his desperation
to get his musical career kick-started, had organised a solo gig at
Colchester Arts Centre. Though essentially Damon's gig, he was
backed by Tom Aitkenhead. 'I did this solo gig at Colchester Arts
Centre. I can't think why. Just trying anything, really. I don't
know about brave; certainly stupid, certainly embarrassing. But
anyway, Graham brought Dave along – they were two of the ten
people in the audience – and he obviously saw something in my
fumblings.'

'He did this little show with his friend Tom,' recounts Graham.
'All tape loops and sequencers and drum machines and it was very
brave really. But I knew he had that about him. I mean, I knew the
first time I saw him perform "Gee Officer Krupke" in *West Side
Story* when he was a kid. The obvious gall of the boy was staggering.
He was a bit of a prat sometimes but every extrovert prat is going
to be famous in the end, leather trousers or not.'

Dave Rowntree was by now well settled into his new shiny-
suited executive desk job, even if it was a strange career move for
a self-proclaimed 'Agit-prop-Marxist-red-flag-squat-punk with a
blond mohican'. While it was not a world he had taken to with
relish, he was certainly glad of the steady and not inconsiderable
salary, and at least he was able to potter around on the computers.
He remembers that Graham had maintained his friendship and
musical alliance with Damon. 'I was aware that Graham had
known Damon since school and that he was travelling to London
to work on Damon's pet project which I didn't know anything
about. I saw Damon's show at the Colchester Arts Centre and
thought it had something. Then one day Graham came back from
one of these London trips with a tape that I thought was great and I
told Graham that he could mention my name to Damon and tell
him to give me a call if ever he needed a drummer.' In fact, as
Damon laboured to build Circus into an ongoing concern with Eddie
Deedigan's help, a drummer was *just* what he needed. Well aware
of Dave's musical pedigree from the Colchester musicians' bush

telegraph, in a moment of high prescience, Damon made that phone call.

'Lo and behold,' remembers Dave, 'one week out of nowhere, I got this call. It was Damon saying come up to London and meet up. It transpired that he had the keys to a recording studio which made him an instantly attractive person. Had he not had the keys I would still have turned up but having the keys meant if he played me a parrot singing I would still have been enthusiastic. I was genuinely keen but a recording studio was a very big deal.'

So, in the October of 1988, Dave Rowntree became the drummer with Circus. To borrow an analogy from the world of safe breaking, two of the tumblers had fallen into place. The big prize had suddenly got considerably nearer, though no one could have guessed just how. At this time, it probably seemed more likely that it was Damon and Eddie Deedigan, the group's main creative engines, whose musical futures were indissolubly knit.

Throughout the winter of 1988, Circus (now a quintet) rehearsed material written, individually, by Damon and Eddie with a view to recording tracks in the New Year or early spring. The Circus *oeuvre* was a curious hotch-potch; a mixture of sundry 80s templates with a touch of Bowie or Morrissey here and a dash of Talking Heads or the literate pop of the Pet Shop Boys or The The there. It was craftsmanlike and songwriterly with the attention to detail that was to characterise the later Blur but without the glowing ember of individuality or the indefatigable momentum of an idea whose time has come. It was, significantly, music that seemed to be created in isolation from the ragged but fertile independent scene of the time, then reverberating to the primitivist noise-pop of The Pixies and My Bloody Valentine and the zonked-out, irrepressible white-trash aesthetic beginning to emerge from Manchester.

Circus were positive and committed and rehearsals went well, the appointed Beat Factory sessions for the mini-album intended to serve as a high-quality portfolio that would hopefully entice major label interests. However, two days before they went into the studio to begin recording, Darren Filkins announced he was leaving. The other members of Circus had known for some time that Darren nurtured ambitions of being a professional photographer: what they hadn't known was that he was on the verge of getting his first professional commission. Somewhat sheepishly, he quit on the eve of the projected recording sessions.

DAVE ROWNTREE: Graham Holdaway had let us use the Beat Factory and given us time to mature and tinker about with a view to getting some really good stuff together. We'd always known that [Darren's] ambition was to be a photographer. But we didn't know he was going to up and disappear just as we were going to start recording. He just fucked off.

The solution to their dilemma was, of course, obvious. Damon was still in regular contact with a gifted musician who both he and Dave had played with in the past. It was just a matter of wresting him away from the bohemian demimonde of cheap wine and invented art movements that he had flung himself into with gusto somewhere across London.

Goldsmiths College is an old independent institution founded in 1891 by the Worshipful Company of Goldsmiths as a centre for technical learning and excellence. Since 1989, it has been a college of the University of London, and has a formidable reputation for academic rigour and artistic innovation. Its visual arts department is internationally renowned and its art shows, music and theatre performances are famed. Situated in New Cross, a savvy, grubby, lively and distinctly urban patch of south London, most freshers live in halls of residence. 'It was a tough college to get into and a cool college,' is Graham's memory. 'All the tutors looked like Trotskyites in their little round spectacles and grey hair and dark clothes.'

Here, then, is a scene probably being repeated in many other campus car parks that autumn morning of 1987. Cars are arriving from suburban estates driven by doting, slightly anxious parents bringing their beloved charges to their new colleges and universities – young, awkward Kevins, Simons and Audreys soon to rechristen themselves Dirk and Rocky and Elsinore and invent more interesting life histories concerning grandfathers who fought in the Spanish civil war and sexual diseases. Alex James, already a little discomfited by a 'weeping mother fluffing around' is furthered dismayed by the sight of Graham Coxon emerging from his parents' estate with his guitar.

ALEX JAMES: I look up and Graham's arriving at the same time taking his guitar out of the boot. We stood there and totally clocked each other. I was a bit sickened, really. I thought he was cooler than

me and better looking. And up till then I'd been feeling pretty cool –
baggy trousers, paisley shirt, floppy fringe – and then I see Graham
who looked like me only cooler and I thought, You bastard. I knew
instantly that he'd be a big part of my life.

The hall of residence they were moving into was in Camberwell
Green, between Camberwell and Brixton in south London. By
another extraordinary coincidence, they were assigned rooms
directly above/below one another on the third and fourth floors.
However, Graham was enrolled on a fine arts degree and Alex had
chosen to study French. 'I'd done physics, chemistry and French A
levels and I was still very interested in physics and chemistry but
French was the option I took because I'd decided I wanted to do art
not science. French was the only art degree I could do plus I loved
France. If you don't really know what you want to do, you should
take something you enjoy. And I was very lucky and met the right
people.' That depressingly cool youth in the car park was one of
those 'right people', but it was to be six or seven weeks before they
met again.

ALEX JAMES: Graham lived above me but, for the first couple of
months, I didn't have anything to do with him. He was doing fine art
and I was doing French. So I felt a bit inferior. He's cool. He hung out
with third years and had the next work space to Damien Hirst although
he was already famous and in a different clique. But there was a fine
art guy, Paul Hodgson, on our floor who I became friendly with, who
was the cleverest, funniest, most inspiring person I'd met till then. The
great thing of going to university is you meet people who have grown
up in cities and who have this sense of what's achievable. Whereas
Bournemouth is a lovely place to sit and do nothing and very pretty
and everything, but there is this vibe that says nothing is possible; a
very restrictive small-town vibe. Paul had grown up in London and he
said he'd work on building sites in order to further his art and I found
that very inspiring. So Paul and I are sitting around eating pasta
sandwiches and getting stoned and he said, 'You should meet Gray.'

GRAHAM COXON: I was loving it; it was an ace time that first year. A
great period of discovering things about life and people. You're
nineteen years old, your own boss, living away from home, smoking
whatever you want when you want, free, and surrounded by kids who
are just like you. And they're free too so you just go berserk. The art
school world is so loose. They gave you a six by six area for your work

and you went there and worked and once a week a guy talked to you for half an hour about what you were doing. So really you're learning social skills. Every day at half-eleven you think, Well, nearly lunchtime, so off to the student union for half a pizza and a couple of Newcastle Brown Ales, and that makes it very difficult to go back to your studio and sit and work. So a lot of thinking went on in the union bar and pondering these beautiful girls who are suddenly in your life.

Eventually though, through the good offices of Paul Hodgson, the two met. Alex remembers Graham's first words to him. 'He said, "How long you been playing the git?" and I said about four years. And then we got drunk together and have been doing it ever since. It's quite sweet that from the moment I met him we were getting drunk together. Of course, a bottle of tequila would last us a week in those days.'

'Alex lived below me,' explains Graham, 'and next door to this really weird, quite square girl who was obviously in love with him. Alex's door didn't close properly. You'd walk past and he'd be just there asleep, completely naked, spread-eagled with all his bits hanging out, next door to this really square odd girl who was infatuated with him and who must have been very freaked out by it. I'd go down in the mornings to drag him up to go to college or whatever or to finish the tequila from the previous night and his door was always ajar. So immodest.'

The pair quickly became inseparable, entering into a phase that Graham describes cheerily as 'total *Withnail* . . . I wore these cheap tweed suits and we were obsessed with cheap thrills'. Their coterie included Paul Hodgson and third year Adam Peacock, who was in Damien Hirst's year. Alex describes Adam as 'this incredible fearless artistic guy who looked like George Coburn and was like mine and Graham's dad'. The gang were often found either in Camberwell Green or round at Peacock's flat a little walk away in Linnell Road. Life was a relentless search for liquid and chemical recreation on a shoestring, the crusade of the student down the ages since Chaucer.

They would engage in sorties and raid other floors of the halls of residence, stealing cheap boxes of wine from the kitchens. Failing that, they would resort to even more desperate measures. Paul Hodgson had given Graham a book entitled *Beers and Wines You Can Make* and this served as the bible for some unsuccessful experiments into home brewing. 'There were recipes for various ciders and punches and one for nettle beer which I always wanted to try but didn't want to go over Camden Road to collect the nettles cos the trains ran by and it looked dangerous. There was something called invalid beer. Specially recommended if your granny's feeling ill. Make some toast then burn it and scrape the carbon off into lukewarm water. Makes you better apparently.'

Invalid beer would have been a good choice for the still sickly Coxon. According to Alex, 'Graham was never very good at feeding himself. When I first went into his room there was all this food that his mum had given him piled up; pints of milk that he'd been too mean to put in the fridge in case they got nicked. All on his window going rotten.'

Graham describes Alex as 'just how he is now but it takes a while to become your own person, I guess, for those characteristics to emerge from the lump of plasticine. I thought he was a very funny bloke, very good fun. He always struck me as being a little bit of a slob: very bright, 143 O levels and all that, but a bit slobby. A typical bloody middle-class grammar school drop-out. But he was just a kid and he was a good laugh.'

Certainly, Alex's memories of the time are fond. 'College was fucking great fun. Everyone should go. We had fuck all money but we soon learned that you can get drunk with hardly any money at all. Let's face it, people who live on the street can manage it so students can.' It was around this time that the pair, along with Paul Hodgson and Jason Brownlee, dreamt up the infamous Nichtkunst movement, a kind of cut-price amalgam of Situationism, Dadaism and The Bauhaus, with no clear manifesto beyond 'staying up all night and getting drunk and talking bollocks', as Alex recalls. 'We'd have these mad, lengthy discussions about art and dreaming up this philosophy which involved a bit of painting and these stunts with balloons and playing Ludo, as I remember.' 'Nichtkunst,' according to Graham, 'was us in our halls trying to intellectualise about performance art. Things take on a surreal slant if you stay up very late. Me and Paul worked out a performance art piece which involved dropping scaffolding from a height into an enclosed hall. It was art, mate, know what I mean.' If a trifle silly, Nichtkunst seems a generally admirable and understandable venture. For what is the point in being an art student unless you dream up your own movements from time to time? And, as movements go, it had every bit as much influence – i.e. none – as the New Wave Of New Wave,

Romo or any other of the vaporous cults that the music and style press conjure up when times are slow.

The first words Graham and Alex had exchanged had concerned music and music formed the bedrock of their friendship. They would repair to one or the other's room with their booty of stolen wine and listen to The Beatles, ELO, The Who and Simon And Garfunkel at Graham's behest, or possibly Alex's enthusiasms – Joy Division, New Order and Prince. Soon, though, they began to look beyond these pre-Goldsmiths favourites.

> **GRAHAM COXON:** The late 80s in London were a bit of a crash course in indie and alternative music for me. We'd go to the disco at the student union every Wednesday, me and Alex and Adam Peacock and his friend Peter, who'd have a tiny bit of speed, and we'd listen to Big Black and The Pastels. Brilliant. I loved that *Up for a Bit With The Pastels* album. 'Address Book' was a good one. Also, I'd go down to the Fountain in Deptford to see McCarthy and Tallulah Gosh who I loved. I don't think any of us were fully *compos mentis* at this period, though. Pernod and cider and speed, I seem to remember, was in evidence a little.

On the subject of original music, Graham remembers that Alex and he would 'sit around with our guitars and try to make up these little songs' but musically his firmest link was still with Damon, who was having a 'horrible depressing time working in the croissant shop at Euston but at least he had this tea boy job at the Beat Factory'. Alex recalls that, 'Graham and I would get drunk and he'd play this song called "I've Lost My Balls Inside My Computer". It went, "Not meant to be a big hero/Wanted to die for a piece of shit that he called his country." Horrible Colchester angst, really. Everyone loved him though cos he was the best drawer and better at music than all the music students. If there's a genius in the band, it's Graham. No doubt about it.'

Six miles north across London, bunkered in the Beat Factory, two other fans of Graham Coxon's abilities had that name uppermost in their minds. In the immediate wake of Darren Filkins' shock resignation, Deedigan and Brolan had been utterly deflated but less so Albarn and Rowntree, who saw the perfect replacement close at hand. Damon quickly got in touch with Graham – he was still in regular contact with him via his part-time course at Goldsmiths – and the guitarist readily agreed to go down to the Beat Factory.

His effect on the sessions was radical in more ways than one. Eddie Deedigan later recalled in an interview with Martin Roache, 'He played this incredible guitar. We were completely blown away by it and then he said, "Is that all right?" Fucking hell, it was all right. We couldn't believe what we were hearing.' The album was recorded and mixed over an intensive four-day session in January 1989. Nothing of these sessions is currently extant but for a handful of titles: 'Salvation', 'Happy House', 'Elizabeth' and 'She Said'. Evidently happy with the finished results, the band arranged for a celebration party to be held for their friends. Graham duly invited Paul and Alex, his Goldsmiths chums. It was to be the first time the four members of Blur were in the same room. Prophetically, the evening had its moments.

ALEX JAMES: Graham had often talked about Damon. He'd say that he was in Hazel Dean And The Carp Enters From Hell and recently he'd talked about Circus and he mentioned his mate Damon and Dave and these various names kept recurring. I got back after the reading week [*an elevated name universities give to half-term to get around the fact that they're not supposed to have them*] – it must have been early 1989, I suppose – and I got back from Bournemouth where Justine was still living and there was this note under my door saying, 'I've been in the Beat Factory studios doing some recording. It was great. Cheers. See you later, Graham.' So at the end of this session he said, 'You've got to come and meet Damon,' so Paul and Graham and I went up to Euston and Damon had the keys to this studio and he was like, 'Ever been in a recording studio before?' and I was like, no, obviously. He played me this tune and it was absolute Brother Beyond bollocks. Now how did it go? 'Won't you come down . . . you won't talk to me.' It was really bad drama school fall-out and he really was giving it large and we got drunk and he was still giving it large and there was a party later and eventually he said, 'Well, what do you think of the stuff then?' and I said, 'Well, it's shit. Why don't you sing about something you care about, something closer to your heart?' I turned very offensive, basically, but I think he liked that.

DAMON ALBARN: And then I met Alex. What was he like? He was . . . he was . . . Well, I thought he was great. Amazingly arrogant but great. He listened to all the stuff we'd just done that we were very pleased with and he said it was shit. Like a lot of other things that Alex has said, they all come back to haunt him. But this time he was right.

Despite Alex's withering assessment, Damon and the others still felt confident enough about the Circus material to consider touting it round the London music business. EMI's Steve Walters was vaguely encouraging but thought the group needed to learn their trade and hone their skills on stage. Thus Circus's one and only paying gig was organised by Eddie Deedigan's wife at the Victoria Hall, South-borough, Kent. For £2.50 the audience were entertained by Circus plus supports from Whale Oil and Annie. Any of the small crowd present would have missed the significance of this first ever on-stage collaboration between Albarn, Rowntree and Coxon.

During a brief hiatus from band activities, Alex, Damon and Graham began to cement as a social unit. They were ever present at student parties, where Graham was normally found 'lying on the floor like a human doormat', in Damon's recollection. On the most famous of these evenings, after bingeing on lager and tequila at a private view at the Slade School of Art, Alex passed out on a night bus and ended up in rural Thamesmead nine miles away while Damon collapsed on Euston Station and spent a night in Holborn Police Station, waking to find he was sharing his tiny cramped cell with a Nepalese Gurkha.

Now 21, Albarn was becoming ever more assured as a song-writer. Moreover, his work was becoming not just more confident and original but more in tune with the times, albeit in an oblique way thanks to his curious nexus of influences which by now included 2-Tone, Kurt Weill, Vaughan Williams, The Cardiacs (of whom more later) and the best of the current crop of indie bands such as The Pixies, My Bloody Valentine and The Stone Roses. The former two exemplified a style of sensual anarchy that was to ensnare Graham Coxon and prove highly influential. But the latter were the ones with the most commercial clout.

As the 80s ended, The Stone Roses dominated British pop, or at the very least, its independent sector. In May, their debut album had charted at Number 32 but was to rechart five times during the next year, their annus mirabilis. In November, they had thrown a cel-ebrated tantrum when exasperated by technical difficulties on an appearance on BBC2's *The Late Show*. Christmas '89 had brought 'Fool's Gold', whose insidious council estate funk and swaggering éclat made it the single of its era. In spring 1990, their Spike Island appearance in Widnes was the Woodstock of the Madchester generation, Madchester being the name given to the explosion of insalubrious but vibrant talent from Manchester. Cool in the early months of the new decade fundamentally meant The Stone Roses, a notion not lost on the future Blur members, though it would be a while yet before the influence would become readily apparent.

In the meantime, though, Damon's accelerated musical development meant inevitable changes within Circus. In later testaments, Eddie Deedigan has put his departure from the band down to an alienation from the group's new direction: 'One day we went from being a melodic pop band to Dinosaur Jr with swathes of guitar over everything . . . It was a very sudden change. It wasn't for me . . . and I had to go.'

But everyone, it seems, remembers it differently.

DAMON ALBARN: Dave sacked everybody. He has his moments, you know.

ALEX JAMES: Dave sacked Eddie Deedigan and his mate. Once or twice a year he'll do something like that with a tour manager or something.

GRAHAM COXON: Dave instigated some sackings. That may not seem like him but he can be quite ruthless. He's not scared to let people know how he feels. He said he didn't like one of Eddie's songs, insulted it in a way, and Eddie said, 'Well, I'm off, then,' and Eddie's mate Dave said, 'I'm only really here to do Eddie's stuff so I'm off too.'

DAVE ROWNTREE: There were two main songwriters in the one group. Eddie and Damon were both songwriters and it got to the point, as it does in every band, that you have to make a decision. I made it clear that Damon was the songwriter as far as I was concerned and that it was Damon's option I was going for. So Eddie left. It's always me who does these things. I wouldn't say that I sacked little Dave but I think I changed his terms of reference in a way that made his position untenable.

So, Circus shrank overnight to the bijou trio of Albarn, Coxon and Rowntree, who were now in need of a bass player. There was, of course, an obvious candidate, provided that certain creases in the social fabric could be ironed out. As Graham saw it, 'I didn't think Alex really liked Damon. They both had that aloofness, that arrogance. They'd got off on a bad foot because they'd both tried to bully each other simultaneously.'

'We all thought Alex was a bit of a wanker,' muses Dave, 'and knew he wasn't a great bass player but he was good-looking and had great attitude. You have to weigh it up: he's a wanker who can't play . . . but he's good-looking with attitude. And after all, it was only pop music. This was everyone's attitude . . . to some extent Alex as well. He came to it a bit like I did in that he thought the music was shit initially but we had a recording studio. What a bunch of fucking mercenaries, eh?'

Much has been made of Alex's supposed technical limitations and it's important to get this in perspective. Even at this stage, he would have fitted comfortably into most pop groups where a bassist is little more than a human metronome. Dave points out that, 'He was OK, just not technically the best. I mean, the other three of us had been playing since we were kids. He'd only been playing since his teens and had only started to get girls, really. That made him very unpopular for a few years until he did get his act together. We were always waiting for Alex to learn stuff. This band has a long history of someone being the outsider for a while. It still happens now to all of us, maybe Damon the least. Alex always turned it round so when in interviews we'd be dismissing him as a non-musician, he'd say, "I'm here to wear the clothes and get the money," which got him lots of brownie points. He's always been the press meister really. It may have been slightly daunting but he's so full of himself and he had a very musical ear and came up with very good parts. He could think music better than he could play it. And now that he can play it as well he's one of the best bass players in the world.'

Alex is characteristically forthright on the subject. 'Paul McCartney tried hard to learn to read music and gave it up when he realised that he was struggling with lessons and "The Saints Go Marching In" when he'd written "Eleanor Rigby". You don't have to have the best vocabulary to write a good story. Music is spoken. It doesn't exist on paper. I wasn't daunted about the fact that they all came from classical sheet music school because I had the best haircut. And they were shit before I joined them.'

And join them he did. In the hall of residence rooms over a few slices of what they had christened Poor Pizza – essentially toast covered with tomato puree and cheese then lightly grilled, if you're following this at home – Graham Coxon asked Alex James to join Circus. 'I think I said, "Do you want to be in a band that's going places?" or something like that.'

Alex had some misgivings. Damon Albarn, he thought, was something of 'a drama school wanker'. Dave, the spiky-haired peace punk, he knew little of beyond the fact that he was 'this ginger cunt with a Mohican who drove a brown car, worked for the council and drank ridiculously', adding that, 'Dave was the scapegoat for quite a while. We were horrible to him but really he's very rock and roll and now I'm very close to him.' Graham he knew and liked. So, all things considered, his decision was a simple one. 'And besides, they had this recording studio. That wasn't something you could turn your nose up at.'

The Waltons it wasn't. But in this tetchy, mercenary stew of mutual suspicion, something rather special was born: a mewling and puking infant that was to mewl and puke its way into the popular consciousness. Like all babies, it needed a name.

3 Seymour

NDOUBTEDLY, THE MOST FAMOUS creation of the reclusive American writer JD Salinger is Holden Caulfield Jr, the sensitive, disturbed, rebellious adolescent hero of *The Catcher in the Rye*. Salinger's considerable reputation and his status as enigmatic guru rest upon a tiny corpus of work – one novel and thirteen short stories – all written between 1948 and 1959 since when there has been perhaps the loudest silence in modern letters. *The Catcher in the Rye* is Salinger's masterpiece, certainly as far as the wider reading public goes, but devotees of Salinger would argue that his short stories, such as 'A Perfect Day for Bananafish', 'Franny and Zooey' and 'Raise High the Roof Beam, Carpenters', are just as poignant in their evocation of a profound yet gentle despair at the superficiality of the adult world.

Each of these stories concerns one Seymour Glass, a troubled misfit World War 2 veteran who attempts to find enlightenment in Buddhism, the company of children and marriage, but eventually commits suicide, unable to reconcile his haunted, questing nature with the phoniness and materialism of 50s America.

Like Hesse and Tolkien before him (and less happily, Irvine Welsh after him), Salinger's works have exerted a powerful hold over successive waves of bright young people. The members of what had been Circus – now slimmed down to a quartet – were no exception. And so, at the suggestion of their friend Paul Hodgson, it was decided to look to Salinger for a name for their new venture. Thus, they became Seymour (after a mercifully brief stint as The Beads) – a very different proposition from the fundamentally conventional pop-rock of Circus. In some ways Seymour was a misnomer. Salinger's ex-soldier was quietly despairing, while Seymour the group were anarchic, chaotic and bloody noisy, as the lower reaches of London's gig circuit were soon to experience.

Alex remembers that the first rehearsal with himself, Damon, Dave and Graham took place on the day before Goldsmiths' winter term of 1989 ended and the college broke up for the Christmas vacation. 'We went to the Beat Factory and we did "She's So High" all together that first time. Ridiculous, really. It came together from some chords that I'd written and some words that Graham had written for the verse. It was the day before the Christmas hols and I went home for Christmas thinking I'm in the best band in the world. Sorted.' So by consulting Goldsmiths archives, we can establish fairly certainly that the first convening of Seymour and therefore, to all intents and purposes, the inauguration of Blur occurred on 18 December 1988. Early signs were auspicious.

'Alex joined,' Damon states, 'and everything changed gear. There was instantly the right chemistry between the four of us. It felt like a real band with a real sense of purpose although wrapped up in all this mad arty stuff.'

Alex was flushed with enthusiasm for the project. 'I was in a band with the coolest person from college and we had access to a studio. We could fuck about whenever we wanted, play music, get stoned. It was all I'd ever wanted.'

Songs were amassed quickly. Remarkably, as we've heard, the very first thing that the four essayed together was 'She's So High' arising, as Graham puts it, 'from this huge long jam that I've probably still got on a tape somewhere'. Other selections came together quickly. During the Christmas break, Damon wrote 'Sing', which was to become probably Blur's greatest achievement of their early period. Years later, it would feature on the *Trainspotting* soundtrack. 'That was the first time, playing as a band, that I thought we really had something.' Graham also remembers that at Seymour's earliest gigs, 'Even people who hated us would come rushing up and say, "What was that song?"' 'Long Legged', 'Fried', 'Dizzy', 'Mixed Up', 'Tell Me Tell Me' and 'Shimmer' all date from this first period of Seymour activity and reflect the curious primordial musical soup that the group were emerging from – everything from Handel's 'Messiah' to The Wedding Present.

'We were quite bizarre really,' Graham reflects now. 'I think we were trying to make scary music at the time with tracks like "Dizzy". I was listening to Dinosaur Jr and The Pastels and I was mad on The Pixies. *Surfer Rosa* was the album for me at the time. I was quite into James from Colchester days, when I'd liked "Hymn From

A Village". Alex was very into New Order and Prince and Damon was off on a Carl Orff kind of thing and this oompah oompah Kurt Weill stuff.'

A small but significant strain in Seymour's music was also traceable to Surrey eccentrics The Cardiacs. Formed in the late 70s and led by guitarist, vocalist and songwriter Tim Smith, The Cardiacs were, by the late 80s, a genuine oddity in the indie scene. They inspired almost complete loathing and malice from music journalists but obsessive devotion from a small dedicated cult which to an extent included Albarn and Coxon. *The Rough Guide to Rock Music* provides a neat precis of their unfathomable style: 'An acceptable dash of prog-rock, a hint of speed metal, some Edwardian-tinged psychedelia . . . [and] a nod towards the Sex Pistols, King Crimson and XTC.' While not as insanely splendid as this sounds, they nevertheless deserved better than the fatuous response they got from the weekly music press guardians of rock credibility – something Blur have never given a fig for. Many years later, at Blur's celebratory Mile End gig, The Cardiacs were invited on to the bill as an acknowledgement of Blur's long-standing admiration for them and a cheery two fingers to fashion. Anyone minded to explore The Cardiacs for themselves is pointed to *A Little Man and a House and a Whole Wide Window* or *Heaven Born and Ever Bright*.

One thing Damon had taken from his abortive drama course was an enthusiasm for a concept known as the 'theatre of cruelty'. The idea, developed in the 30s by the French dramatist Antonin Artaud, became fashionable again in the 60s in England and remains a prime influence on experimental directors. It was in essence anti-literary and anti-civilisation which, according to Artaud, repressed and inhibited us. Artaud's vision was one where drama would force us to confront the extremes of human feeling – madness, violence, perversion – via shock tactics on stage such as sensational effects, chanting, screaming, giant puppets, spectacular lighting and the like. In this way we could get in touch with primal emotions and our true uninhibited selves. Whether this was possible or desirable third on the bill at the Bull and Gate in Kentish Town on a rainy Tuesday in front of twenty indie kids was far from certain, but it was Damon's intention to give it a go with the infant Seymour. As he puts it, 'We were an art band, very much so. And it's come back again now into our music which is great. We are what Seymour would have evolved into.'

DAVE ROWNTREE: We knew how we wanted it to feel but we had no idea how to achieve that state, no concept of how to make it work, so the nearest we could get for a long time was to turn everything up, play really fast and mad with stupid chord changes and tons of shouting and lots of bashing things. It got us a great deal of attention. We'd bash something once too often and it would break. Remember that this was around the time of the Manchester explosion and it was very different from the norm. Everyone was pretending to be the Happy Mondays and we were doing this weird incomprehensible thing. We always gave the impression that we knew what we were doing though. Damon would talk about the theatre of cruelty and it sounded like we had some theoretical basis for all this craziness.

Seymour's first actual gig in the sense of public performance (some sources suggest it was actually performed under dire monicker The Beads) was at Chapel Viaduct Station some five miles outside Colchester. In front of an audience of about 100, who sat in a Tube carriage, the band played a short set which began with 'Long Legged'. Alex remembers the event as an Albarn family celebration. 'Our first gig was Damon's dad's 50th birthday. Also, his sister was eighteen and he was 21 so the Albarns threw a big party. We went and played for the grannies. Graham's friend Adam Peacock actually filmed it and I've still got it somewhere. Damon's got this spiky hair and looks like someone from Stump and we used Damon's dad's old strobe light from the 60s. But that doesn't really count, I suppose. The first proper gig is the degree show at Goldsmiths at the end of our first year.'

This well-documented performance in the early summer of 1989 was to celebrate the final-year shows of the third year – this included Graham's friends Adam Peacock, Peter and, of course, Damien Hirst, who afterwards declared to Alex and Graham that they were the best group since The Beatles. Among the audience were such later notables of the YBA (Young British Artists quasi-movement) as Sarah Lucas, Michael Landy and Angela Bulloch.

DAMON ALBARN: It was always a real advantage that Graham and Alex were well known at Goldsmiths and my sister was at Hornsea Art College so we became a focus for the students there – the cool ones, anyway. Our early gigs were automatically parties.

Seymour never gigged extensively – allegedly as few as ten in their whole career, it seems – but they soon fell into an enjoyable and productive regime of sporadic gigs and lengthy nocturnal sessions at the Beat Factory interspersed with college studies, computer work for Colchester Council and bartending at the Portobello Hotel.

ALEX JAMES: Damon would be telling us that Ian McCulloch was in last night or Tina Turner so he's staying up all night being offered cocaine and slammers with the rock aristocracy of the time. It was good practice for celebrity although his parents were no strangers to it. Damon's dad once did this art show and Princess Margaret came and he said to her, 'All right, love,' and got a real dressing down. Good mush, Damon's dad. Nothing like Damon. And at weekends if we couldn't get the Beat Factory and needed to rehearse for a party or a gig we'd play in Damon's mum and dad's. Rugs on the walls, oak tables; an artist's house. Damon called them Keith and Hazel – very right-on and hip. We'd go up there and his mum would make lovely food and Graham and I would share his sister's four-poster bed. My mum and dad thought it was great what I was doing but didn't want me to expect anything to happen because no one in their ken had ever been in a newspaper. As soon as we got in the *Guardian* and the newspapers that their posh friends read they were, 'Wow!' I'm not dissing them at all; they were very encouraging. But Damon's dad had managed bands, his mum had been in theatre, so they knew it wasn't a pipe dream, whereas my parents came from working-class backgrounds and were less sure.

During the summer vacation of 1989, Adam Peacock moved into a squat adjacent to Goldsmiths on New Cross Road, opposite rock club The Venue. When it was found that the whole block was empty, it filled with Goldsmiths students, and Alex and Justine took the ground-floor flat of a building that became the focus of a culture of squalid bohemianism. 'Magic mushrooms and druggy reprobates round all the time. We had no money. Horrible. Eventually the whole house was real *Withnail and I.* Justine moved up and we took the bottom flat with this disgusting little garden full of slugs. Justine didn't know what to do, she was pulling her hair out surrounded by these lunatics doing mushrooms and hot knives. Tennents Super for breakfast, hot knives for lunch and mushrooms for supper, and the odd gig at Dingwalls. Graham and I would walk to Euston from New Cross, we were so skint.'

Meanwhile, Seymour continued to gig in a leisurely fashion. 'George Robey all dayers and the like,' says Graham, referring to a popular, low-key indie haunt of the time. 'Damon used to tell us we had a gig and then we'd get there and we'd realise we weren't actually on the bill and by then we'd carried all our stuff in so we'd force ourselves on to the bill that way. We used to drive around in Dave's Montego estate; all of us and all the gear.'

Seymour's gigs were clearly events and to understand this we need to see them in the pop context of the day. The 80s as a decade is still loosely defined by Martin Fry's lamé suits, Phil Oakey's fringe, Duran Duran's bandannas and Boy George's cosy transvestism. There flourished a knowingly superficial camp glamour, a thought-through artistic response that twisted the rampant materialism of the era – the 'Greed Is Good' mantra of Gordon Gecko – and both celebrated and parodied it in a pastiche of affluence and style. At least, the smarter groups did this: Tony Hadley was clearly just a berk who liked wearing tablecloths.

But by the end of the decade, ideas were at a premium. A random dip into the charts for summer 1989 finds the upper echelons dominated by Kylie, Jason, Jive Bunny and bubbly Scouse epiphenomenological curiosity Sonia. No worse than the state of play at the time of writing – Robbie Williams, All Saints and a slew of interchangeable pectorally enhanced boy bands – but hardly the barometer of a musical scene flushed with creativity, at least from the group's angle. True, dance music was in the ascendant and Black Box's 'Ride On Time' was one of the summer's big records, but if your tastes lay towards rock – what we would have called underground music in the 60s and 70s and alternative or indie now – then the characteristic mood was one of torpor. Madchester had created a hegemony of sorts and no one could doubt the visceral greatness of the early Stone Roses and Happy Mondays, but even then the nascent stars of this scene celebrated ordinariness. The fashions were those of the terrace and the council estate; a virtue was made of the proximity to 'the street' and of a lack of airs and graces beyond pugnacious self-belief. Bands aspired to a state of downbeat insolence and apathetic cool.

Something of this was to surface in the early Blur, not least in Albarn's contrivedly anodyne and disengaged lyrics. By contrast, Seymour, at least in their live performances, were men committed if not entirely to the 'theatre of cruelty' then at least to a kind of orgiastic, therapeutic slapstick.

ALEX JAMES: We used to get as drunk and stoned as we could, pour wine all over ourselves, then go out and see what we could do. It was all about being as uninhibited as possible, saying, 'Look at me! We are out there and we are HAVING IT!' We'd make ourselves feel as pumped up as possible, like Henry Rollins does with his natural drugs. Get as ridiculous as possible and be brilliant and loud and energetic. Be something very . . . purple.

GRAHAM COXON: We had melodic things, songs like 'She's So High' and 'Repetition', but sometimes we wouldn't get beyond the third song. Damon was into this theatre of cruelty thing and he'd jump on Alex's shoulders and come giraffing over to where I was and everything would get destroyed so we didn't play for very long. At the Borderline we did three songs and couldn't carry on. We thought we were really exciting and the reviews were quite nice and we got asked back to places. The Borderline had us again supporting Five Thirty. I'd like to have seen us. We might have been awful. The in-house sound men would hate us and want us to turn down. I'd think, What does this guy in a pony-tail and tight black jeans know? We'd also get pretty drunk; a few ales and a few bottles of wine. And we could deal with it then. We were very skinny and ultra-energetic then. It's different now. We're more conscious of our own mortality now.

The most celebrated Seymour appearance of the time was their first London outing, supporting Mancunians Too Much Texas (of whom nothing is remembered now but that singer Tom Hingley went on to sing for the Inspiral Carpets) and New Fast Automatic Daffodils at London Dingwalls. For reasons that aren't fully understandable – the minor cachet of New FADS or a sticker and graffiti campaign by Seymour – the gig was spectacularly well attended by a host of industry insiders, journalists and the like. At least one major opinion former could not gain admittance, but more of this luckless soul anon. As for the gig itself, it went off in typically eventful Seymour fashion. As was often the case, their set ended prematurely in a drunken shambles. Adam Peacock, refreshed and taken by the mood, began to act 'boisterously', recalls Alex. 'I remember him drinking a bottle of neat pernod and saying to the singer of Too Much Texas, "You've got a tasty little packet", and then grabbing his balls.' After this assault on, presumably, Tom Hingley, Adam dropped his trousers and began waving his genitals around indiscriminately. Security staff panicked and a bouncer sprayed the band with Mace, the anti-personnel tear gas derivative. Blinded and in agony, the band accidentally flagged down a police car in the street. Later, in casualty, an old lady berated them for drinking vodka in the waiting area. Much later, the evening's events formed the basis of 'Mace', the B-side of "Popscene".

Among the crowd that night, though, had been the Irish rock journalist Leo Finlay, who wrote a glowing notice for the group in the trade paper *Music Week*. Obviously dictated over the telephone, the group were unfortunately mistakenly billed as Feymour. A mistake somehow in keeping with the band's unconventional approach, what mattered was that they had received their first press – a rave, at that – from an established music publication. 'This unsigned and unheard of Colchester band played a blinder which swiftly endeared them to the Dingwalls' disaffected. There could well be a gap in the goofy market and Feymour have the charm to fill it.' Finlay's review was the beginning of a close friendship between him and the band – they once asked him to manage them, to which he replied curtly and sensibly, 'Fuck off' – that lasted until his tragic untimely death in 1997.

Mid-1989 then, and the mood was contented, as Alex recalls: 'I thought we were Talking Heads. It was great. That twelve months or so was spent going to the Beat Factory whenever it was empty and watching *The Blues Brothers* and eating all the food in the fridge. It was great, being at college and going to the studio most nights, making art and sonic terrorism – there must be miles and miles of tape of us going as mad as we can – and playing these mad gigs.'

Good word of mouth and snippets such as the above meant that what the music biz would call a 'buzz' began to circulate about Seymour. As mentioned, one minor industry mover and shaker hadn't managed to get into the Dingwalls gig but was sufficiently interested in the group to persevere and track them down at their next engagement. But to get to the roots of this story, we need to employ the Vaseline fade beloved of the 1940s film director and come up again on the dark, rainy streets of Liverpool. And note that the fluttering calendar pages read 1978.

*

Undoubtedly, if punk rock had a single, distinctive voice it was the over-enunciated and withering drawl of Johnny Rotten or the pedagogic, phlegm-inflected battle cries of Strummer. But if punk was born within earshot of the Bow Bells, the north worked the really cool variations on the basic simplistic template of yobbish bravado. In Manchester, The Buzzcocks, Joy Division and The Fall gave punk an intellectual gloss and made the really lasting music. Similarly in Sheffield and Liverpool, where gaunt young men in demob jackets and long overcoats were soon artistically outstripping the taproom antics of Eater and Gene October.

David Balfe was one of the first Liverpudlians to embrace the new cultural ferment. A band called Big In Japan, named after their one decent song, were one of the town's main punk attractions and central to the group's appeal was visually striking front person Jayne Casey. Other members included such future luminaries as Bill Drummond (later of The KLF), Ian Broudie (of The Lightning Seeds) and Holly Johnson (of Frankie Goes To Hollywood). Johnson, a camp punk elf, fitted the group's ethos but was never going to challenge Jaco Pastorius as a bass virtuoso. Thus, in 1978, he was sacked and replaced by Dave Balfe. By now, the primitive tenets of punk looked increasingly laughable, though, and a new breed of Liverpool 'face' as exemplified by Pete Burns, Pete Wylie, Ian McCulloch and Julian Cope (a Midlander who'd located to Liverpool on a teacher training course) were in the ascendant. Cheekily, such musicians, in their various early incarnations as Nova Mob, Mystery Girls and Crucial Three, once petitioned (literally) Big In Japan to split up but failed to secure enough signatures. Out of this incestuous reservoir of talent and braggadocio emerged The Teardrop Explodes, Echo And The Bunnymen, Wah Heat and many others. Interested parties may like to know that the whole 'scene' is recalled in two lively memoirs of the period: Holly Johnson's *A Bone in My Flute* and Julian Cope's splendid *Head On*.

On the dissolution of Big In Japan, the twenty-year-old Balfe and the ever entrepreneurial Drummond set up their own label, Zoo, to reflect Liverpool's post-punk fecundity around Eric's night-club. They produced and managed the two standard-bearing bands of the city, Echo And The Bunnymen and The Teardrop Explodes. In June 1979, four months after the release of their acclaimed *Sleeping Gas* EP, organist Paul Simpson left The Teardrop Explodes to continue his studies – promoting a minor crisis in the band.

> **DAVE BALFE:** Bill and I had Zoo and were producing and managing the Bunnymen and The Teardrop Explodes. The Teardrops were starting to get their name known and then the keyboard player left and I filled in for what was supposed to be four gigs and turned into four years on and off. Then in '82 or '83 they split up in a lot of acrimony. Bill and Julian had fallen right out.

Anyone disputing this last statement is advised to listen to the track 'Julian Cope Is Dead' ('I shot him in the head . . .') from Drummond's solo album *The Man*. The Teardrops' life was a colourful odyssey through the outer reaches of pop, but they are remembered fondly. *Melody Maker* once said of the group: 'Had they not been composed of three or more certified screwball psychopaths, they might have been bigger than The Beatles.' Hyperbole aside, there's a grain of truth in this. A seemingly glittering career had foundered in a sea of drug-induced madness, lunatic self-indulgence and seething personal hostility. This is worth bearing in mind in view of Balfe's dealings with the beleaguered Blur of the early 90s.

Just prior to expiring conclusively, the moribund Teardrop Explodes had been a duo comprising Balfe and Cope and briefly managed by concert promoter Paul King (not the singing policeman and MTV VJ). Balfe and King had become good friends and in the wake of the Teardrops' demise, they entered into a business arrangement.

> **DAVE BALFE:** I said, 'Give me the use of a desk, a phone and a secretary and I'll start managing people again and give you 50 per cent.' So we formed Balfe–King management. We managed a couple of bands, including Strawberry Switchblade, the one-hit wonders. Then I said I wanted to do a label on the same basis: 'I'll pay for everything but I'll give you half for the use of office.' I had zilch money but enough to find bands, make singles, get a vibe going then sign them to a major and recoup the money – which is basically what we'd done with Teardrops and Bunnymen. So I put out records by The Woodentops and Brilliant. And that's how Food was formed.

Another of Food's early acquisitions was cartoon rock god Zodiac Mindwarp. Balfe had heard the buzz about him but couldn't secure a tape. 'Eventually I bumped into him on the 38 bus and he himself gave me a cassette. He didn't even have a guitar at this point. So I fixed him up with a guitar and we put together a band and put out these singles 'High Priest Of Love' and 'Wild Child'. Around this point I got Andy Ross involved.'

Ross had been involved in music since his college days in the late 70s, when he had formed a band called The Disco Zombies with Dave Henderson, now a publishing magnate with the EMAP Metro group. They released a clutch of home-made singles, championed by John Peel, and one of them, 'Drums Over London', is worth twenty quid today should you have one mouldering in the attic.

At the time that he came into David Balfe's orbit, Ross was working in a London tax office and freelancing for the now defunct *Sounds*. During the last days of the Teardrop Explodes, Balfe had bought a house in the Buckinghamshire countryside. 'About as far out of London as you could get without actually being in Cheshire. Very impractical for a bachelor with most of his activities in London.' Balfe began a relationship with a woman who had previously been living with Ross – indeed, they still shared a flat platonically while Ross was looking for somewhere else – and it was in this way that the two became friendly

DAVE BALFE: I didn't have a big network of friends in London because I'd grown up in Liverpool. In London I wasn't clocked in to what was going on whereas Andy knew journalists and people in the business. I said, 'Look, I can't afford to pay you anything but I'll give you 25 per cent of the company if you come and work with me on A&R.' He'd come to me with a demo or a new act and I'd go, 'Yeeuch' normally, but I did sign Voice Of The Beehive on his recommendation.

It soon became apparent that Food would need a serious and substantial cash injection if it was to become any kind of player. 'I'd put the odd bit of money in but I was by no means a rich man,' explains Balfe. 'But then I sold this house in Buckinghamshire at the height of the 80s' property madness and made about ten grand profit. I was making a bit here and there. Over two years I put in about thirteen grand. At that point the record company arm was a bit of a loss leader for the management business. I bought another house and got a nice bit of equity on that and took a twenty grand overdraft at the bank.'

The initial plan for Food was to find a couple of bands, sign them and then do some kind of label deal. The general idea, according to Andy Ross, 'was to concentrate on making a few acts successful –

we've never done it the Alan McGee way.' Balfe was fairly optimistic, since the last two bands he'd signed had both provoked a bidding war. A fixture of music business life, the bidding war has a self-perpetuating logic and energy. The potential of such groups is often negligible. It matters not. 'Anyway, we thought let's start to do this properly – find bands and get four or five album deals. So with this in mind we found Crazyhead and Diesel Park West.' Assiduous followers of the British music scene and press may remember these two groups. The former were a ragged and greasy though infectiously enjoyable outfit from Leicester, resplendent in names such as Kev Reverb and the Porkbeast, and the latter were a craftsmanlike pop-rock outfit in the Crowded House mould. Neither were to achieve much although Food succeeded at the time in whipping up minor interest in both.

> **DAVE BALFE:** Crazyhead were part of this so-called grebo movement and they were a fantastic garage-rock band. If it had been two years later and Guns 'n' Roses were around, it might have happened. Diesel Park West were always going to be a major label band – they were this Byrdsy, Stonesy, U2 style group, although to the ungenerous ear, they were quality pub rock. But we were getting indie Number 1s with Crazyhead and most majors were interested in us. At this point, we were still operating out of Paul King's office. Meanwhile he'd picked up Level 42 and Tears For Fears and he'd got this massive office building near Cambridge Circus by The Ivy. At some point, though, his fortunes started to decline and he decided to amalgamate his interests. He was happy to carry on but he wanted to kind of swallow us and we didn't want that. Luckily, he said that to us at just the right juncture. He said, 'If you want to go, fine.' So we went and took the fledgling Food: Zodiac and Beehive and Crazyhead and Diesel Park West.

Only one major label offered Food the kind of deal they wanted: 100 per cent ownership and therefore complete financial support coupled with autonomy for the smaller label. That label was EMI. 'At that time they had a very successful top end with Queen, Pink Floyd and the Pet Shop Boys but they had no street-level vibe at all so they needed us too. It was a perfect hand in glove fit.' The complexities of the financial deal are frankly too dull to recount in full here – suffice to say that Food became an entirely owned subsidiary of the Parlophone label division of EMI. 'And it all worked out. It didn't work too well with Diesel and Crazyhead but the next two along were Jesus Jones and Blur.'

Ironically, in view of future events, it was Jesus Jones and not Blur who were viewed as Food's obvious potential superstars. If Jesus Jones are now a footnote in British pop, it is a significant footnote. Arguably, their cocky merger of techno-styled beats and rhythms with Madchester stylings and student chic was to influence the whole tenor of British indie music of the period. They convened in the Wiltshire town of Bradford-upon-Avon in 1986 and while nominally always a group they became, increasingly, a vehicle for the talents of leader Mike Edwards, a bright and charismatic self-publicist. They signed to Food in late 1988, some six months into the label's deal with EMI, and Balfe has a vivid recollection of his first contact with them. 'It was a classic A&R moment. I was just going off to lunch and Andy came in with this early demo of 'Info-Freako' which he stuck on and before they got to the end of the first chorus I said, "We have to sign this group." It got to 42 which was quite a big deal then for an indie group and it got them a lot of attention. Then the first album did about 100,000 worldwide which, if not a great deal, certainly made them contenders. We were all very excited.'

Singles like the influential 'Info-Freako', 'Real Real Real' and 'Right Here Right Now' and the album *Liquidizer* were critical and commercial successes and pointed, seemingly, to a stellar career, particularly in the US where 'Right Here Right Now' was to later become a gung-ho Gulf War anthem. For now, Jesus Jones are notable in Blur's history in that the initial success was to exert a distorting pull on the orbit of the nascent Blur since Balfe, in their eyes, seems to have regarded Jesus Jones as the template for any successful act of the period. This may be an exaggeration but certainly he was, at the onset, bullish about Jesus Jones' potential.

Back at the Beat Factory, things were also looking good for Seymour. Their very first rehearsal had produced a song called 'She's So High', which all were keen as mustard on. It remains the most democratic track they have ever recorded, in a manner never to be repeated. 'Alex came up with the chord sequence, I came up with the verse and its lyrics and Damon did the rest,' remembers Graham. 'She's So High' was the stand-out track of four included on an early demo which found its way on to the desk of Andy Ross. 'It arrived via Maryke Bergkamp who, along with Graham Holdaway, seemed to have some kind of management and production contract with Damon in some way. I thought parts of it were great. You could definitely hear something there.'

> **DAVE BALFE:** Andy got hold of a tape first and played it a few times. I quite liked it but wasn't bowled over. Reports sometimes say that Andy loved it and I was reluctant. Well, it wasn't quite like that. Andy wasn't unreservedly mad for it. Plus you've got to see it in context. Once a month there was a band to consider signing and you don't always dive in like we did with Jesus Jones. So we started to watch Seymour play live but I don't know how interested we were. There was absolutely no interest from anywhere else.

Importantly, Damon's contract with Graham Holdaway and Maryke Bergkamp was about to expire. He didn't want to renew it and was hoping to find interest elsewhere.

> **DAMON ALBARN:** The funny contract I was under was about to elapse. We were rehearsing there at the Beat Factory still and it was a great set-up in some ways but I felt I had to move on. I didn't feel that bad about it because they were not and never would have been part of the world we needed to move in. It wasn't a good time and I felt a little ungrateful but I was very glad to be free of it. At that point I had to show my intent about what I wanted to do.

No longer attached to Holdaway and Bergkamp, Seymour continued to perform various under-attended gigs to tepid receptions from the industry, if not from fans. But Andy Ross was sufficiently interested in the curious Brechtian/My Bloody Valentine-inflected art outfit that by the infamous Dingwalls gig he decided to venture forth to see them and found himself left on the pavement.

> **ANDY ROSS:** I get cheesed off with them when they say I missed the gig at Dingwalls because I was pissed. I wasn't. It was eight in the evening of 13 November 1989. They were supporting the New Fast Automatic Daffodils. I was a friend of the manager so I was on her personal guest list but when I went straight up to the front of the queue the bouncer was having none of it. 'What makes you think you're so special?' and all that. There was obviously some mix-up with the guest lists, maybe because New FADS were quite a big deal at this point. So consequently I missed the gig. Not an auspicious start. So I guess

the first outsider, as it were, to lay claim to discovering them was Leo Finlay.

GRAHAM COXON: I liked Creation as a label. I thought they were cool and everyone talked about them. I'd never heard of Food but then I wasn't big on labels or the business side of things at all. But Creation's A&R man really hated us. Damon went in with a tape and he couldn't bear it. Damon had talked to Food on the phone. He told me he'd been speaking to 'Andy Ross from Food records which is an indie label'. He was very concerned that I knew it was an indie. Then he felt he ought to tell me that it was run through EMI. But my attitude was, well, whatever. I wasn't that staunch. A deal's a deal. So Andy tried to come to Dingwalls but there was some confusion over the guest list and I think he was a bit drunk. But he got along to see us quite soon after that.

In fact, it was two weeks later when they played the Powerhaus in Islington, a regular haunt of indie acts, journos and the like. This time, Ross got in. He was intrigued by what he saw.

ANDY ROSS: I went with some American girl and she didn't get it at all but I thought they were great. They were shambolic, certainly. There was a lot of stupid jumping around of the kind that Damon has refined and honed over the years to an art. It was extremely frantic and a bit hippy-dippy weirdo but within it all some really good stuff. You could hear something in there. But it was art rock without a doubt. Big elements of The Cardiacs, who Graham's always been a big fan of and who ended up playing at Mile End. And of course there was Dave Rowntree and the famous pyjama trousers which were going to have to go, as well as some of this peripheral music. But what stood out was that they could all play. This was the turn of the decade. The era of Annie Lennox and Phil Collins was coming to an end but standards of musicianship in the indie sector were very low. They were obviously very solid musicians – Graham in particular is a phenomenal player – and great songwriters despite all this tomfoolery. To an extent it's my job to see through that and spot the talent.

Food's courting of Blur went from coy to passionate with unseemly haste and ardour. Ross's appetite was whetted by the Powerhaus gig but he was not yet convinced. He made two more trips to see them. One was at the Cricketers Arms at the Kennington Oval, Graham's first meeting with Andy Ross. 'Low ceiling and very hot. We were getting increasingly confident each time we played. I remember that gig because of meeting Andy and because this big rocker bloke offered to be our road manager and he said, "I'll drive you to Leeds for a bottle of Jack Daniels," which terrified us.' Ross also saw them at the Ladyowen Arms, Highbury and Islington, with Dave Balfe. Dave Rowntree recalls meeting the pair for the first time: 'Andy and Dave Balfe had been talking to Damon but the first time I met them was at this pub gig in Highbury. We were playing with The Keatons on some all-day thing with a whole bunch of bands. I think talks were quite advanced at this stage. Balfe went round us all individually and asked us what we were doing and did we want a record deal. We thought it was the end of a long road rather than the beginning of a rather longer road.'

Andy Ross explains that, 'I was very much the junior partner in Food and had to convince Balfie. So we saw Seymour at the Ladyowen Arms, which doesn't even exist any more, and then at the Cricketers at the Oval. Dave took a bit of convincing. He likes things to be quite solid and corporate and these lot were definitively indie. Dave looked down on that a bit. I was more readily persuaded.'

One of the gigs that sticks in Alex's memory was at the Camden Falcon. Knowing that Food were going there to see them, they had 'papered the house' with their healthy college following. 'I'd never met record people before. We did this brilliant gig at the Falcon to this great crowd. Afterwards I found Balfe and asked him what he thought. He said, "You're Talking Heads meets The Cardiacs," which I assume was meant as criticism but went down all right with me. I was very enamoured with Balfe. I mean, come on, he played the "Ba Ba Ba Ba" intro to "Reward". And the first time he came down to the Beat Factory he did it and we all went "Fucking hell, that's so cool . . . Dave Balfe from The Teardrop Explodes," and then three months later he came again and went "Ba Ba Ba Ba". And this time, we were like, "You fucking sad cunt."'

DAVE BALFE: I thought we'd seen them half a dozen times if not more. Gigs with three or four people there who were pissed off there was a band on at all. That little place near the Angel. Absolute basic Wednesday night pub gigs. We used to define them as having two very different sides – a Cardiacs side and something more appropriate. That weird side would later emerge in many popular album tracks and B-sides; that disjointed semi-Brechtian thing. But it was stuff that Andy and I found discordant and anti-musical. I'm still not a massive fan of that side of Damon's musical personality. We kept on trying to prise that out of the set. But they had a lot going for them. Alex and Damon were very good-looking and they had the right hip attitude. They went mad onstage. Well, all except Alex, who has that strangely louche vibe that no one's been able to pull off like that since Brian Jones. But, to my horror, it still wasn't that far from shoe-gazing.

'Shoe-gazing' was a term coined by Andy Ross which had gained great currency in the press of the time. It described a style of ponderous, neo-psychedelic rock that was prevalent in the clubs of the capital, if not the provinces, who have always liked their pleasures a little more vital. According to your viewpoint, it was either an exciting new development – ambient soundscapes married to the dynamics of rock championed by writers such as *NME*'s Dele Fadele and *Melody Maker*'s Simon Reynolds, who would talk of 'sonic cathedrals' and 'blissing out' – or it was posh Home Counties kids who couldn't play but had expensive sustain pedals slumming it in their gap year. Slowdive, Chapterhouse, Swervedriver . . . the names mean nothing now but for a summer they held court on the covers of the indie press. To be honest, Seymour did have something of the shoe-gazers about them, chiefly in the loud, distorted guitar textures beloved of Graham and which he admired in My Bloody Valentine, majestic gurus of the shoe-gazer generation.

However, despite Balfe's misgivings and 'mild intransigence', he was eventually convinced of their worth, perhaps because by now other labels – notably Island – were showing an interest. 'We had loads of chats and I was teetering on the brink and eventually I thought, Oh, let's do it.' But there was a further, indeed final, stumbling block. Unimpressed by the erudition of the Salinger reference, Ross hated the name Seymour. A meeting was called at their usual rendezvous, Soho Pizzeria on Golden Square, south of Oxford Street. For ever after, Food's habit of taking them for pizzas was to fuel the band's half-joking accusation of meanness.

DAVE ROWNTREE: There were several items on the agenda. Andy said, 'Seymour's a pretty crap name, in our opinion. It makes you sound like an indie anorak band. A gay indie anorak band.' Then he stopped and looked around, horrified, and said, 'None of you are gay, are you?' That was when we realised it was going to be a laugh. I think we'd been a bit terrified up to that point of stepping into the unknown. Being an unsigned band is quite easy in some ways. There's no responsibilities. I don't think any of us knew what we were letting ourselves into. It was a world of people with job titles we didn't understand.

A whole list of alternative names were suggested including The Government and The Shining Path (the Sendero Luminoso Maoist guerrillas of Peru), both of which Graham rejected as 'too scary and Fascistic'. Sensitize and Whirlpool were similarly dismissed although Balfe and Ross must have been mighty pleased with these inventions since they foisted them on later Food signings.

ANDY ROSS: They didn't take kindly to it. No band likes being told to change their name because it suggests they weren't up to it in the first place. I'm pretty sure it was me that came up with Blur although I'm sure they'll say it was them. There were sheets of A4 full of names that we and they came up with and by process of elimination we arrived at Blur. It's a great name. It took the band forward but still reflected what they were up to. A bit arty but not obscure.

So what opinion of each other had these two parties arrived at over their grissini and mozzarella salads? The band remember distinctly an element of good cop, bad cop: Andy appeared more obviously matey while Balfe seemed more distant and, though not unfriendly, dominating. But, as Damon says, 'That might have just been that we were in awe of him. I'd been a huge Teardrop Explodes fan and now one of them was signing my group.' Dave remembers Ross giving them 'the spiel I've seen him give a million times since to other people'. Alex's memory is that, 'We were really rude to Andy and Balfe cos we were so confident of our greatness. We'd stayed up all night so many times with each other, we thought we were pop stars before we'd even played a gig. You have to have that belligerent self-belief even if unfounded.'

DAMON ALBARN: We knew that between the four of us we had something really strong. We knew that it was working. And now there was a feeling of our hour having come; that this is what we, certainly what I'd, been doing it for. And now we had Dave Balfe interested who picked up on my ambition and hunger. We were very excited about Balfe – The Teardrop Explodes and everything. It's pretty mind-blowing when you're nineteen. We all felt, Oh my God, it's all happening.

The Food directors had discerned both the group's cohesive culture and ethos – art, craziness, booze, vulnerability – and their clearly delineated personalities. 'They were all strong characters,' says Andy Ross. 'I mean, what do we know about Bonehead or the drummer in Oasis. But in Blur, well, Dave is into computers and then flying and is very down to earth and sorted, Alex is the bohemian, Graham is the coolest person in rock and Damon is the leader and the chief songwriter. The others aren't yes-men by any stretch of the imagination but Damon's always been the leader, always pointed them in a particular direction. That's as it should be. Total democracy in bands never works. There's a tendency to drift.'

Dave Balfe concurs with this assessment. 'It was pretty much like it is now. Damon was the leader, Graham the second lieutenant, Alex this louche, debauched bohemian and Dave the pragmatist. The big difference between then and now was that Dave was a big, big drinker, although not a painful drinker as Graham became later. But we dealt with them as a band because bands always want to be perceived as democratic, at least at the start. Later, they can't give a toss.'

It was time for the uncapping of pens and the popping of corks. Once the decision was taken to sign them, Dave Balfe was very keen. 'And at that point we were only signing a band a year so it was a big deal. The deal was we had to consult EMI but as long as things fell within a certain budgetary level, we didn't have to get their approval. I suppose we dragged someone down to see them. I seem to remember that we definitely wanted a seven-album deal because we were not expecting them to get away straight away. That wasn't a negotiating ploy, it was because they were kind of weird. As it turned out, "There's No Other Way" popped up before too long and sounded very now. But as was proved by subsequent releases, that was a bit of an anomaly. However, it's one of their strengths that no matter how experimental they get, a pop instinct comes through.'

The rechristened Blur signed to Food records in March 1990. Andy Ross remembers the initial advance being for £5,000 though Balfe puts it higher. Dave says it was 'definitely £7,000.' Whatever, it was certainly no king's ransom. 'We were certainly prepared to offer them more than £5,000 but in the end they signed because there'd been several months of bonding and they trusted us. They've sold enough records now that the advance becomes an irrelevance but it still rankles with them.' 'Rankles' may be an understatement. 'We got four grand or something up front for seven albums,' says Alex, disbelieving even at this remove. 'I wouldn't dream of signing a band to my label for that. Up until *Parklife* we were bunking the tube.'

DAVE ROWNTREE: I think it was one of the worst record deals in history as it turned out. Years later, we were renegotiating the deal at the time of George Michael's court case and that had fucked it for everybody or so it was thought. In a meeting with our lawyer, he was wringing his hands saying, 'Oh my God, why didn't he leave well alone? No band will ever be able to get out of their record contract ever again.' Pause. 'Except you, of course.' Ours was so bad that it would have been easy to extricate ourselves from. Typical. I don't know if they realise that to this day we could have taken the money and walked at any time. But it didn't do us any harm signing for a pittance, I guess. At the time it seemed an enormous sum. I remember holding the cheque in awe. Damon nearly got arrested when he tried to bank it. It said 'Pay Blur' and no one knew what to do. Damon said, 'I'll pay it into my bank account and we'll take it from there.' So he tried to bank it and they nearly called the police. They thought he'd nicked it. Luckily his auntie was an accountant and she said, 'No, you've got to open a bank account called "Blur".' She saw us straight for a while. None of us had a clue. We didn't keep accounts or anything . . . which was very prophetic, as it turned out.

Still in their second year at Goldsmiths, Alex and Graham naturally had to curtail their studies. Graham went to see Goldsmiths director John Smith. 'He said he'd seen it all before. "Take a year out and see how it goes then come back and finish off. Cheers and good luck and good on you." He was really nice. Goldsmiths were used to quite wacky people. Mum and Dad were really understanding. They were glad I'd gone back to music, I think. They dug it. Later, at my 21st birthday, we were playing at the Marquee and they came to see us and saw how exciting it was and they really liked Uncle Andy Ross. They were happy after that.'

To mark their signing it was thought appropriate that the group, with Balfe and Ross, should celebrate at the Portobello Hotel,

Damon's nocturnal workplace. The evening turned into a monumental session which ended in confusion and, for Graham, at least, near disaster. 'I ended up walking through Notting Hill without my jacket and got knocked down by a car. It was quite nasty. He came out of nowhere and then drove off. I was in hospital most of the night. The next day my face was all scarred and I was limping around and we had to meet at Food's offices in Piccadilly to do something. When I got there it was all, "What the fuck happened to you?" Everyone was laughing but very concerned.'

At some six hours, Graham Coxon had almost had the shortest career of any signed artist in the history of rock. It was a strangely appropriate way for Blur to commence their entry into the rock business.

4 The Poverty Jet Set

FTER CHAMBERLAIN'S FAMOUS SPEECH of 3 September 1939 (. . . and no such undertaking having been received, I have to tell you that this country is at war with Germany), many Britons thought there would be fireworks and air raids, beachhead landings and anti-aircraft fire immediately. When there weren't, they began to talk of the 'phoney war'. In an infinitely more trivial way, Blur too had their phoney war. Signed to Food in the March of 1990, it was nearly nine months before they released any material, an unusually long gestation for a pop band. Blur had, unsurprisingly, wanted to put something out forthwith but Ross convinced them it would do them more good to hone their craft to an even greater degree, particularly outside the capital, and thus consolidate the still untried line-up.

'Things happened quite slowly,' says Dave Rowntree, given that Blur had already attained the status of, as he puts it, 'One rung above absolute filth – we were playing two or three gigs a week, anyway.' A creeping sickness of the pragmatic/mercenary 90s was the "paid support". Far from being a gracious leg up to the struggling neophyte, it had become widespread (and still is) for support groups to have to buy their way on to tours and the like. It was a morale-sapping ignominy Blur managed to avoid. 'We never paid to play. We always came away with at least 50 quid. If there were three bands on the bill, we'd be second. You could say we had middle-ranking connections. Then we got an agent and things got a lot busier. We started to get supports to bands we'd actually heard of.'

The first of these – indeed, the first gig actually performed as Blur, according to Graham and Dave – was at the Brixton Academy ('a bit scary . . . big wooden stages after all those sticky carpets') supporting the boisterously undistinguished weekly music paper stalwarts Mega City Four and The Cramps, an 80s curio from America best described as *The Rocky Horror Show* with A levels.

'It was very scary,' remembers Dave. 'I think we had to go on stage before the doors opened. People were coming in going, "Is this the soundcheck?" and putting their coats in the cloakroom. By the time we'd finished, there was one row of people going, "Who are these idiots doing this indie rubbish? We want The Cramps." The Cramps' tour manager told us they were in a bad mood and said to stay out of their way. "Don't leave the dressing room, don't look at them and don't make any noise." We weren't allowed in catering. We spent the evening creeping around. I collected a sequin from Poison Ivy's see-through dress and stuck it on my laminate pass.'

Food had consciously elected not to release any material for several months, preferring instead to build up a 'vibe' around the group. Thus the group were gigging outside London by early 1990 and the first tiny flickerings of interest were illuminating the music press. In various early mentions of the band, we learn that Dave is 'the Dark Destroyer', Damon is 'a loud-mouthed funster' and Alex is 'dishy'. The first substantial attention given to the group was a compact live review of their January Manchester Boardwalk gig, printed in the student paper *Pulp*. Reviewer Simon Cole devotes half of the already bijou review to a detailed description of the lighting rig but also asserts, in splendidly unadorned prose, 'They're from Colchester, they're energetic and they're good! . . . The band seemed genuinely pleased to be there and, quite frankly, I think the singer was stoned.'

Under the small and prosaic heading 'New Food signings' tour dates', *Sounds* dated 14 April carried details of a handful of dates across London and a couple of exploratory ventures north of Watford: Dingwalls April 9, Manette Street Borderline Headspin Club April 10, Powerhaus April 21, Cambridge The Junction April 26, Dudley JBs April 27, Bull and Gate Kentish Town May 4.

In terms of their music, Blur were clearly a different proposition from the uncategorisable Seymour who were, according to Alex, 'The more radical, non-bite-sized, unfriendly face of Blur.' Damon further explained that 'Seymour were our obtuse side'. The first reviews from these early Blur gigs confirm that the group might have toned down some of the conceptual excesses of Seymour but the orgy of manic on-stage energy and convulsive dancing remained. Every one of their earliest reviews mentions the group's, and in particular Damon's, crazed gymnastics. They were noticeable enough anyway, but in the context of the accepted stage demeanour of the time – static pimply youths in black Levi's hiding behind immense fringes who played ambient dirges while nodding imperceptibly – they were bona fide nutcases. They would end each set with a demented, accelerating version of the punkish 'Day Upon Day', always threatening to end in explosive self-destruction. As Damon puts it, 'A lot of people came to see us just in case I killed myself.'

Sounds reported their 40-minute set at the Manette Street Borderline gig under the headline, 'The Madcap Grins and Jumps About', the paraphrase of the Syd Barrett album title picking up perceptively on a treasured influence. The review itself was enthusiastic. 'There's a new mind-bending substance on the scene that's fearsomely addictive . . . Blur.' Along the way, writer Nick Griffiths describes Alex's 'Emo Phillips fringe' and points out that 'Uncle Dave is a stately 25' – although he was actually an even more magisterial 27.

The band were throwing themselves into their art with abandon if not awareness. 'We knew nothing about equipment,' explains Graham, 'so we stuck to the same stuff. I was using amps that couldn't deal with what I wanted so that was frustrating and made me go even madder. Balfe would say, "Go and buy yourself a guitar," but I didn't know which I liked. I hadn't got a clue. It takes a long time to find out what you like. So I had this Aria Pro 2 which I broke at this mad night at the Bull and Gate.'

'The antics of their vocalist have to be seen to be believed,' said the *Melody Maker* of this particular outing, where Damon ripped his hand open and smeared blood around liberally. 'He's obviously been eating too much cheap beef,' chortles the reviewer before concluding sniffily and not entirely sensibly that the 'melodies are disappointingly easy to follow . . . and don't offer any sort of challenge'. Given that Blur at this stage would be devouring every printed mention of them, this must have been particularly galling to a group who prided themselves on their confrontational artistic intensity. Within the month Damon was explaining to *What's On* magazine that Artaud's 'theatre of cruelty' was a prime shaping influence. 'I like things to repulse people . . . to upset them and move them . . . I want to give them a crisis.' In a grandly daft rhetorical flourish he concluded, 'I don't have any records and I'm not interested in any other bands.' Bemused, the article compared them to

'Iggy Pop fronting The Monkees'. Blur's first response from rock's great and unforgiving readership was swift. A witty correspondent to the *NME* in early June took Damon to task for his espousal of the 'theatre of cruelty': 'At no point did Artaud ever say we could purge Western society of its repressive duality by playing crappy tinny psychedelic riffs for ages.'

The peace of the phoney war finally and completely collapsed in the early summer. It was the summer of Italia 90, of Pearce and Waddle's ineptitude and the nation's agony. Blur's first serious tour was scattered across the country's medium-sized venues throughout the month of June, beginning in Camden and the relatively familiar pastures of Bath and Oxford and then heading north to Sheffield, Newcastle, Walsall, Glasgow, Leicester, Manchester and on and on. A report of the Camden show in *Sounds* did neatly characterise Graham as 'a cross between Jim Reid and Hank Marvin' but declared, 'Whether they're any good or not is still a matter for debate.'

Consciously aloof reviews like that were a natural reaction to Blur's manifest cockiness. They were beginning to simmer nicely and kept the heat up with regular bolshy pronouncements in the press. They were going to be huge, they wouldn't release a record till they had been given the cover of a magazine and, in Damon's words, 'I've always known I'm incredibly special and if I didn't think we were the best band in the universe I wouldn't bother.' Of course, Blur were clever enough to know that this was mere bluster without the evidence of a record. As Tamla Motown's Berry Gordy had observed twenty years before, 'It's what's in the groove that counts', so while Blur would publicly express a cavalier disregard for procedure, in private they were itching to get into a studio. And so they did, even as Robson's worthy dolts were still marching proudly towards their German nemesis.

Even if you never play a note there, perhaps *especially* if you never play a note there, recording studios are curiously romantic places: huge, wonderful train sets for a particular kind of boy and girl. Sarm West, Sun, Kling Klang . . . names glamorous and exotic, but even in Britain we have some impressive examples. If studios were tourist attractions, AA guide books would award rosettes to the rowboat ride that is the only access to Cornwall's Sawmills, the band room at Monnow Valley with its glass wall overlooking the meadow and the glass-bottomed cubicle at Real World where the river swirls below the producer's feet.

Battery Studios in Willesden lacks this kind of Arthurian charm but to the Blur of 1990, experienced in only the friendly but bijou surrounds of the Beat Factory, it was a step up into a different world, not least because it was where The Stone Roses had recorded 'Fool's Gold' a year before. Stone Roses comparisons abounded during Blur's first year of existence, particularly after the success of 'There's No Other Way'. In truth, Blur's tastes generally ran to more esoteric stuff than the Mancunian quartet but, without a doubt, 'Fool's Gold' had been the record that had set the cultural tempo of the first year of the new decade. Partly because of the clothes – smock-like hooded tops and voluminous flared loons – and partly because of the musical style and typical demeanour – indolent, sloppy, casually unconcerned – it became known as 'baggy'. The cream were The Stone Roses, Happy Mondays and The Charlatans. Beneath were reservoirs of the blandly forgettable: Northside, My Jealous God, The Bridewell Taxis and scores of others now mercifully forgotten.

The Stone Roses had been around since 1984 but their unremarkable goth pop had consistently failed to ignite any real interest. By 1989, though, and the release of their startlingly good first album, they had found their voice and, more importantly, it had become recognised as the authentic voice of a new street-level movement – the meshing of spotty white student rock with the vibrant energy of Britain's revitalised club scene. Manchester became a nexus for both the rock heritage – boys with guitars, vaguely politicised and philosophical, white – and the new dance culture – multi-racial, druggy, hedonistic. 'Fool's Gold' embodied this in one tremendous artifact, a lengthy, loping rock-funk excursion worthy of Hendrix or Sly Stone, propelled by what was to become the most influential drum pattern of the next two years.

GRAHAM COXON: The Stone Roses were 'it' so there was a feeling that we'd arrived just because we were recording in the studio where they'd done 'Fool's Gold'. We'd done some early demos for Food whilst I was squatting in Camberwell – 'She's So High', 'Explain', 'Fool' – but they were crap, worryingly crap. But this time it was great being in a proper posh studio. There was a table tennis room and a huge live room where you could set up and play and you got your food cooked for you. And we were working with these two blokes who obviously knew what they were doing. We finished the recording and they said, 'Right, now we'll make it sound like a record.' And they did. It sounded like a real record, not a shitty demo.

'These two blokes' were in fact Steve Lovell and Steve Power, something of a rock curiosity in that they were a production duo. Balfe knew them from his Liverpool days, Lovell having worked on material with The Teardrop Explodes and Julian Cope – something which scored highly with Blur. (Power, incidentally, enjoyed huge success in 1998 with Robbie Williams.)

ALEX JAMES: From being this weird outsider art thing, we were suddenly in the thick of the mainstream and were suddenly something else, but it all felt very right. Success always fits; it never feels odd. We really felt stuff was starting to happen. But we had to learn how to make a record. Previously we'd done everything completely live or been bashing stuff out in these mad jams. Now it took two days to set the drums up and a day to do each bass track. A big posh studio has a lot of toys. A lot of distractions. Including the World Cup.

Progress was slow. The drum tracks took a week. Lovell and Power had serious doubts about Alex's ability and insisted on 'looping' the bass: recording short fragments which are then repeated as often as necessary. Eighteen-hour days were the norm. Nevertheless, two tracks stood out instantly – 'I Know' and 'She's So High' – and despite the practical difficulties, there was a very positive atmosphere around the young band. Just as they had predicted with the breezy arrogance of youth, they now found themselves emblazoned on the cover of a weekly newspaper, still without any recorded product to their name. Under the headline 'Young, Loud and Snotty' in the *Sounds* issue of 7 July 1990, their champion, Leo Finlay, again sang their praises, invoking The Who, The Kinks and The Beatles. Alex summed up the difference between Blur and Seymour thus: 'Seymour were just this great big esoteric thing ... The difference between Blur and Seymour is Blur are going to be hugely successful.' It's not unheard of for a band without any records on release to feature on a music paper cover. Frankie Goes To Hollywood had done it before them and Suede – ironically – would do it after. But it is a rarity. However, it is one we should see in perspective. As Dave Rowntree points out, 'Andy Ross did write for *Sounds* at the time so we can't really brag too much about that and Food also had Jesus Jones who were going really well, so we were sold a bit on the back of them.'

None the less, it was an indication of the band's growing reputation, and they became the first band to headline the 1,000-capacity University of London union without having released a record. That record, and much else, was to happen between now and the year's end. For one thing, they were to formalise their relations with two men who still loom large, in very different ways, in their history. Two Mikes, coincidentally: Smith and Collins.

Mike Smith is, or rather was, 'a good middle-class boy who did what his mum and dad wanted and went to college in Manchester to study history and politics instead of going to art school which is what I wanted'. He soon lost interest in his academic studies and, in the mid-1980s, left to gain a toehold in the cliff face of rock by going to work for Mancunian music entrepreneur Gareth Edwards, later the manager of The Stone Roses and at this point running the International and International 2 rock clubs. After a year or two of managing various unsuccessful bands, the young Smith went down to London, 'green as the hills', to further his ambition of becoming an A&R man, the much-maligned but hugely important industry position responsible for the scouting of new talent and handling song publishing, often the most lucrative part of a band's finances. He wangled himself a job in the post-room at MCA and was soon operating as a counterfeit A&R man, blagging into gigs with a fake pass he had knocked up and, as his confidence grew, actually organising meetings with bands and their managers in the post-room of the MCA building. 'It was all going very well until I brought in the Darling Buds [Welsh indie poppers, then much touted] who twigged that I was the post boy. They and their manager were extremely fucked off but it did get me a job as a talent scout for their publishing wing.'

Throughout 1988 and 1989, Smith strove to convince his bosses – fixated with dance music, as were many in the industry – that far from being defunct, there was creative life in the guitar sector. 'The penny dropped in early 1990 when The Stone Roses and The Charlatans began to have success. My bosses realised I knew all about this stuff. Everyone was very excited about Five Thirty [now forgotten indie hopefuls] and we tried to get involved. When I tried to sign Blur I got lots of support cos we were on the Five Thirty rebound. MCA felt it had to get one of these bands. I was very half-hearted about Five Thirty, I have to say. Blur was the first thing I got really passionate about.'

> **MIKE SMITH:** I wish I could say I saw them as Seymour in '89 but it was February 1990 when they'd just signed to Food. I saw an ad in Camden Record Exchange advertising 'Food's new signings at the Bull and Gate'. They had some kind of residency there on Fridays. I have a very strong memory of my first impression being that they were strikingly good-looking and were obviously punk rock but were going down this baggyish route that didn't seem to sit right with them. Damon was going completely berserk, climbing up the walls and ceiling, and I couldn't work out if it was genuine or contrived. There was incredible energy and Damon was undeniably a star. But I went away not really sure. So I went back the following Friday and this time the music was better and tellingly I remembered every single song. I got drawn into Graham's tricks, all the changing tones and stuff. They were still trying to challenge and freak the audience out with this fuck-off noise and it was obviously not contrived and the baggy thing was a complete irrelevance. They were very compelling onstage. Alex looked like someone of unfathomable sexuality from an Evelyn Waugh novel. Damon was really confrontational, hanging from the ceiling and dropping on to audience, getting really worked up, running behind the drum kit and throwing up. I thought it was great. I didn't know whether it was the sort of thing we should sign but I loved art-school punk rock and that was what it was. Andy Ross took everyone to a Spanish tapas bar after and I met them. Damon was very approachable and very curious about the business whereas Graham was quite introverted and even a little sullen. Alex and Dave were just so happy to be in a rock and roll band. They all seemed fearless and unfazed. They'd been signed for virtually no money at all but had such an excitement about this being their future. So different from some bands you meet today. Blur had this real lust for life.

At this stage, Blur were without management as such, although Food were getting them gigs and fielding press enquiries. Damon himself went to Smith's office to discuss the possibilities of a publishing deal. 'He was talking on a very strong intellectual level about the music and what he wanted to achieve. He was very keen on this "theatre of cruelty" idea and I genuinely thought he was fantastic after dealing with people who didn't know about anything beyond The Beatles. I liked the combination of intellectual theory and primal rock, which is what they made. And he was also very earnest and humble. I really liked them and wanted to spend as much time with them as possible. And I wanted to sign them.'

Spending time with the band at this stage meant tagging along with them on their summer jaunts around the country. With no management and no tour support as yet – financial backing for touring coming from the record company – transport facilities were ad hoc to say the least. Their friend Jason from the East End rehearsal studios The Premises would drive them to gigs in his VW van. Mike Smith remembers long drives to York and the like followed by longer drives back to London in the small hours with 'Dave slapping Jason at the wheel to keep him awake. A little later EMI gave them some tour support and they got the legendary Gimpo aboard as tour manager. Alex was always quite reserved initially but he was very, very stoned. He smoked joints all day, hiding behind this cloud of dope smoke. But they were all very charming. Dave was loving it and drinking a lot. They used to carry a fridge of acid on the bus and go off tripping on the Yorkshire moors and Gimpo would encourage this. Graham had all these tapes of Tallulah Gosh and My Bloody Valentine. And I can remember him getting tremendously excited about the guitar line from "And Your Bird Can Sing".'

While not quite rock's hottest property, a definite bidding war was in the offing over the rights to the group's songs. Mike dragged his then boss Paul Connelly to see one of their shows. 'He loved them but was unsure about Damon's voice. That was very frustrating to me in the era of Ian Brown and Mark Gardner. Nowadays you've got singers like Thom Yorke but then I felt that Damon's voice was one of the few with any individual character. We had a lot of battles not helped by the fact that there were no demo tapes. It was summer at least before we got a five-track demo of "She's So High" and some live tracks from a gig in Leeds.'

By now, several companies were sniffing around the group. Virgin had become interested and were courting them with canapés and fine wines in Scottish castles. Mike Smith, shrewdly, was keeping the higher corporate insanity and the top brass at arm's length from the group, figuring that Blur were more attracted to his own genuine enthusiasm and a sense that he was on their wavelength. He figured right. Blur signed on Smith and MCA's dotted line in August 1990 for £80,000. Mike Smith's recollections of the day are vivid. 'One of Alex's old bands were playing the King's Head in Fulham and our offices were on Fulham Palace Road. I remember Damon ringing his mum excitedly, declaring, "I've signed my publishing!" Then we all went off to see Alex's former band and Damon hurled abuse at them.' And then, in what was by now a ritual, it was on to the Portobello Hotel, where all concerned became fearsomely intoxicated and the evening ended with Graham running over parked cars in the street.

Though modest by today's standards, Blur's deal with MCA was healthy enough for 1990 and doubly so when compared to the meagre advance they had received from Food. Importantly, the various elements that made them a real group – as opposed to the protean outfits that proliferate up and down the country – had nearly all fallen into place. They had a full complement of committed members. They toured regularly if shabbily. They had a record contract and a publishing deal. True, they had no manager, but that was soon to be rectified. All they needed now, the icing on the cake, was to actually release a record.

As stated above, the two clear stand-out tracks from the World Cup sessions with Lovell and Power at Battery were 'She's So High' and 'I Know'. The former, while obviously of its time and fashionably supine and detached, was glacially slower than the shuffling indie dance hits of the day. The powers that be, both at Food and MCA, preferred 'I Know', a self-consciously trippy exercise in baggy pastiche, which Graham now acknowledges they 'used as a stepping stone to get us noticed'. 'There were lots of arguments about that first single,' Mike Smith remembers. 'Whether it should be "I Know" or "She's So High". I was always personally wary of baggy. I was a sucker for "Day Upon Day" and "Won't Do It" and the white noise side and I said so. This was very annoying for Food who didn't want that element encouraged. They wanted it suppressed, particularly in Graham. My bosses at MCA were all for "I Know".'

DAVE ROWNTREE: We'd done 'She's So High' and 'I Know' at that first session and Food were very keen on 'I Know' because it fitted perfectly with the baggy scene and they knew it would get us press and such but we were keen to pursue the long term as well so we wanted 'She's So High'. I think Balfe had his sights so obviously set on the US where singles don't make a fuck of difference anyway that he let us have our own way or at least a compromise.

'She's So High', Blur's opus 1, was released on 15 October 1990. It maintains a central place in their affections as can be seen by the fact that, much to their girlfriends' chagrin, it is still in their live repertoire today. This may owe more to its historical significance than its lasting worth but it proved a masterful debut. For one, its daringly unhurried tempo and ghostly melody set it apart from the flotsam and jetsam of the day. Ostensibly simple to the point of the simplistic, it has hidden depths. The controversial bass section is deceptively detailed and Graham's backward guitar treatments are highly individual. Lyrically, though, it was negligible to the point of irritation, as Damon would now agree, though the image of 'crawling all over her' was odd and memorable.

A couple of months prior to its release, trade paper *Music Week* had gushed, 'This column has been known to rave about London guttersnipes Blur and having received a rough cut of their debut single that time has come again . . . it's quite simply brilliant.' Now, on its actual release, acclaim was, if not unanimous, then widespread. The *NME* made it single of the week, claiming, 'If some backwoods Simon Napier Bell had decided to put together a calculatedly post-Roses record with just the right pre-pubescent psychedelic feel, it would sound like this but a lot crapper.' The ever-loyal Leo Finlay, writing for *Sounds*, was extravagant to an almost embarrassing degree. ' "She's So High" stands comparison to anything produced in the last five years. Blur are the first great group of the nineties.' Many other reviews were to mention the Stone Roses comparison while generally applauding the single. On the margins of the national media, there were some less generous voices: 'She's so high, she's so high . . . he's so high, more like, or the band were when they wrote it. A mind-numbing repetitive chorus in a mind-numbing repetitive single. No chance,' concluded the *Leicester Mercury* bluntly.

The single received similarly short shrift, albeit couched in sardonic terms, when it was shown on the revamped *Juke Box Jury* BBC TV show. The original *Juke Box Jury* had been a Saturday teatime favourite of 60s Britain, where the buttock-clenchingly 'square' David Jacobs would goad Thora Hird into saying something idiotic about The Rolling Stones. The 90s incarnation, hosted by Jools Holland, was the latest in a line of doomed attempts at resuscitation, and this is where Blur's first video, a memorable directorial effort by one David Balfe, was shown. 'I directed the first two videos. For "She's So High", the concept was that there would be no lighting whatsoever apart from the set itself which was this weird loop containing 100 little neon rings.' The effect was that it appeared that the band – modishly vacant-looking with Damon in Penguin Books T-Shirt and bowl cut – were performing inside a gigantic electric cooker hob. New Order's Bernard 'Barney' Sumner dismissed it as 'a bit "we are weird"', while Jonathan Ross, now of *Film 99*, made a coy reference to 'the size of the singer's pupils', an entirely unfounded reference to the hip new drug Ecstasy which must have meant nothing to 90 per cent of viewers. 'Jonathan Ross said they looked trendily drugged or words to that effect,' remembers Balfe. 'That was the only TV showing it got. Shame – I still like that video.'

Power and Lovell had done 'a magnificent job', according to Balfe, and this, coupled with the warm praise from the admittedly hysterical London media, meant that most concerned were deflated that the record only made 48 in the charts. 'I was pleased,' contends Dave Balfe. 'Very pleased with that although slightly disappointed because it got incredibly good reviews.' The truth was – indeed, still is – that even though Britain is the most press-led rock market in the world (Americans are routinely astonished by the power *Q*, *NME* and the like wield when compared to their own country where radio is king), purple prose in Carnaby Street or Long Acre often means little to the cost-conscious punter in Worksop and Whitehaven. That said, it is important that we put 'She's So High''s chart showing in some historical context. The 'indie' or 'alternative' sector was still just that: alternative. It was to be many years and with much sterling work by the likes of Blur themselves before we arrived at the not altogether healthy situation where, at the time of writing, a middling indie pub act like The Stereophonics can enter the single chart at Number 3. The group, however, were dismayed. 'We were all gutted,' confirms Alex. 'It meant we wouldn't get on *Top of the Pops*.'

'It got to 42, didn't it?' muses Dave Rowntree inaccurately. 'There's a rumour that Alex's mum went into her local record shop and bought twenty copies which showed up somehow on the sales figures so the chart adjudicators knocked us down ten places cos they thought it was a buying team in operation. That was the rumour, anyway. Maybe it was respectable with hindsight but I definitely didn't think it respectable at the time. We were all very impatient. I was mortified it hadn't gone Top 40. Being in the Top

40 was the pinnacle that would top my career to date. I thought that was the ultimate.'

Deflated or not, there was little time to mope. A raft of press was scheduled and a longish autumn tour beckoned – bringing the band's lack of a manager painfully into relief. Food, or to be more accurate, Andy Ross, had handled the day-to-day running of the group until the release of 'She's So High'. Then, according to Dave, 'One day we had some big falling out. We were grumbling to Andy – "Why did you make us do this?" – and Andy said, "Well, it's not my job, anyway. If you want to shout at someone get a manager."'

ANDY ROSS: At this time, they had no manager, no press officer, nothing. I'd taken most of that on. Balfe and I looked after stuff like getting them gigs and getting them from A to B. After a while we felt they required a manager. Frankly we couldn't be arsed to do stuff any more. We saw two candidates, maybe more. We saw Chris Morrison and a guy called Mike Collins who had managed Wire, who were a very arty band and this appealed to Blur. He was very avuncular and the band were still somewhat insecure. So there's Chris Morrison, ex-manager of Thin Lizzy with his Midge Ure gold discs on the wall, and this guy who's into Wire and art who's a very nice chap or at least it appeared so. So Blur went with Mike Collins, with the touchy-feely as opposed to the corporate. He probably genuinely is a nice chap. It just turned out further down the line that he didn't seem to keep receipts.

Graham remembers meeting the two management candidates. 'Mike took us to Fred's and we had veggie bangers and mash and he seemed very calm. I liked him. Chris had this very old-school 70s decor. He was a wheeler dealer, shouting on the phone behind his desk, "Send us some coffee!" I found him a bit frightening.'

'Chris,' remembers Damon, 'had the dregs of the 70s roster all around him in his office: lots of Ultravox and Thin Lizzy stuff and salmon-pink sofas and to us at that time Mike seemed cooler.'

'We had no idea,' admits Dave. 'We didn't know what a manager did so, "Ho ho ho, typical Blur, let's see who buys us the best dinner". That seemed as good a criteria as any and Mike bought us the best one by far. We should have realised it's the one who buys you the worst dinner and talks the most and has the most to say rather than the one most interested in the wine list. Wire was another reason why we agreed on Mike Collins. But it all did go very sour and to an extent we blamed it on Balfe and Andy cos we didn't know any better. Chris Morrisons's parting remark to us was, "It's up to you, guys. Choose whoever you want. But choose wisely." '

Alex is sure that among other contenders for the managerial job were various former managers of Pink Floyd and founders of EG Records. 'The Wire connection didn't mean anything to me. I didn't know who Wire were. But Mike Collins bought us the nicest lunch and told us the best stories.' And so Blur gained a manager. With the benefit of hindsight, which is never less than 20/20, Alex remarks waspishly, 'We had signed the worst recording contract in the world over the worst pizza in the world. And now we had the worst manager in the world.'

'Collins,' in Mike Smith's opinion, 'seemed incredibly plausible. Art-school type, well dressed, had dealings with Wire and Propaganda. He came on board after the publishing deal was done, probably to his annoyance cos he didn't see any money. He seemed totally convincing and he seemed to fit perfectly with what they wanted. Only later did people begin to say to me, "Oh, lovely man but no manager." '

The group threw themselves with gusto into the 21-date tour that would promote the single. That tour and its concomitant merchandising paraphernalia of posters and T-shirts drew widespread attention to something many might have missed – 'She's So High''s artwork, a reproduction of 60s pop artist Mel Ramos's celebrated image of a naked woman lounging casually on the back of a hippopotamus. As the poster began to appear in more and more places, so the entirely predicted and entirely welcome controversy harrumphed into life. Hackney Council complained to Food, London Underground banned it and at colleges and polytechnics all over the country, it inflamed passions. Women's groups at Liverpool Poly picketed the hall. At Warwick University, irate feminist students attacked the merchandising stall and tore down the offending posters and T-shirts. At Coventry Poly, under an edict that would have been comical if it wasn't so sinister and illiberal, anyone wearing the T-shirt in the Steve Biko Bar, where the band were appearing, was ejected from the gig, presumably by stewards who were 'only obeying orders'. New manager Mike Collins remarked perceptively, 'It seems very odd when you would find the same picture in a book in their library. It's definitely not a sexist thing, just a piece of kitsch art.' Damon added that he was surprised that the presence of a hippopotamus had not alerted the student body to the possibility of irony.

> **DAVE BALFE:** We'd got together with Stylorouge and designed both the Blur logo and quite a lot of other Food packaging. That was my best time ever for getting sleeves together for Blur and Jesus Jones. I was very pleased with the artwork for 'She's So High', that huge double poster of the girl on the hippo. It did get us into a bit of trouble; just the right amount, really. It upset a few feminists at various universities. I thought it was naughty but nice, really, and had a real degree of artistic merit.

Andy Ross gives perhaps the most pointedly accurate verdict on the kerfuffle. 'It got banned by just enough student unions to get us news stories, which is what you need really.'

Being in the news was Blur's natural habitat in the late autumn of 1990. A major *NME* feature with fellow Colchester native Steve Lamacq found the group, or at least the Colchester contingent, berating their home town in a way that would win them no friends among the civic dignitaries and pressmen of that town in the coming years. Graham claims to have taken photos of gravestones when asked to take pictures into school about what Colchester meant. 'It's death for young people, this place,' Damon stated. 'I used to get beaten up quite a lot when I lived round here but maybe I asked for it because I sound quite arrogant when I talk. I'm horribly cynical. I don't suffer fools gladly.'

A week later, in *Sounds*, journalist George Berger asked, 'Are Blur full of shit or what? . . . The latest in a long line of bands who think they're the best in the world.' The group broached the subject of drugs for the first time, with Damon eulogising acid. 'It made me relax more, with bigger landscapes, bigger sounds, more lush sounds.' 'E's crap,' offered Alex. 'E's shit.' Damon agreed. 'It's more of a cocaine trip whereas acid is more a dope mentality. It's not celebrating that worldy up feeling. It's more panoramic.'

Thus fortified, the tour rumbled on, supported by The Keatons, an anarchic five-piece whom Blur were very keen on. The Keatons' forte was bizarre and outlandish confrontational antics. They would swap instruments between every song. The singer, as well as manip-ulating an eccentric puppet show, would charge into the crowd

Coming Alive

27/10/90

hurling honey, then flour, thus coating the audience in a kind of pastry.

MIKE SMITH: It was all very Cardiacs and very like Blur's extreme side but more so. It was great that Blur took them out but halfway through the tour it became obvious that they were very wrong. Colleges and venues were getting hugely annoyed with this mad person throwing honey at punters and leaving the stage in a horrific mess. So they got thrown off the tour. But that was the tour when I realised Blur could be as big as The Stone Roses. Walking out of a gig in Sheffield with Alex, there were girls screaming and he was grinning and holding his head high, absolutely relishing it. You got his sense that all the boys wanted to be their mates and all the girls wanted to shag them.

Mike Smith also remembers the formation of pockets of intense fervour and loyalty that remain true to this day, chiefly in the West Midlands. There were mad scenes and stage invasions at Dudley JBs and Birmingham Burberries. 'The provinces loved us,' asserts Graham. 'Birmingham, Leicester, Dudley, Walsall. It was insane whenever we went. Got 90 quid each once from Dudley JBs and were blown away. It meant we could buy new jeans. London were snobbish, we felt. They took a while to get it.' Further north, too, the response was often cooler. At The Duchess of York in Leeds, Damon took to the stage announcing, 'We're from London.' 'Well, fuck off back there, you cunt,' came a voice from the throng. Just before Christmas, at a gig at Bath Moles club, Damon sustained a fractured nose from Alex's swinging bass. A version of 'Day Upon Day' from this gig was to surface on the B-side of their next single.

But that next single was some time in coming and its birth was not an easy one. In late 1990, the band went back into the studio to produce the follow-up to 'She's So High'. The main candidates were 'Bad Day', a passably attractive pop song written by Damon while suffering from a streptococcal viral infection during a brief tenure in a Hampstead flat, and 'Close', an undistinguished tune later released as a fan-club-only single. The sessions did not progress well.

ALEX JAMES: We were in the studio with Steve Power trying to make something of these two obviously commercial things we had – 'Bad Day' and 'Close'. Steve Power had Graham playing the bass because I couldn't play it. I was coming home thinking, What the fuck is going on here? Eventually everyone realised it sounded shit and it was shelved. Balfe came down with the head of A&R from EMI just before Christmas. He was very scary – all aftershave and sharp suit. What we'd done was shit and he said, 'This isn't really working, is it?' So the position is that the first single's not been a hit and we've gone in to do another and got nothing. It was quite desperate; a touch-and-go point, really. EMI could drop us if they wanted because at that point there was no albums option.

A momentous meeting was at hand, though; one that would shape the course of British pop in the 90s and create the shiny, mod-casual beats they would later call Britpop. Bernard Sumner and Jonathan Ross may have been less than enamoured with 'She's So High' on *Juke Box Jury* but one viewer in front of the telly that Saturday teatime had been impressed. Watching the show at home with his wife, Stephen Street turned to her and said, 'This is great!'

STEPHEN STREET: I started out in music playing in various bands in the late 70s and early 80s. As we did demos, I began to realise that it was the studio side of things, the recording and production, that I liked. It became apparent that the band I was in was going nowhere so I decided to try to break into the world of studio recording and production. At the time, the really interesting new producers who were doing new-wave music and alternative music – people like Steve Lilywhite, Martin Rushent and Martin Hannet – came from a background of studio engineering rather than the classically trained producers of the 60s. So that's how I decided to start off – by trying to get some studio experience as an engineer. I wrote letters to every studio in London asking for a job and eventually I heard that there was a job going at Island, who had this little demo studio in the basement of their building. I managed to talk them into giving me a job. I started off as an assistant and worked my way up to house engineer over two years. That's where I was when I met The Smiths.

The Smiths went to the studio where Street worked for a session. They immediately hit it off, the band being taken with his enthusiasm, even though the 24-year-old Street was in awe of the group who had made 'This Charming Man'. Street recorded 'Heaven Knows I'm Miserable Now' with them and it was the start of a close working relationship that Street acknowledges as his big break. Armed with the cachet of being The Smiths' producer, he went freelance and became a name producer in his own right. He also co-wrote the songs on Morrissey's first post-Smiths work, *Viva Hate*.

'That was a useful step for me because it showed people I had more musical credentials than just being a knob-twiddler.' His next venture was an abortive record label with the rock journalist Jerry Smith. 'It was a bad time to start a label, the end of the 80s when Rough Trade and others were going under.' It was a difficult phase for Street and an uninspiring time musically, particularly in the capital. It is perhaps no surprise, then, that, Blur's performance that Saturday teatime on *Juke Box Jury* fired his imagination.

> **STEPHEN STREET:** They obviously had that certain something. They looked like a group; they had presence in that way that The Smiths did. My manager Gail Coulson also managed Jesus Jones so there was a contact with Food there and I told her to let Dave Balfe know that if Blur were ever looking for a producer I was up for it. It was the first time I've ever done that. Without being big-headed, usually tapes come to me. Anyway, they said thanks but they were going to stick with Steve Power. But the next single hadn't worked out so Balfe did call me and I went to meet them at the old Food offices in Brewer Street, Piccadilly. We all went to The Crown at lunchtime and chatted. Even then I could tell that Alex was the most *laissez-faire* and that Graham was more intense. He obviously wasn't going to endure any bullshit. They seemed very tight knit. I also knew they'd be a handful but I was very taken with them. They gave me the once-over and invited me on board just before Christmas and we went into the studio, Maison Rouge in Fulham, just after.

The band, all Smiths devotees, were delighted to have Street work with them. Mike Smith remembers that, coincidentally, the band had had a drunken conversation with him the day before Stephen Street's message had come through in which Damon had expressed his desire to be 'to the 90s what The Smiths were to the 80s – the defining band'. In one 'damn good' session, the band and Street put down 'Come Together' and a song called 'There's No Other Way'. The latter, a lightweight groove dashed off fairly quickly by Damon, had never been earmarked for greatness within the band. However, in the studio it began to take on a definite dynamic of its own. As Balfe puts it, 'It got a little baggier in the recording.' According to Street, 'Balfe thought some of demos we'd done sounded very 60s garage band and he didn't want that at all. Indie dance was what he wanted. He was adamant that he wanted that housey Jesus Jones production with heavily looped rhythms.' As they began to construct it, 'There's No Other Way' had two immediately attention-grabbing elements.

First, a terrific rhythm track. Alex states: 'It often happens that you can just hear the drums and bass and tell if a song's a hit. Not always, of course; sometimes the rhythm track is shit and you can still get a good song out of it. But that was monster straight away.' Street didn't go as far as Steve Power did, 'but I did put down a drum loop over which Dave played live drums'. Mike Smith remembers how Dave Rowntree, to whom the idea of looped and sampled drums had previously been anathema, suddenly became wildly enthusiastic when he heard the results.

Second, and perhaps more important, it had a guitar riff that ensnared the listener immediately: a bluesy double-string lick in the song's root chord of E achieved by a high glissando at the twelfth and fourteenth frets. 'Graham wouldn't play in the control room with me as he would now,' relates Street. 'He sat by the amp in the playing area. I remember thinking what a great guitar riff it was and pretty soon I realised that this was the best guitarist I'd worked with since Johnny Marr.' This is not just high praise. It's positively vertiginous. But Street certainly had a point, and in a climate where one lazily strummed chord elongated and made panoramic by Japanese technology had become the musical norm, Coxon's playing, like that of John Squire, was electrifying by comparison.

Little else of note occurs in 'There's No Other Way'. The lyrics suffer, as indeed most of Albarn's did at this time, from a kind of wilful banality. In part, this was an intentional artistic device; a rejection of rock's usual bluster and an ironic 'celebration' of the vacancy of contemporary youth culture. But more importantly, Damon couldn't be arsed writing anything better. However, add the most simplistic two-note organ figure imaginable and 'There's No Other Way' sounded suspiciously like a hit. A very palpable hit.

Blur, in 1999, have little complimentary to say about 'There's No Other Way'. They haven't played it live for years and Graham in particular is scathing about it. So let us sing its praises for them. While neither ground-breaking nor particularly original, 'There's No Other Way' is right up there with 'Fool's Gold' and 'Step On' as the apotheosis of the baggy *oeuvre*. It can still twitch the foot even at this remove – and it's only that bloody organ that really irritates.

Balfe and Ross were delighted with the results, as was Stephen

A very young Alex hits
the bottle

Damon, 1990 (Jeffrey ▶
Davy)

Damon models orthodox 1991 indie bowlhead cut

Alex endures Phil Oakey phase

A remarkably alert-looking
Dave Rowntree

Graham during Joey
Ramone period

(all photos: Zanna)

British Image 1: streetwise casuals, 1993 (Paul Spencer)

British Image 2: dandyish fops, 1993 (Paul Spencer)

On Sugary Tea tour with Melody Maker journalist Ian Gittins, Newcastle, 1993
(Matt Bright)

Immediately before Alexandra Palace show, 1994 (Paul Postle)

London, 1998 (Kevin Westenberg)

Blur, London, 1998 (Kevin Westenberg)

Street. 'It's not their favourite tune, I know, but I'm proud of it.' Balfe thought it just the sort of track that would break them both in Britain and in the States, the latter being a market he was fixated on, according to the group. As it stands, he was partly right. It was a minor college hit but it was in the UK that 'There's No Other Way' hit pay-dirt. Radio stations fell over themselves to play it and it was also helped, albeit imperceptibly, by another Balfe-directed video, this one a suburban Sunday lunch homage to David Lynch, in which Damon pouts at the camera from beneath a faintly silly pageboy haircut. Amazingly, when Damon had it cut, Balfe and Ross were concerned that they'd lost 'a commercial asset'. 'We thought this was going to be a problem.'

On 27 April 1991, the group gathered around their radios to hear that it had entered the chart at Number 20. Graham recalls the momentous occasion. 'I listened to the chart round at Damon's and was on the phone to my mum at the same time. It was outrageous that we were in the Top 20.' In those healthier times, singles still actually had a career and went up the chart rather than enter at some ludicrous position and then fade away. So, in the coming weeks, it rose to 11 then to 10 and finally to its highest placing of 8. This, too, as Andy Ross rightly states, 'in the days when indie bands didn't have hits at all so it was a real breakthrough'. Overnight, literally, they had become pop stars.

The success of 'There's No Other Way' ushered in a period of frenzied activity for the band. As the record scaled the chart, Blur were trekking around the country on an extensive tour of smallish venues. In the middle of this, they drove back to London for their debut performance on *Top of the Pops*, always a significant moment in any pop career.

DAMON ALBARN: We were doing *Top of the Pops* and Balfe gave us an E. It would have been a fantastic experience anyway but obviously after the E it looked amazing. I remember just before we were on, Vic Reeves, who was in the charts with 'Born Free', was on the other stage and he was doing this big crooner thing and suddenly all this glitter fell from the ceiling and Alex and I were at the side of the stage just looking at each other going, 'Yeah, this is it! Come on!' It was a beautiful moment.

ALEX JAMES: Electronic were on which was unbelievable for me because New Order and The Smiths were the reason I wanted to make music in the first place. It was fantastic. The drink really started flowing at this point. When you've had a hit, there's drink everywhere. It was a big round of parties and booze and dodgy kids' TV and then there was the tour, the first one that all your ex-girlfriends come to and snog you again. It was great. Get up in the morning, have a few beers, go to the town centre of wherever we were, hang around and get recognised, then get on a bus and go somewhere else. Gimpo, the tour manager, would say, 'Do you want your PDs [*per diems – daily pocket money*] or do you want acid?' We had so much energy. On tour then, we'd get up early and say, 'Let's go somewhere in the van.' Then later we'd be standing at the bar at the gigs, saying, 'Come on, here we are, in your fucking town.'

By his own admission, Alex became 'insufferable' at this point. A big-headed arsehole. My girlfriend didn't want to know me. I was smug and unbearable. Shades after dark and all that kind of thing.' This was very much how he was represented in an article in a now defunct Scottish magazine that must hold some form of record for the most splenetic ill-considered diatribe in the annals of hackery. 'In their bass player Alex they have a dickhead of such magnitude that even Gazza seems bearable . . . I've been intimidated by worthier fuckwits than you, scumbag,' he concludes, hinting at a hidden agenda and unmentioned hostilities.

During that same tour, hairline cracks began to appear in Blur's rapport with Balfe. From his point of view, 'I wanted to get the presentation of the band right. We paid a lot of attention and money to this. We spent two or three grand on this elaborate pop-art illuminated backdrop, all slides and stuff, and it was just too overwhelming because the band weren't visually too exciting at that point.' The matter is open, it seems, to interpretation.

ALEX JAMES: Balfe made us spend a lot of our publishing money on a stage set which is definitely something that comes out of record companies' tour support money. We only used it once. There were all these lightboxes that people had to come on and change and these transparent drapes, all for the Pink Toothbrush, Rayleigh, or wherever. Stupid. And then he had the audacity to buy them off us for something else he was doing at a quarter of the price. He had absolutely no sense of style or largesse but to be positive, he was very good with Damon. Damon's a hard person to disagree with a lot of the time. Meetings would just degenerate into scraps between them. Balfe would say, 'Damon, you dickhead, you can't do that,' or he'd say to all of us, 'You can't get that fucking drunk. Be a bit clever – pretend you're that drunk.' He was the wheels of industry and we weren't in it for that. But maybe he was right. The stumbling block was that he wanted us to be Jesus Jones really.

The band spent the late spring working both on what would become the *Leisure* album and their burgeoning social profile. Their ubiquity on the party scene led to the *Daily Star* describing them as 'Britain's top sex and drugs band'. This was the work of the gossip columnist Linda Duff, whom Dave Rowntree remembers as an ally of the band. 'She quite brazenly made any old crap up about anybody. I really liked her; she was very funny. She'd bump into you and say, "Oh, I've made this great thing up – New Lads – and that's you, you're it." Little did she know she changed the history of the world. Everyone picked up on New Lad. It became government policy.'

It was at this time that Damon acquired a girlfriend, Justine Frischmann, the trainee architect daughter of an ennobled military man. She also played guitar in new band Suede.

DAMON ALBARN: The whole thing with Justine was that I was with some friends, Mike Smith and Ben Wardle, actually, and they said, 'Do you wanna go and see this band tonight? One of them's a public schoolgirl and she brings all her really nice friends along.' So I thought, Great, and off we all went down the Falcon. I saw them but didn't really pay much attention to them and then we were scheduled to do a gig in Brighton and their name came up as a support so we did the gig and she asked for one of our posters and I said she'd have to pay for it like everyone else. She just stayed in my mind and early the next year I got her number from Ben Wardle and asked her would she like to come out.

Damon and Justine, the rest of Blur, Linda Duff and indeed the rest of pop London had discovered a new haunt in the spring of 1991. If you wander down to 68 Oxford Street now, as no doubt a few obsessed Britpop archaeologists still do, then you will find a dully impersonal metal and glass doorway opening on to the shabby vestibule of a language school; or perhaps by the time you read this, a discount leather goods shop or noodle bar. But if you had ventured there one Thursday night in the spring of 1991, you would have found . . . well, a dully impersonal metal and glass doorway opening on to the shabby vestibule of a poky, subterranean club that was briefly the hub, the very fulcrum, of London's music scene. No band played live at this strange lair beneath the pavements of one of the world's major shopping thoroughfares. It was just, as Alex would have it, 'a hang', but it was a good one. Three quid would get your hand stamped at the cash desk with its lurid ultra-violet light and you would emerge into an L-shaped room with a tiny dance floor around the dog-leg and nearest the entrance, a bar that was little more than a Formica counter, a few beer kegs and pile upon pile of canned beers which retailed at some idiotically low price. This was Syndrome, and it became synonymous with an incestuous rag bag of bands (Blur is the only one any modern rock fan would recognise), promoters, journos and the odd desperate rock tourist from Tokyo or Telford clutching their *NME*. Because of its nightly visibility in pubs and clubs, its engaging sociability and daffy youthful self-regard, it became known as The Scene That Celebrates Itself.

ANDY ROSS: Every Thursday without fail we'd all go to Syndrome. Lush, Swervedriver, Courtney Love and Kurt Cobain on a couple of famous occasions. You knew you'd meet people there. London hadn't had a music scene for years, which seems daft now but there was no focal point. So in the months after Blur signed they threw themselves into it. They were there every week with Damon's pudding bowl haircut and after. I came up with something called the universal riff. Virtually every indie song at the time you could go 'wo wo wo' through all the songs so we would go on the dance floor to this. Highly mature stuff. It was very important in that we were bonding and they were being seen and feeling like a band. And hanging out with these luminaries like Chapterhouse and Moose.

The band remember this period, as do most of Syndrome's habitués, with great affection. Damon describes it as 'an amazing place'. 'I've got a picture of me and Justine and Bernard Butler all with three drinks each, completely out of it, hugging each other.' 'We decided we'd go there every week,' says Alex, 'and be seen together. We drank Pernod and cider and got wrecked. Everyone went there. I met Courtney Love in a bathroom at the MTV awards in Los Angeles last year and she asked me about Syndrome.'

'There was always someone there you could get drunk with,' remembers Graham Coxon fondly. 'The Senseless Things or Lush or someone. I'd have my Red Stripe and Damon would drink these horrible Pernod and cider concoctions. You could take your records down there on white label and Neil and Jared would play them. Girls would look at you. Maybe because we were being spoilt brats but they'd look at you all the same.'

DAVE ROWNTREE: We thought of ourselves as the poverty jet set. We had twenty quid a week and we had been living on five so twenty was quite good but we had to go somewhere where drinks were bloody cheap and you could get in for nothing, so we played on our minor pop stardom and went to Syndrome. You could get smashed for a fiver. Anything alcoholic was a pound and there was usually people there who you knew. So you'd spend a fiver and then blag three more drinks. All the bands would look at each other warily and then when you were pissed you'd talk but there was no punters and that meant you could get pissed with no hassle and talk to people with common interests. Then word got out and the address got printed in some mags around the world and Syndrome was on well-off kids' must-do lists whilst in London. The outside world's perception of Syndrome was cocaine and limos and us falling down the stairs to take coke off young girls' spines. But in reality we were all wondering if we could afford another drink and wondering whether we could keep enough money back for the night bus. The real irony was that we were quite big in Japan and with Japanese audiences even though we'd never been and to all Japanese tourists we were major league rock stars but they were coming over with £10,000 thinking, What are these scumbags doing in this grotty hole? They should be at the Ritz. We had less money than the tramps on the pavement probably. 68 Oxford Street. The one with the sick outside. Dele Fadele would be there with a carrier bag and his Walkman on. And that was The Scene That Celebrates Itself.

It was good that the band were enjoying themselves. Because it was later than they thought.

5 Annus Horribilis

THE FIRST SIGN THAT anything might be going awry in Blur's predicted rise to the broad sunlit uplands of perpetual stardom came with the release of 'Bang', their third single, on 29 July 1991. The other notable release of the month was hostage John McCarthy. 'Bang' had been written in fifteen minutes at The Premises rehearsal studios and, to the ungenerous ear, it sounded like it too.

Prior to that, things were moving on apace. The group were preparing for what was to be a reasonably triumphant first festival appearance at Reading and sessions for their first album were going well, albeit in a rather fractured way. 'They were putting *Leisure* together and rehearsing at The Premises in east London,' recounts Mike Smith, 'and I'd sit in on rehearsals sometimes. Damon and Graham would be in there together, Damon playing very rudimentary bass and them knocking around ideas. You could hear some very exciting stuff. They were working on "Fool", a kind of rejection of an old girlfriend, and that was great, and "Birthday", which was a real jawdropper, and "Sing". It was so obvious that there was phenomenal talent here – very removed from knockabout thrash. So it was all going well. They'd just started going abroad for gigs. And everyone was very excited about "Bang" because it sounded like another "There's No Other Way" basically. But then when it came out there was a sense of things somehow slipping off the rails. With hindsight, it was a bit like Britpop circa 1997. It was the dying moments of that particular scene but we just didn't know that at the time.'

'There's just something about "Bang" which is shit,' diagnoses Damon now. Similarly severe, Alex states, ' "Bang" is and was rubbish.' Dave says that he would like it to be legally asserted that 'Bang' is not to appear on any Greatest Hits. This is all a little harsh

I Want To Be Asleep

27/9/91

but certainly if 'There's No Other Way' had been an exemplar of its particular art, as perfect in its own way as the Maglite, the Walkman or the Pot Noodle, then 'Bang' was the Panda Cola, the own-brand chicken tikka masala; perfectly functional but inert, even a little cloying, in its desperation to please. Its saving grace is some inventive bass playing by Alex and Graham's spirited hammer-ons at the song's intro.

> **GRAHAM COXON:** At the time we all thought it was good. Not as good as 'There's No Other Way' but stupid and catchy. We did it on *Top of the Pops*. When we'd done our first *Top of the Pops* for 'There's No Other Way' we were very elfin and very good boys. By the time we did 'Bang' we were very different. Damon was waving this plastic chicken around on stage and I was refused entry by the doorman because I was really pissed and scruffy. I had these old ripped baseball shoes on and dirty clothes and I was staggering about.

'Bang' was produced by Stephen Street who, on the completion of 'There's No Other Way', had left for New York for six months to work on a new Psychedelic Furs album. 'I wasn't really in the frame for the album because Balfe had this downer on me for some reason. I knew they were still looking around for producers and wouldn't commit to me. So when I came back it was really nice to find out that not only had "There's No Other Way" been a big hit but they'd saved half the tracks on the album for me to do, one of which was "Bang". Balfe put a lot of pressure on during the recording. He was very hands on. He sat next to me during the mixing of "Bang" and made suggestions and stuff which I found very odd.'

Balfe acknowledges this trait. 'I'd been a producer and a musician so I always interfered in arrangements – "that bass line's not happening" or whatever – but by and large I thought my contributions were positive.'

While pointing out that they still shout for 'Bang' in Italy, Andy Ross concedes that, 'Whilst it wasn't an own goal, it didn't do as well as it could.' In fact, it reached 24, a huge disappointment after 'There's No Other Way''s Top 10 status. And there was more disappointment to follow. Though the band enjoyed the recording of their debut album at Maison Rouge ('Cheese and pickle sandwiches and chips every day for lunch. Table football. Nice parties,' remembers Graham), there were smouldering disagreements.

STEPHEN STREET: I'm proud of my bits on *Leisure* but I felt really put under pressure from Food. They wanted indie dance, they wanted something as programmed as Jesus Jones. And the band really didn't want that. They were much more into that darker, Syd Barrett style that came out on the B-sides around this time. So though we got on well, maybe they thought I was a bit poppy and I think they wanted to try other things like they did with Mike Thorne. Balfe wasn't convinced about me. He never had any faith.

This fundamental fault line – Food's commercially motivated faith in indie dance and baggy beats on one side and the band's predilection for weirdness on the other – is what makes *Leisure* such an unsatisfying curate's egg of a record. It fairly glows with potential but it frequently irritates. The lack of cohesion is partly due to the proliferation of chiefs and paucity of Indians on hand at the time. There are no less than four production credits on the sleeve: Lovell and Power for 'She's So High', the band themselves for one track, the bulk by Stephen Street and three by US-based British producer Mike Thorne.

Thorne was, according to Andy Ross, 'a moody arty fucker by reputation' and had been brought in at Balfe's suggestion to work on the darker works in the Blur canon. If truth be told, it was probably also partly a concession to the group's arty nature. He had produced Soft Cell's huge hit "Tainted Love" but also Marianne Faithfull and Wire's superb first trilogy of albums (*Pink Flag*, *Chairs Missing* and *154*), which endeared him greatly to the band. 'He looked like Billy Bigget from *One Flew Over the Cuckoo's Nest*,' says Graham. 'Really nice bloke. He'd jog home from the studio every night and get lost. A pretty Zen producer. Pretty out there.'

Thorne's three tracks are 'Fool', 'Birthday' and 'Wear Me Down'. 'Fool' is slight but charming ('Damon trying to be Morrissey,' jokes Alex) and the noisy instrumental break at 1.30, featuring Graham on drums, is appealing. 'Birthday' – written on the morning after the infamous Slade School preview and Damon's night in the cells with a Gurkha – was initially well thought of by Balfe, Ross and Graham Coxon ('I thought it was the greatest little song I'd ever heard'). It is a sweetly eerie tune marred by the faintly vacuous nature of the lyrics and the pointless explosion of grungey ensemble noise at 2.42, which was considered dubious even at the time by Damon. Thorne believed 'Wear Me Down' could be a single, clear evidence of his peculiar outlook since it sounds not unpleasantly like Black Sabbath having drunk a bottle of Actifed.

Street's tracks are usually more fastidiously neat and saleable. 'High Cool' takes its name from a setting on the air-conditioning unit at The Premises. 'Repetition' – the weakest song on the album – is an old Seymour number, whose only distinguishing feature is Graham's guitar hook whereby the note is bent and then the pick-ups are quickly switched on and off, thus giving the interrupted tone. The lyric, incidentally, is inspired by an incident in Damon's youth and is an exercise in Beckettian nihilism. 'Repetition' was the only track on *Leisure* attempted by both Street and Thorne. Alex liked neither but in the end Street's was chosen. 'Slow Down' is a My Bloody Valentine homage while 'Bad Day', whose genesis was mentioned in the previous chapter, is a decent enough song boasting a pretty melodic intro and some ultra-baggy drums. 'Come Together' is raucous enough if unmemorable.

Singles aside, this leaves one track unaccounted for – undoubtedly the best. 'Sing' was a demo recorded at the Roundhouse in Chalk Farm, and rightly regarded as good enough to be included on the album in this version. Production is by Blur themselves and the track's significance is that, more than anything else on *Leisure*, it indicates deep reservoirs of talent and imagination rather than the shallow ponds of baggy opportunism that glisten elsewhere on the record. 'Sing' is a vast, plaintive mantra revolving around endlessly reiterated minor chords of E, F sharp and C. The memorable bass motif consists of two looped patterns while a sampled snare whacks along for most of the song's six minutes. Disorientating and gravely lovely, it was not the kind of track Northside were likely to come up with.

The evident quality of 'Sing' was remarked upon in most of *Leisure*'s mixed bag of reviews when the album was released on 27 August, the Monday after their well-received Reading show at which the undoubted stars were Nirvana. The *Melody Maker* gushed about 'guitars like forests of burning pylons' and Blur's naked ambition and star potential. Other reviewers, though, balked at the lack of focus and dynamism. The broadsheets were muted, perhaps reasonably, though the *Independent*'s attack on 'Sing' smacked of sheer cluelessness. However, Andrew Collins in the *NME* infuriated the group by identifying Blur as symptomatic of English rock's contemporary malaise. 'There is no mystique to Blur: they are standing next to you at the Moose gig, they spend less on clothes than you do . . . Blur are really pretty good. But it ain't the future. Blur are merely the present of rock and roll.'

Andy Ross is spirited in his support for the maligned debut. '*Leisure* gets an unduly hard time. The problem is that when critics got into Blur after *Modern Life is Rubbish* the feeling was that the boat had been missed and we'll have to acknowledge that but we'll explain away our actions by saying that *Leisure* wasn't very good.'

These are fair points but the inescapable truth is that *Leisure* isn't very good. It's every bit as good as a debut album can be by a group caught between their fixation with My Bloody Valentine and half-digested philosophic movements and their record company's straight-forward desire for mainstream success. The result is that both endeavours, the commercial and the artistic, feel half-baked. The pop isn't poppy enough and the weird shit too obvious. The inclusion of 'Inertia', 'Uncle Love', 'Mr Briggs' and 'Luminous', the B-sides of the singles on which they were given their head, would have made it twice the record. But let's hear the verdict of the protagonists.

GRAHAM COXON: We were very happy with *Leisure*. It was definitely the best we could have done at the time. I'm sure the *NME*'s was the only lukewarm review we got. It said we were the present rather than the future of rock. Isn't that what a record's meant to be – a snapshot of the present, you know, a slice of now? I listened to it round at Andy Ross's not long ago and for the first time in years, because we sort of put it to the back of our minds. After a few glasses of wine I thought it was ace. Rocking.

DAMON ALBARN: *Leisure* has no identity at all. It wasn't allowed to have any identity at all. If we'd been allowed to put our B-sides out as album tracks, 'Luminous' and the like, it would have been a really interesting record. It seems ridiculous now but we were being told what to do continually. That's why the relationships with Balfe soured very early. We felt we knew better than him which we did really.

DAVE ROWNTREE: In terms of style, *Leisure* is a touch of My Bloody Valentine and Dinosaur Jr, as well as the Manchester thing which was enormous; The Stone Roses were all-conquering. But there was no common thread. It took a few records for people to work out the Blur sound. There's a whole bunch of reasons for the way *Leisure* sounds. It was being pulled in different directions. Graham was worried about being too pop at the exclusion of Seymour-style weirdness which he got off on. Balfe was worried that that Seymour side was going to make us enemies. He wanted us to put out very simple messages: this band are like this. He thought that was the key to mass markets and Damon, I think, was trying to keep everyone happy and push us into a more song-led direction. He wasn't sure whether you could build a career on this unpredictable wildness we had live so he was trying to move the whole thing on to a more songwriterly, musicianly basis and I was with him on that. Alex wanted to get drunk and shag girls. He was very into *Smash Hits* and limos and wanting to be Duran Duran. So everyone put their ten penn'orth in and made sure their vision of the band was represented. So the album's quite, shall we say, eclectic.

ALEX JAMES: We'd done some great B-sides but Balfy was trying to make us a baggy band; that was the market. So it was a hotch-potch. With four different producers' credits, it was never going to have any cohesion or homogeneity. If we'd gone for some of the tracks that ended up being B-sides it would have been a lot cooler. It wasn't a case of, 'What kind of record do you want to make?' It was, 'I'm Dave Balfe and I'm holding the purse-strings. This is the album you're going to make.' But it's unusual for first albums to be that good anyway. *Leisure* is half-decent but it's neither one thing nor another. But albums are where the international merryground starts and then it's 'Welcome to New York!'

Welcome to New York for most British first-timers means JFK's infamously officious and bureaucratic immigration officers, the ones who didn't get the joke when, having asked G. K. Chesterton the standard query about 'whether the purpose of his visit was to overthrow the US government' received the reply, 'Not sole purpose of visit.' Blur made their acquaintance in mid-November 1991 when a short tour of the States began in New York at the Marquee club. They'd already ventured abroad playing dates in France and Italy with Pulp and Lush but there's always a certain significance in a British rock group's first trip to the States. There's always the vaguest cultural echo of The Beatles descending those runway steps in an electrical storm of flashbulbs.

Contrary to most reports and significantly in view of later events, Blur's first visit to the States was an enjoyable one for all, including Mike Smith. He was becoming rapidly disenchanted with his position at MCA, having tried and failed to sign a variety of bands, the latest being Teenage Fanclub. His growing disillusionment with the corporate rock world was furthered when despite the presence of two of their acts on the bill, Slowdive and Blur, no one from the American label SBK bothered to go to the show in New York. According to Smith, it was their loss. 'It was the gig of my life. Here was a band that you'd followed from the Bull and Gate and now they were selling out New York clubs. The crowd were going mad for them. There was this enormous sense of expectation, a lot of gossip about SBK spending a million dollars on breaking Blur. "There's No Other Way" was poised on the edge of the Hot 100 and it looked like they were going to follow Jesus Jones and EMF. The band were very optimistic and positive about their new material like "Popscene" and "Oily Water" and "Turn It Up", which felt like a new direction. They charged on, Graham in this deerstalker, and played "Popscene". Dave Balfe was down the front pogoing. It was a brilliant evening.'

Socially, the trip was everything a young band wants from their inaugural US jaunt. 'The band were on cloud nine,' says Smith. 'It was a whirl of limos and late nights at the Paramount Hotel. Drinking with Peter Buck and Martika running barefoot through the corridors. The band holding court in the whisky bar, Alex and Dave Balfe with a couple of models on each knee. It was a kind of rock and roll dreamland.' But Smith also knew that he no longer wanted to be in the business and that this was his swan-song before, he thought, breaking the news and going to art college. He could also see that things were going badly wrong administratively. For one, their manager seemed increasingly disorganised and antagonistic. 'Mike Collins was obviously losing it. He was getting very drunk and seemed to be always berating the band.' For another, relations with the US record company SBK were deteriorating badly. 'The group's schedule was ridiculous,' explains Smith. 'They were playing shows at night and then unwinding obviously and not getting to bed till the small hours and then were expected to do photo calls and meetings at 8 a.m. and then they started complaining about Alex turning up reeking of booze. Well, come on, he was still drunk from the night before.'

ALEX JAMES: That first US tour when 'There's No Other Way' was threatening to be a hit was something else. You're a long way from home on a tour bus in America and America has always been so good at mythologising itself. So you wake up in Chicago or Sunset Boulevard and it's all magical. But there were some real downers too. Let me be very clear about SBK. If we thought Balfe had business over taste, then SBK were the biggest bunch of inept, soulless, artless fuckwits you could ever meet, a company founded by lawyers selling Jesus Jones records on the back of the Gulf War. They thought they could make hit records and then sell the company. They were the most horrible and contemptible bullies and idiots and they just did not know what to do with us. In fact, they just had no idea at all and eventually the company folded.

Before that day, though, Blur's relations with them were actually to worsen, as we shall see. However, on their return to England, things still looked reasonably good. The mood at Food Records was buoyant, as Dave Balfe recollects: 'We'd had two Top 10 singles in four months with the two bands. We'd done about 100,000 of the first album. We had our little poky offices in Brewer Street and we took on two girls. And then Jesus Jones's next album did two million worldwide and they were very big in America, if not here, so we started making money.'

Since mid-October the band had been furiously demoing new material at Matrix Studios, Little Russell Street, with John Smith. The strength and originality of these new songs ('Popscene', 'Oily Water' and 'Resigned' were the first to be essayed) had invigorated the band and pointed a way out of the baggy cul-de-sac. Indeed, these were the seeds of what would become their sophomore album, *Modern Life is Rubbish*. No one, however, could have known that that record would be nineteen harrowing months hence although clouds, some of them no bigger than a man's hand, were beginning to gather. Their drinking was escalating beyond the merely spirited. Worse, Balfe was unimpressed by their new direction. 'I wanted them to conquer the world. There's more to life than getting *NME* and *Select* covers,' he explains.

None the less, Mike Smith found the band in good spirits at Matrix when he turned up to break some difficult news to them. 'Out of the blue on returning to England I'd been offered a job at EMI and I thought, Fuck it, I'll do it. I went down to Matrix where they were demoing with John Smith and told them. Damon was very upset but really supportive. Graham's attitude was, "Great, now we can be mates." Mike Collins, though, was furious. I remember him ranting, "Fuck, fuck, fuck! Why did they sign to you? They could have got so much more money from someone else." I was seeing them a lot socially. I was living above a super-market in the West End and Alex moved up from New Cross to live in Endell Street next door to a tramps' hostel, though Damon didn't think living in Covent Garden such a good idea in view of Alex's temperament. He was a lot sharper and more focused since Justine had managed to convince him to pack up dope, but it's true that we were both in love with the Soho drunk Jeffrey Bernard myth.'

On 10 December, Smith and the band celebrated his new job – despite Mike Collins' irritation – in The Plough on Museum Street, their local whenever they recorded at Matrix. They all went on to see Pulp at North London Polytechnic, apart from Graham who returned to the studio with Smith to add guitar parts to a track in progress. When the others returned to the studio later, they found a very drunk Coxon banging haphazardly on a chair leg. 'Michael!' he shouted in greeting to Smith as he spotted him. Both the drunken percussion and the salutation can be heard on the finished track 'Miss America' on *Modern Life is Rubbish* (Dave does not play on this track and on the album sleeve is credited as 'The Plough, Bloomsbury').

Such sessions brought forth several other tracks that would later be released. One, 'Badgeman Brown', later the B-side of 'Popscene', brought about one of many confrontations between the band and their record company. The track was intended as part of an embry-onic Blur soundtrack to a film by Storm Thorgerson, half of the legendary Hipgnosis design team and old friend of Blur guru Syd Barrett, whose distinctive musical style the song apes blatantly. 'It was a big idea about a man leaving his house and just vanishing but it was a castle in Spain, a pipe-dream,' explains Alex. Balfe hated it and, in an angry argument, reminded the band that Pink Floyd soundtrack albums had sold nothing. Ross, though more philosoph-ical, also thought the track stank. 'If ever Blur got too cocky or we began to think too highly of them, we'd play them "Badgeman Brown" to remind them they were only human.' Such differences were forgotten when, on the Saturday before Christmas, Food held a party at the Brixton Academy. Jesus Jones headlined, and Diesel Park West and Blur played, as did Sensitize and Whirlpool, Food having found bands to go with the names they were so keen on.

As the year ended, Damon cast an appraising eye back on 1991 for the benefit of *Melody Maker* and celebrated the death of baggy, bemoaned the 'punk nostalgia' of the Manic Street Preachers and Bryan Adams' sixteen weeks at Number 1 and objected to the Gulf War and the Soviet coup while celebrating the release of the Beirut hostages and Anthony Hopkins' performance in *The Silence of the Lambs*.

Who doesn't know the sickening, empty feeling in the pit of the stomach when, on dropping by the hole in the wall to pick up cash for the Saturday evening revels, we glimpse the chilling bright green minus figure balance on the screen before the card is discreetly sucked from sight and we are told to 'contact our branch'. Hasn't the pay cheque gone in? And what about that 200 quid balance we had on Thursday? This can't be right.

These are the thoughts, though scaled up by several indices, that raced through Blur's mind when they found, early in 1992, that they were penniless. Worse than penniless, in fact. Much worse. Blur's pay cheque really ought to have gone in. They had recouped the couple of hundred grand spent on *Leisure*'s recording reasonably promptly. Despite aesthetic misgivings, the album had, after all, gone straight in at Number 7. They had hit singles to their name. They were pop stars of a fledgling kind. Unfortunately, their bank account told a different story. £40,000 was missing from their accounts and they were £60,000 in debt. Practically all of the money earned from *Leisure* had gone and, worse, creditors were springing up everywhere like Hydra's heads.

The realisation that their finances were lain waste dawned on them slowly. In Mike Smith's view, Mike Collins' days were numbered after his behaviour in New York. Now, as the band's accountant Julian Hedley began to uncover the true extent of the band's financial disarray, there were some hard questions being asked of him.

DAMON ALBARN: I don't remember how we got the first inkling. It wouldn't have been the band who noticed. Julian Hedley our accountant and Alistair George our lawyer must have realised that no one was getting paid. I've no idea why. I've heard wild rumours since but I can't see why it should have been malicious.

DAVE ROWNTREE: The way things worked was that whenever we needed money we'd go and see Mike and he'd give us some. Then we hired an accountant and a lawyer and one day our lawyer asked the accountant for a financial update. The accountant said, 'I can't tell you anything because Mike hasn't given me any details.' That rang alarm bells. Mike had always said to me on Friday or whenever he wouldn't see us for a few days, 'Could you sign a few cheques?' so I'd been signing blank cheques away. I didn't know any better. When it all came to a head and the lawyer requested photocopies from the bank, to my horror and embarrassment virtually every cheque had my signature on it. I resolved it would never happen again. Now I'm the one that reads all the contracts and legalese and it all stems from there. It really scared me.

Alex and Graham can both now recall the warning signs; the winking dashboard lights that should have told them the wheels of their car were about to fall off. 'I remember our tour manager saying, "So, do you think Mike's all right?" recalls Alex. 'Looking back, some people were trying to tell us. I remember turning up to the start of some British dates one time and we couldn't get the gear out of the studio because nothing had been paid for and cheques were always bouncing. The VAT hadn't been paid and that brought things to a head. Luckily we had a new accountant and lawyer and they got on the case because you can go to prison for VAT.'

Graham now feels that they should have known something was wrong. 'We were flying club class to France and drinking nice wine on the plane and then we'd get home and have no money for cigarettes. We'd recouped on *Leisure* but where had all the rest gone? Then we started remembering signing all these blank cheques, mainly Dave, who was very upset, but you don't realise it's stupid.'

It's unlikely that we'll ever know how Blur's finances got into such an unholy mess but it would seem reasonable to say that Collins was not keeping on top of the situation. The moot point, i.e. whether he acted – or rather omitted to act – out of incompetence or malice, is something that has baffled the group and those around them for years. In a touching testimony to the forgiving nature of the human spirit, nearly everyone is now prepared to give him the benefit of the doubt. 'After all these years,' reflects Dave, 'I think it may simply have been human error but he should have at least gone for help. When you're in a position of financial trust, you have to do that. You have to declare if you're in over your head.' Mike Smith quotes an instance that supports the simple incompetence explanation. 'Mike thought it was important not to take tour support. But that money comes from a marketing budget, it doesn't come from the band's money. It's there to be spent with no comeback . . . and he didn't bother taking it.'

'He was doing some really daft things,' says Graham. 'I don't think he was evil but he was rubbish and he shouldn't have been managing us.' Damon regards him as 'someone to be pitied rather than despised'.

Balfe and Ross and accountant Julian Hedley are now similarly generous and willing to attribute it all to poor business sense. 'When money is unaccounted for,' muses Balfe, 'there's always two explanations. It's either been misspent or it's been spent appropriately but someone foolishly hasn't kept proper book-keeping and receipts. One is very bad and one is just bad. I think it was probably the latter.'

Seven years and several million albums sold later, the Blur camp are admirably relaxed about what was at the time a near-crippling disaster, although they still aren't quite ready to laugh about it. Actually, that's not entirely true.

DAVE ROWNTREE: There's a guy called Mick Conroy who I'd known since Colchester days. I used to walk home from school with him. He went on to be in quite big stadium bands in America. Anyway, I knew that Mike Collins had managed a band he'd been in so when Mike Collins' name came up as our potential manager I took Mick quietly to one side and asked him about Mike. He said, 'Oh yeah, he's all right.' So when it all blew up I went back to him and said we had a funny business with Mike Collins and ended up losing all our money, and Mick said, 'Really? Blimey, that happened to us as well.'

As Andy Ross pertinently observes, 'I don't think Mike stole money but whether he did or he didn't they didn't have any money.' Emergency surgery was required immediately. Collins was called to a meeting with Julian Hedley, Alistair George and Damon. Collins denied knowledge of any money not in the account. Moreover, he became upset and angry, accusing the others present of being a Stalinist cabal intent on scapegoating him. None the less, he was summarily sacked. At this point, the future of the band hung in the balance. If it was to survive, it needed expert help. In Hedley and George they had this calibre of professional, but they now needed a manager and quick. Someone who understood the business; someone who might have salmon-pink sofas and Midge Ure gold discs in his office but who could be relied upon to get the best for the band and to make things happen. Blur, rather sheepishly, had to admit that they knew just the fellow.

Pete Frame probably remembers mid-60s college band The Dissatisfied – guitarist Jim Cregan later played with Rod Stewart and married Brit soul chanteuse Linda Lewis – but their thread in rock's rich tapestry is a slender one. But they were Chris Morrison's first tentative steps into the world of rock and roll. A Scot by upbringing (he left when he was fifteen but retains the faintest burr behind the transatlantic vowels), he met the band at college and was dragooned into managing them.

> **CHRIS MORRISON:** The first thing I did was get their nightly fee up from £5 to £25 so they thought I was a hero. Then things developed from there. I worked out of the front half of a disused fish and chip shop with a domestic cleaners agency. Then I went to work for an agent called Tito Burns. You can see him in *Don't Look Back* trying to negotiate a TV deal for Dylan. He was a big impresario. He had The Searchers, the Stones, Dusty Springfield, The Zombies. Then I went to work for Giorgio Gomelsky and through him I started to do the Brian Auger Trinity and I think I was pretty crap. But I carried on moving around and then I picked up Thin Lizzy, first as their agent in '71 and then as their manager in '72. They had their big break in '73 with 'Whiskey In The Jar' and I managed them till Phil died.

Through the 70s, Morrison's roster included The Sutherland Brothers & Quiver and John Cale. At the end of that decade, he enjoyed major success with Midge Ure and Ultravox, then later Visage, Dead Or Alive and Living In A Box. But by 1990, the year of his first contact with Blur, he was best known in alternative circles for managing the uncompromising Jesus And Mary Chain, essentially a vehicle for the excoriating rock and roll vision of the brothers Jim and William Reid. 'Geoff Travis of Rough Trade approached me and my US partner about them and we went to meet them in Dublin. I said to Jim and William, "I don't know if I'm right for you," and they said, "Look, we're chaotic on stage and as people. Behind us, we need someone who's organised."'

At Food's instigation, a selection of managers were approached with a view to the Blur job. Morrison was keen. 'I really wanted to manage them. I'd only heard one thing – "She's So High" – but I'd got a real gut feeling about them. I was mortified when I didn't get them; really disappointed. Later I asked them why they chose Mike Collins and they said it was because he took them to lunch and bought them loads of brandies. Since then I've always taken potential artists to lunch. Really, I'd never put much importance on schmoozing, we offer a business service and a relationship and I thought it would be enough. There was more to it than that too. The Wire connection worked in Mike Collins' favour and I think they thought of me as a bit of an old fogey.'

So Morrison watched, peeved, as 'There's No Other Way', 'Bang' and *Leisure* established Blur as one of the white hopes of their generation. But he had other responsibilities, namely The Jesus And Mary Chain. The Mary Chain, as the industry knows them, had emerged from East Kilbride in a squall of feedback and a blur of shades and leather in 1984. With demos recorded in a portastudio bought with their dad's redundancy money, they caught the attention of Alan McGee, whose typically astute handling of the London media made them the toast of 1985. Their debut album, *Psychocandy*, was rightly hailed as a classic: a squalid and romantic union of Spectoresque widescreen with punk monochrome. Radio One DJ Mike Smith had made a fool of himself over them by refusing to play their single, 'Some Candy Talking', on the grounds that he suspected dark drug references. Radio One DJs performed these acts of conceited idiocy periodically and no doubt will soon do so again. It may even be stipulated in their contract. Since then, however, the band had done little of note and were in danger of being absorbed into the body politic of alternative rock as elder statesmen. Morrison sought to up their profile and that of the quiescent indie sector generally with a tour project openly borrowed from the successful Lollapalooza package jaunts instigated by Jane's Addiction's Perry Farrell in the US.

CHRIS MORRISON: The alternative sector lagged a long way behind the mainstream in sales and profile. The best that indie bands sold was around 150,000. The Stone Roses, who were regarded as global superstars, had only sold 800,000 worldwide. Bear in mind that Michael Jackson thought *Bad* had flopped for selling 30 million. The idea behind Rollercoaster was to find a vehicle for the Mary Chain, something that would create excitement. They'd been around a while, they weren't such an event, and they never bettered *Psychocandy* in terms of profile. So let's do a tour which they headline each night and we take with us three other characters who we rotate underneath and we'll take the whole thing out of the clubs and on to bigger-sized venues and show these bands could play arenas or bigger halls. Blur were very enthusiastic and co-operative. Funny because the Mary Chain didn't think anyone would want to play with them. And there were some problems. My Bloody Valentine were a nightmare. Kevin Shields and his sister, who was looking after My Bloody Valentine, seemed to think everyone was out to screw them. Kevin Shields wanted to know why the Mary Chain had to headline and I said because it's our party. But everyone got equal money and equal facilities.

According to Morrison, he had already lined up Blur as potential guests on the tour, and it was an enquiry to their lawyer Alistair George about this that told him they were managerless. 'Alistair George said, "Can you deal with me from now on and not Mike Collins cos we fired him today." I said, "Sure. So what are they going to do for a manager?" He told me that they'd really like to talk to me but they were embarrassed. My attitude was no need to be. I must have done a bad presentation. I screwed up and someone did a better job. I'd love to meet them. So Damon and I had a one-hour meeting and he asked me to manage Blur.'

In Morrison's opinion too, Collins had 'not deliberately defrauded the band'. None the less, Morrison began 'a hell of an investigation'. They were roughly £60,000 in debt with £40,000 unaccounted for. Morrison bullishly declares that he's grown used to taking on artists and finding 'an atrocious level of previous management'. 'It's often not difficult to shine . . . but Blur's predicament was an appalling situation for an artist. But not insoluble. The first thing we had to realise is that the group could not exist beyond next week as things stood. So I started to look into things. They'd done a number of tours and when touring, the first thing you do is send your accounts and budget to the record company and get some money up front. This had never been done. Nothing had ever been presented to the record company. So I got this moving and we'd got £25,000 in about ten days.'

Then Morrison and Julian Hedley really began to earn their money, going into overdrive in order to try and pull the band's finances round and extricate the group from a seemingly intractable mire. Hedley began horse-trading with the various creditors, keeping them diplomatically at bay and negotiating various deals in order to defer repayment. 'They were overtrading,' explains Chris Morrison, 'meaning that had anybody called in their debt, they'd have gone bankrupt. But we kept them at bay and Julian Hedley negotiated to reduce debts and I negotiated with Julian Hedley to reduce his fee.'

DAVE ROWNTREE: Julian took over the day-to-day financial running of our affairs and sent letters out to that effect. He started getting letters back saying, 'As you're dealing with the band perhaps you can settle this bill for £10,000.' It turned out not only was there no money in the bank but not a single bill had been paid – debts for full PA hire for tours, not one bill. These bills were of such a size that if any one creditor had wanted to, they could have had us declared bankrupt which would have instantly meant the end of the band. So it was a good job we'd charmed everyone up till then. Everyone liked us and they helped us out. Julian ran around everyone doing deals and, praise the Lord, they accepted the terms. Otherwise we were completely finished as individuals as well as a band.

We started legal proceedings against Mike Collins but it turned out all his assets were in his wife's name. So he declared himself voluntarily bankrupt. We took out court action that as registered creditors we were entitled to any future money. He had to come to us and ask permission to be bankrupt. I've never forgiven him but I think the whole episode turned him into a broken man so I bear no ill will. In terms of interpersonal management, making sure everyone felt OK and focused and all those bullshit Americanisms, he was very good. He made us an awful lot of friends. He was a great guy, he knew everyone and told great stories and jokes but he had no business acumen whatsoever. He should have been a press officer. As Chris proved within a week, there's all sorts of ways for a working band with a deal to get money. So it was all for nothing really. I think Chris did say 'I told you so'. I would have done. He and Julian between them saved this band from extinction.

GRAHAM COXON: Lucky Chris didn't hold a grudge really. We were going to do Rollercoaster and kept it quiet that he was our new manager because we didn't want people to think something funny was going on. He was much more efficient and ruthless and that had put us off before but now it seemed very attractive after all this blithering. We thought, He's going to work hard and get us some money for food and cigarettes and he did. He scraped stuff together really quickly. And he's got the most outrageous laugh which was sort of cheering.

Unlike the Passenger Pigeon and Opal Mints, Blur had evaded extinction by a whisker. They still had almost a year of bitterness, booze-addled rancour, violent confrontation and misery ahead of them, but right now it was, hey, show time!

However beaten and bloodied the band were feeling on the eve of Rollercoaster, Damon was talking a good fight. 'Without wishing to sound really crap, I think Rollercoaster is the most exciting thing we've done. We usually look forward to the next two weeks on the road with a sense of dread and loathing but none of us can wait to get on this tour. To be honest, I'm a bit starstruck by it all. I'm delighted that we're gonna be playing with them even though we're very different to all of them in our outlook and in the way we try to present ourselves.'

If it weren't for Blur's presence, Rollercoaster would be rarely mentioned these days. Not that it was a failure: it was a bold idea, well received at the time. But whereas the Lollapalooza model was a travelling circus of side-shows, theatre and music, Rollercoaster, in essence, boiled down to three rather lugubrious if credible indie bands and one bunch of cute art punks off their nut and going for it with the abandon of a group whose career is unravelling.

ALEX JAMES: No manager, no money and nobody liked us. Yet Rollercoaster was fucking great. We were on the road with our favourite bands and that was the booziest tour ever. The others might have seemed a bit miserable but we were four serious drinking bands. There was always someone in the hotel bar, always someone to get drunk with. That's when the punching game came in, that's when we started hitting each other. Graham would pass out in his chair and we'd put him in the lift. It was all Chris's idea – a sort of tacky Lollapalooza. It was fun but it wasn't a big success.

That said, it was by no means a failure. Sizeable shows at the Brixton Academy, Birmingham NEC and Manchester Apollo all sold out and reviews were generally good. But a vague sense of disappointment hung over the venture. Chris Morrison feels that, 'To an extent it worked, in that we were playing to up to 4,000 people a night. That's pretty successful but the problem was half the acts, My Bloody Valentine and Dinosaur Jr, didn't have anything out. If they had new material out, it would have been huge, but basically all the excitement was generated by Mary Chain and Blur, who towards the end had "Popscene" out.'

Mike Smith is firmly of the opinion that Rollercoaster was 'a fantastic tour' for the band. 'Blur seemed like the token pop group but it confirmed their status as a rock and roll band. It was a very surly time. They used these films which were great; fast epileptic strobing things. There was a long piece about cows turning into meat then turning into shit. I remember Damon dropping his pants at Brixton Academy. Looking back, there was a manic exhaustion there. I was too close to notice that it was going horribly wrong.'

'Rollercoaster was OK,' is Graham's verdict. 'It was a lot more boozy than I would have thought. I thought the other bands would be more laid back. My Bloody Valentine seemed so lazy and grown up but they were the opposite. So it was an exhausting tour and all the while we knew that we had to get things together. "Popscene" didn't help.'

Pop music isn't cricket. Reducing it to statistics and averages tells only half the story. Marketing men and cynics who contend that records that don't 'ship units' are worthless trinkets for anoraks may have a small bitter point but anyone with a heart, anyone who's ever been passionate about pop, knows that some of its greatest moments went almost unnoticed at the time. Nick Drake's *Five Leaves Left* or the Scott Walker solo albums, some of pop's most cherishable moments, failed miserably to trouble the chart scorers when first released. Thus, 'Popscene'.

'Popscene' was one of the new songs that had fired Blur with creative zeal before the loss of all their money, the sacking of their manager, the negative responses of their record company and the exhausting Rollercoaster tour had frayed their nerves to ragged edges. But 'Popscene', Blur's first single in almost a year, was going to make everything all right; of this everyone was sure. It had been debuted at the Kilburn National Ballroom on 21 October of the previous year and they had performed it on the risible Channel 4 pop show *The Word* shortly after. It had become their explosive opening number on stage. The version released as a single at Easter 1992 had been recorded at Matrix Studios in February with Steve Lovell, Street being inexplicably out of favour with Balfe, and was the first instance of the group using brass on record.

A scathing attack on a culture and industry they felt increasingly

Dave Relaxing After The Word

20/12/91

at odds with, 'Popscene' is Blur's great lost single, perhaps even the great forgotten British pop song of the decade. It begins with a curdling guitar note played through a flanger and then picks up an ominous, thundering bass line and a drum rhythm modelled on Can's 'Mother Sky'. It remains a tremendously original and unorthodox single; vibrant, sharp, laceratingly intelligent and utterly at odds with the musical culture of the day, which then was swamped by the horrid, horny-handed witlessness of American grunge. Such music had become feted by practically every British pop journalist and consequently they dismissed 'Popscene' with an ignorant flourish. The *Melody Maker*, barely believably, mocked it as 'a directionless organ fest in search of a decent chorus'. Since the writer could not even tell an organ from a horn section, it was no surprise they were so wrong about the record, one that they would be venerating in two years when it was fashionable to do so. Worse, it failed to connect with the record-buying public and only limped to 34. This was a grave disappointment to all concerned. Even Balfe thought it was a winner and blames its poor showing on the tame nature of pop radio then. The resentment over 'Popscene' lingers to this day.

DAMON ALBARN: 'Popscene' was the beginning of a new phase in our music. It had an edge and presence that we hadn't had before and that no one was attempting at the time. I think it's a great song, I still think it's a great video and I still feel very disappointed it didn't do a lot better.

ANDY ROSS: They had this track 'Popscene' which we thought was great – this fucking song is a huge hit. Then it went in at 34 and we thought, Ah, this isn't going right at all. They had a song called 'Never Clever' that we thought was equally brilliant and the cunning plan was to have a big hit with 'Popscene', capitalise with 'Never Clever' and then we'd all be rich. But it didn't happen. 'Never Clever' didn't come out as a single and it was back to the drawing board. With hindsight, the world wasn't ready for punk rock with a brass section.

DAVE ROWNTREE: In a way, it was no surprise that 'Popscene' flopped because no one gave a fuck about us. But it's still a milestone for us. Steve Lovell did it in a few days at Little Russell Street, Matrix. We came up with the most powerful, amazing sound, just right for before you go out to the pub or club. It still sounds amazing now. It hasn't dated at all. But no one got it. The music press in England are a bit like the sixth form at school. The new bunch of journalists have to mark their own territory and say 'We're very different from the old guard', so we fell foul of that.

As a matter of principle, 'Popscene' has still never appeared on an album. 'Though that might change,' laughs Dave, presumably alluding to any future Greatest Hits. When *Modern Life is Rubbish* was released a year on, it wasn't included because the band felt, as Graham puts it, 'If you didn't fucking want it in the first place, you're not going to get it now.'

The failure of what was easily their best record to date only compounded the group's growing sense of desperation and isolation, not helped by their now punishing and near-suicidal regime of drinking. Graham had settled into a routine of a bottle of vodka a night during the Rollercoaster tour. Dave's drinking was beginning to worry many around him. They were poised on the edge of the abyss. For the remainder of the year, it was downhill all the way.

Blur's 44-date American tour beginning May 1992 is perhaps the greatest single shaping influence on them. In the same way, albeit much more seriously, that certain writers or film directors will return constantly to Vietnam in their work or Billy Bragg, Ken Loach and Ben Elton will never truly forget the miners' strike, so Blur's perspective of the world around them for the next five years would be forged in the blood- and vomit-spattered odyssey of their ten-week tour of duty through the baffled, unforgiving heartlands of the United States. Rueful exaggeration, of course, typical pop writer hyperbole, but if each year's Glastonbury Festival is routinely and feebly compared to the Somme, then let's compare Blur's '92 tour of America to a trip up river along the Mekong Delta to the heart of darkness.

Rita Rudner once said of the Pope 'I have great respect for him. I admire anyone who can tour without an album.' Why were Blur returning so soon after their last trip *sans* new material to a country which had no great yearning for them? Money. As part of Chris Morrison's swift and decisive package of emergency measures aimed at keeping the group afloat, he had landed a lucrative deal with a merchandising company. They were willing to advance some of this money on condition that the band return to the States for another tour which SBK were very keen on. This, however, puzzled Chris Morrison. 'I'd had no previous dealings with SBK. So I was surprised

Waiting For The Big One

4/1/92

that they wanted us to tour again to promote an album that was a year old. They said that they believed in really working a record. Getting the most out of it. OK, I thought, great.'

But that meant returning to America and a gruelling lengthy slog cross-country, SBK allocating them two days off in 44. Across a country, more to the point, where they meant nothing. America's soon to be christened Generation X were in the thrall of Nirvana, whose move from Seattle indie Sub Pop to baby boomer corporate label Geffen, with subsequent sales of nine million for their album *Nevermind*, was the touchstone moment of the era. Languor, indifference and morbid self-absorption were the order of the day. Later they elevated it to a movement, 'slacker', and its 'Do I have to tidy my room?' petulance to a creed.

'America had found its voice,' Alex observes, 'and no one wanted to know about these bouncy, floppy-fringed indie kids on the tail end of this failed Jesus Jones/EMF so-called British invasion. Balfe, though, was so keen on breaking in America that we were shipped off on this mind-bogglingly tedious tour of a country where nobody had heard of us. Nobody had heard of the biggest English bands. Nobody had heard of The Stone Roses so why the fuck should they have heard of us?'

DAMON ALBARN: We were doing two and a half months in America basically to sell T-shirts to pay off our debts. This whole massive tour was a direct consequence of the previous managerial shit we'd got into. That second tour changed everything. For one thing, we were drinking obsessively. Ridiculous amounts of booze every day. So I don't remember that much beyond the fact that we were very drunk at most gigs and we smashed up places all the time and there was very bad behaviour and it was relentless and depressing. It was hell and it just didn't stop.

GRAHAM COXON: It was a horror story. We hated every minute of it. We'd have these gruelling day and night drives to towns and cities where we meant nothing to the people there. I smashed all the mirrors on the tour bus in one of these emotional outbursts I was having. I was drinking too much and having this awful homesickness, completely at the end of my tether. We all felt the same. Me and Alex came to blows out of sheer misery and frustration. We had a fight in the car park at some godforsaken place and then we had this three-hour drive to the next gig. There'd been this scrap and Alex had really tried to break my nose and I started to cry and I decided to say the word 'arse' every five seconds for the whole three-hour journey. It was stupid and horrible. We meant nothing over there. We'd be drunk on radio interviews and would end up getting thrown out of radio stations and making people really angry. And the record company didn't understand our humour at the time which was very dry and, er, humourless, especially after a few drinks. We were very, very close to imploding.

There were new horrors at every turn. Damon's habit of throwing water into the crowd saw them chased from the stage by security guards and audience members more than once in the first week. *Vox* magazine reported that their gig at the Venus De Milo club, Boston, was 'a full-scale rock and roll riot featuring every rock and roll cliché in the book: promoter switches power off, audience destroys hall, band assaults bouncers who chase band into broom cupboard, band escape via window to waiting car, run into blood-soaked fans and so on.'

When the band arrived for their first meetings with the detested SBK label, they found that the label's talk of repromoting the *Leisure* album was disingenuous. There was, indeed, a new Blur product to be issued: namely several new mixes of 'Bang' under the appalling title 'Blur-tigo'.

'We didn't know,' explains Chris Morrison, 'but they were about to put out this version of "Bang" no one had ever heard. Damon was upset about this but I didn't know how upset really. My attitude was more pragmatic. I thought we should just let them stick it out.'

Alex has a clear memory of visiting SBK's offices and seeing teetering piles of these loathed artifacts arranged around the room. 'What the record company had done was commission these unauthorised remixes of "Bang" and the promotional gimmick was if the radio station was, say, 99x they got 99 of them, if it was 209 FM they got 209. So there were millions of these fucking Blur-tigo things waiting to be shipped out. And they were odious. A bit housey but in a really cheesy, six months out of date way. They had no sense of aesthetics, these people, they were just after a fast buck. You know how if there's a cool, fashionable pair of trousers you can buy in good shops then Carnaby Street will sell you a shit version of it six months later? That's what SBK were like. They just counterfeited the cool stuff. We all went back to the hotel in despair. We hadn't seen *Spinal Tap* at this point but looking back it was total *Tap*.

They were total Artie Fufkins. And on and on it went, playing these pubs in Wichita, Kansas. You can drink a lot at that age too so we were steeped in alcohol. Booze is fine but if you drink all the time for ages you turn into a nasty aggressive piece of work. If you're in a band in Los Angeles there's lots of things to do but when you're in Wichita and Topeka . . . Balfe's advice was take more drugs but SBK would be whining if I even turned up in the office having had a drink.'

The tour had a profound influence on Damon Albarn, who began to suffer, as did all four, from constant, gnawing homesickness. 'I started to really miss simple things. I missed people queuing up in shops. I missed people saying "goodnight" on the BBC. I missed having fifteen minutes between commercial breaks. I missed people having some respect for my geographical roots, because Americans don't care if you're from Land's End or Inverness. I missed everything about England.'

Dave Rowntree today is a wry and reasonable fellow with a lucid perspective refreshingly free of hyperbole and rockbiz bollocks. But even he is at pains to impress that Blur's account of their second US tour is no lurid self-mythologising. If anything, he doesn't think they adequately relate the soul-destroying trauma of it. 'It was really horrifying stuff. I went to sleep one night and Graham had smashed the whole bus up, every available pane of glass, and I hadn't even woken up. Slept right through it. The level of drinking was phenomenal. The crew actually nearly left us which is extraordinary – the crew are usually the worst. But the sound engineer had actually packed his case and was on his way to the airport. One of us had to go and stop him and tell him it would all be OK. But these weren't good-time antics; it was pure misery. An appalling time. The worst time. We were taking it all out on each other. There were permanent punch-ups. At one point we all had black eyes. Me and Alex would just be sitting there and suddenly he'd throw his drink over me and that would be it, another scrap. We were unbelievably pissed and upset and depressed all the time.'

This whole sorry chapter in the band's history is captured in lurid, vomit-flecked detail on the *Star Shaped* video, directed by Matthew Longfellow, and required viewing for anyone interested in the band. By the end, they were so unhinged, according to Mike Smith, that there was talk of replacing Dave Rowntree with Senseless Things drummer Cas, who was seen as 'more of a pop star'. But all things must pass, as George Harrison rightly said (though at tedious length) on his 1970 triple album. Eventually, the tour was over. Incredibly, The Senseless Things, who had accompanied them on this trek, had loved it and decided to stay on an extra month. But Blur were coming home. Psychotic, alcoholic, bloodied, bruised and on the verge of hospitalisation but coming home none the less.

That's when things really started going badly.

6 British Image 1

'ALL THAT WORK FOR NOTHING,' reflects Dave Rowntree on that now legendary tour. 'By the end of it, still no one had heard of us in America or cared about us and by the time we came home everyone had forgotten us here. We thought we'd have to pack it in. We weren't even hated – just forgotten.'

Although Blur were hardly helping themselves with their erratic behaviour and prodigious drinking, certain causes of Blur's malaise of late '92 were out of their hands. Two other groups in particular had cast a pall over them; two very different propositions but two groups whose ascendant stars were blinding everyone to what Blur had to offer.

Nirvana had formed in the late 80s in Washington State and signed to the Seattle label Sub Pop. The preferred musical style of the Sub Pop roster – loud, unkempt sludge-metal topped with angsty teenage lyrics – was something of a joke among music critics at the time. It seemed that every few months the same ad – Mudhoney, Tad, Nirvana. Doors 7.30pm – promoting the same package of acts could be seen in the back pages of the music papers as they touted their unwholesome wares around the grubbier end of the London music scene. From the start, though, it was apparent that Nirvana, led by the haunted trailer-park misfit Kurt Cobain and featuring his bleakly raging songs, were vastly superior to their hirsute, plodding peers in the fledgling 'grunge' movement. In 1990, they signed to Geffen and in October '91 released the epochal 'Smells Like Teen Spirit'.

'Smells Like Teen Spirit' was recently voted the best single ever made by the readers of Q magazine. It isn't that good, but you can see their point. It's perhaps wrong to say that there had been nothing like it before; you can hear the same melding of pop sensibilities with metal's characteristic morbidity in Black Sabbath's 'Paranoid', a group for whom Cobain had immense admiration. But 'Smells Like Teen Spirit' both defined, celebrated and reviled America's young in a record that was both structurally original, awesomely powerful, genuinely despairing and bloody catchy. It had crashed into the Top 10s of both the US and UK in the winter of 1991, ushering in the grunge era, a kind of musical dark ages, at least in this country.

For, as is often the case with influential records, books or films, 'Smells Like Teen Spirit', excellent in itself, spawned a rash of truly useless imitators such as Alice In Chains, Screaming Trees and Pearl Jam, each peddling their hoary rock and its attendant world view of self-pity, apathy and pomposity. As Blur dragged themselves across America, MTV had become a 24-hour rolling grunge network and the nation's indifference was withering and total.

Even here, though, grunge held sway. The *NME* put the utterly and rightfully forgotten Superchunk on the cover pretty much for having plaid shirts and lank hair. A dull earnestness that punk had done much to dispel began to creep back into pop culture – for what were Soundgarden and Stone Temple Pilots if not the Uriah Heep and Deep Purple of their time? People forgot how to dress – even those who had ever known how – and shampoo was anathema.

'Popscene', of course, and the new material Blur had been working on in the early part of '92 were a rejection of all this, a celebration of British vim and vigour. But while Blur had been schlepping around an uninterested United States (remember that they had been there twice already this year) another new pretender had emerged and seduced the few English rock journalists not addled by Seattle. They were to prove another millstone around the ailing Blur's neck. And unlike Nirvana, this time it was personal.

We began this book by positing the theory that all rock and roll is suburban, the craving of the commuter-belt kid for the anonymity and glamour of the big city. Nowhere is this seen more clearly than in the story and music of Suede. Their nucleus lies in the youthful dreamings of Mat Osman and Brett Anderson, two boys from lower-middle-class families in Haywards Heath, an anonymous dormitory town some 40 miles away from London. They met up with guitarist Bernard Butler after he answered an advert in the *New Musical Express* and initially played as a trio using a drum machine. An early rhythm guitarist – though this tends to be written out of the group's history now – was Justine Frischmann, and some credit her with giving the band its name. She left, however, before any recordings were released. Initially dismissed by the bulk of the media, who were infatuated with slacker rock, more discerning critics began to hear of them and their fame grew. They soon became the talk of a London media desperate for new sensations and were cover stars of both the *NME* and *Melody Maker* before they had released a record. Even the more sober and august *Q* monthly ran a cover story on them before an album had been released – a then unheard of extravagance.

Hyperbole abounded, as in *Melody Maker*'s, 'The most audacious, mysterious, perverse, sexy, ironic, hilarious, cocky, melodramatic and downright mesmerising band you're ever likely to fall in love with.' However, as stated before, even music press exorbitance contains a kernel of truth. Suede's early singles – 'The Drowners', 'Metal Mickey' and 'Animal Nitrate' – were bravura reawakenings of long-dead impulses in British rock, namely glamour, decadence and a kind of corrupt beauty. They winningly combined both a cocky swagger and the wretchedness of the English underdog. And, very simply, they had good tunes, strongly Bowie-inflected and heavily dependent on Bernard Butler's rococo guitar work.

More than anything else, it was Suede's unexpected dominance of the London music scene that galled Blur on their exhausted return from America. Justine Frischmann, an ex-girlfriend of Brett Anderson's and now living with Damon Albarn, was an obvious source of animosity. But there was more to it than that: Blur also felt that Suede had appropriated Blur's nascent cockney stylings and made them their own. Alex explains. 'The Suede thing was hard to deal with cos of the Damon Justine thing and Bernard Butler was a bit of a cunt and they were always rude to us in the papers.'

DAVE ROWNTREE: We were in a terrible depression. We'd very broadly been seen as the next big thing but in the sense of London's answer to something or other, we'd never had anywhere near the type of praise we thought we deserved. Then Suede came along and everyone said they were the best band in the world and there was these rumours that a tape of the *Modern Life is Rubbish* sessions had got to Bernard Butler. All bollocks probably but little rumours were circulating and we thought they'd nicked our sound. And we were into

Mike Leigh and they started to talk about Mike Leigh and Englishness and we thought, Hang on, that's us. So we were fucking well narked, I can tell you. This band was not only getting the praise and attention we thought we deserved but was getting it by saying the things we thought we'd invented in the first place. We had invented England!

To be fair, Suede's excellent early singles have little in common with *Leisure*. But there was more common ground between Suede and the new material Blur had been demoing and playing live, which would form the basis of *Modern Life is Rubbish*. And there's no doubt that Blur had steadfastly maintained a uniquely and unfashionably English viewpoint for some time. Add to this a feeling in some sections of the Blur camp that Bernard Butler had plagiarised Graham Coxon's guitar style and, *voila!*, a rank brew of mutual loathing.

DAMON ALBARN: When we came back from America, things got even more precarious. While we'd been away Suede had took off so I find that I've been away and when I come back, we're not very popular and the band of the moment is your girlfriend's ex-boyfriend. It was horrible. And it got stoked up by the fact that Brett Anderson was so fired up about being chucked. He was a man possessed. Brett Anderson was very angry and out of that came that burst of inspiration. All those songs on the first album which are about the two of us.

These songs, it has been suggested by sources close to the parties involved, were 'Animal Lover', 'Metal Mickey', 'Pantomime Horse' and 'Moving'. The air of hostility was not helped by some nasty exchanges in the press. Bernard Butler said the lyric to 'Bang' was the worst he had ever heard. Rather more seriously, Damon accused Brett of using heroin, for which 'he was a fucking idiot'. Creditably, he was later to admit, 'Every time I got drunk I got very nasty about Suede. I just couldn't see the woods for the trees because of Justine.'
While Suede held dominion over the music press, Blur came home to a creative impasse. Actually, their first visit to a studio on their return was in late June to record a version of Rod Stewart's 'Maggie May' for the *NME*'s 40th birthday triple CD, *Ruby Trax*. Still angry and humiliated from their US experiences, they were in no mood to treat the 1971 hit with any decorum or respect. The version they laid down with Steve Lovell at Matrix is desultory. Alex refused to play on the session because of his dislike of Rod

Stewart and the bass is supplied by a keyboard. The fact that Food considered this as a single shows the growing gulf between their and Blur's conception of what the group were about. This was to become more apparent as Blur's accumulation of new material neared completion. Frenzied activity on the demo front had produced over 30 songs, many now reflecting Albarn's antipathy towards the banal, swamping nature of American culture. These songs showcased a very different Blur from the fey noiseniks of *Leisure*. Sharp, quirky and steeped in British rock values, they had fired the band's sense of worth. Balfe, though, was hugely sceptical and Andy Ross was conscious of EMI's anxieties. 'There was a real possibility of them being dropped. The boss of the label at that time, Andrew Prior, was a very nice bloke but the figures were not adding up. The scenario was not good and he was concerned. But he relented, they didn't get dropped and for now they were spared. No one knew they were going to sell 1.2 million copies in the UK of the next album.'

That was not even a pipe-dream at the time. Things looked bad. To add to their woes, their drinking had now reached a near suicidal pitch. In Damon's words, 'It had got to the stage where we couldn't hold our instruments.' And it was drink more than anything which contributed to the fiasco which proved to be Blur's lowest ebb, their nadir, and in some ways a turning point.

The *NME*, in association with the homelessness charity Shelter, were organising benefit gigs that summer under the banner 'Gimme Shelter'. One such gig, at the Town and Country Club (now The Forum) in Kentish Town, was to be headlined by Blur with 3½ Minutes, Mega City Four and Suede as support. At this point, many would have disputed that billing, feeling that Suede should have been headlining. In fact, the running order was to work in their favour, as is often the case. Particularly given Blur's performance. Blur's preparations for this prestigious gig were to start the day with afternoon drinks at The Good Mixer. This drab Camden pub weaved itself so tightly into the weft of what became Britpop that it's worth taking a moment to tell the story of how it became a bona fide London tourist resort.

ANDY ROSS: Food had moved to Camden in March 1992 and it was very important that we had a local. We'd conducted a good deal of our 'business meetings' at The Crown when we'd been in Brewer Street so we needed a place like that. Quite arbitrarily, because it's near the office, it became The Good Mixer. Camden, you see, knows its indie pop, and we needed a pub where you could have peace and quiet and a few beers without the indie tourists hassling you. Within the Camden area it became quietly known that this was a cool pub to hang out in. Sufficiently tatty and a bit run down to have some kind of tarnished glamour. Two pool tables, draft bitter and a jukebox with Tom Jones and Nancy Sinatra and screaming out to be hijacked by us. We went in one day, opened the door, and there was three of Madness having a drink and Morrissey sitting on his own and no one else in the pub. Bizarre. Moz came quite a few times and Madness hung out there a bit. So from summer '92 right through '93 it became a place we could hang out, Graham and I the most. Savage and Best the publicists were next door to us on Arlington Road so they started doing interviews there so the writers would get a bit of atmosphere. So Pulp and Suede and the Auteurs would be down there too but then the journalists starting bragging in print about being down the Mixer with Blur and Moz and so the readers all got to know about it. And when the Japanese *NME* readers came to 'do' London they decided it would be great to hang out. Before you know it, it's mobbed every night and all the pop stars have fled.

The Good Mixer now is merely a crowded student indie pub but in the summer of '92 you could pop in and still find the indie glitterati having a quiet pint and a packet of smoky bacon crisps. On the day of the infamous Gimme Shelter gig, Blur no doubt started out in this calm fashion. 'The Mixer had become our base,' says Graham. 'We'd soundchecked and were killing time and Alex and I went into the Mixer for a couple of drinks. Andy came later then Dave and Damon.'

Ask Dave Rowntree about the day now and he will still blench. 'OK, here's what I remember. We were sharing the bill with Suede and they were the darlings of the time and that made us pissed off and depressed. We'd gone from feeling we could do nothing wrong to feeling we could do nothing right. They'd been supporting us for years and suddenly they were bigger than us. So we all went out in the afternoon and got right royally pissed up. Damon had bought a new shirt and tipped a bottle of wine all over it so I offered to go home and wash it and meet them in a couple of hours.'

The session got more and more punishing as the afternoon wore on . . . or wore off, more accurately. Alex and Graham actually got lost in Camden, Graham's neighbourhood. 'Ridiculous but that's the state we were in.' They decided to visit every pub in Camden and miraculously wound up at one directly opposite the Town and Country Club.

Here, not surprisingly, accounts vary. Andy Ross thinks, 'I turned up at six and all four were pissed. They were an absolute shambles. At the time I was their mate and not talking to Balfy so I sat down and had a few drinks with them and they were completely and shockingly pissed.'

Dave insists he was not at the pub. He remembers next seeing his comrades at the venue. 'I got back a couple of hours before we were due on stage and everyone was in the dressing room by then. I'd left them narked but jolly. When I came back the mood was pure poison. You walked in the room and knew that this was a place that no right-thinking person would want to spend time in at all. If there had been guns in the room, everyone would have been shot. They'd been in a pub across from the T&C all afternoon. People could barely walk. But everyone was fully compos mentis and fucking angry.'

Damon drunkenly wandered into Mega City Four's dressing room swigging from a bottle of spirits, where he proceeded to lecture the group on the evils of American culture, as their singer Wiz later reported. 'He just kept saying how much he hated the place and how all Americans were wankers and how he fucking hated gigs and he was trying to get us to agree. We just sat there listening and I remember thinking, We're not from the same planet as you, mate, and then one of our band just opened the door, pointed him towards his own pissed-up dressing room and pushed him out.'

The band staggered towards the stage, nearly insensible. 'Before we left the dressing room,' recounts Dave, 'I thought, I've got some catching up to do here, and necked drink after drink, but even then I was still comparatively sober by the time we got on. I could see my instrument. We walked on stage and Damon said, and I quote, "We're so fucking shit you might as well go home now. This could be the worst gig you've ever seen." And he was right.'

Damon's opening announcement – so refreshingly different from 'Are you ready to rock, Cleveland?' – has now passed into legend. However, there are some dissenting voices who seem to recall a ramshackle but bracingly punkish set. Indeed, Blur authority and Graham's drinking partner Biffo claims it is still the best Blur gig he has ever seen. Graham is similarly enthusiastic. 'It's very frustrating when your brain wants your fingers to do certain things and your fingers won't. You know when you write phone numbers down in pubs and you get home and you can't read it? Great show. I'd like to have seen it.'

'It was a real low point,' reflects Alex now, 'but it did us a lot of good. That was the point when people saw we weren't just arrogant upstarts, that we had something sort of real and intense. I think it was great in an insane way.'

Insane is *le mot juste*. Instruments and drum kits were trashed, gymnastics were attempted and failed miserably, and Damon tried continually to shoulder-charge a speaker cab off the stage. Several times, Alex and Graham collapsed in Buster Keaton-style pratfalls. Contrary to some later versions of events, the crowd did not leave en masse. Indeed, many lapped it up. It was funny and electrifying and unforgettable but in a rather desperate tragi-comic way. It was a band on the edge of a nervous breakdown. No, it was a band having a nervous breakdown right before your very eyes. Mike Smith remarks, 'I didn't think it was that bad. I'd seen them so fucked up before. Damon was leaping on Alex's back and then they'd all fall over. But of course Suede were on such a roll that it reflected badly on Blur. I dragged a girl along that I was trying to impress and she was like, "What the fuck is this?"'

Melody Maker's Jon Selzer seems not to have noticed that the band were near demented with drink and instead used the space to deliver a pompous, unintentionally funny diatribe against the youth of Britain, or at least that rather small section of it who might be reading his words, 'Blur are one long gloat, they offer nothing but contempt and you lick it up like all the shit shovelled your way because you're too numbed to care.' *NME*'s Keith Cameron characterised it more pungently as 'Carry On Punk Rock'.

DAVE ROWNTREE: It had attitude but a bad attitude. I was thinking, Please, somebody break something so I can get off stage. We ought to have apologised to the homeless. That was a low. But not isolated. It was fairly common for us to be so drunk we couldn't play. There were times, fairly frequently, we'd turn up, drink the rider and make them get us more before we went on and then drink that. Some nights it worked and was mad and enchanting and lunatic. But that night it didn't.

Chris Morrison straightforwardly asserts that, 'They were appalling, fucking dreadful. They were in a complete mess backstage before and after. I said, "There's no point discussing it, I'll talk to you tomorrow."'

Dave Balfe, horrified by what he had seen, demanded a similar post-mortem. Ironically, on the way to it, a builders' van drew up alongside them and the driver wound down the window and shouted at the group, 'Best fucking gig I've ever seen.' Less pleasantly, it was then on to Arlington Road and a meeting with Balfe. Damon remembers it well. 'Balfe said, "I've seen all this before with The Teardrop Explodes. It's all going to collapse and go wrong. I'm washing my hands of you." It was a tough meeting. Essentially he told us that we were probably going to be dropped.'

By the time the band got to Chris Morrison's offices just over the Thames in Battersea, a chastening hangover was upon them. 'Balfe had a conversation with them that lasted hours, telling them their careers were over. In my meeting they walked in and said, "We know, we know. We've arrived at a rule. No beers till half an hour before we go on." I said fine. If they'd come and tried to justify their behaviour to me, I'd have known there was no point me continuing. If people want to commit suicide on stage, which is my memory of what they did, then you have to let them. But they sat on the couch and admitted they'd been stupid and said they wouldn't let it happen again. They are intelligent lads, after all.' The band still value Chris's supportive attitude. Damon points out that, 'Chris said we were fucking idiots but he also made it clear he was on our side. Chris had seen a lot of these problems in his time with Thin Lizzy – problems with drink and drugs.'

'He said, "You can't build a career on this,"' remembers Dave. 'Perfectly right too. We were at a stage where we couldn't have too many shows like that. "Popscene" had flopped and everyone was watching expectantly. We had a very hungover meeting and we all agreed to ban alcohol before the show apart from one beer half an hour before. I think that was at Chris's suggestion; he thought you do need something to steady your nerves. That was very reasonable. I think we were very worried that the gist of the meeting might be, "I no longer want to work with you and now we have to go to the police station because you killed a granny last night."'

'We just liked drinking,' Graham touchingly puts it. 'And Andy encouraged us. Everyone did. When someone said, "Who wants a drink?" we all went, "Yeah". I didn't know much about it cos I was in cuckoo land all the time but apparently we were near to getting dropped. Balfe had meetings with Damon and said how familiar it was after The Teardrop Explodes. He thought it was all pointless. We were going to split up.'

Beleaguered is a word that best sums up the band at this point. The situation with Balfe and EMI, Food's parent company, was to worsen still, but Blur's one motivation was that they were sure they were finding their own voice musically.

ALEX JAMES: Artistically the tide really had turned. After all this shit in America we were keen to get back in the studio and get the new record done. It was good in a way that the American company were so inept and shit because it forced us to forge an identity. I'd been waking up and thinking, I don't want to do this, but now we'd been forced into something and it turned us back into revolutionaries. So Damon's seen the future and it's not shopping malls in Michigan, it's greasy spoons and cafes. Remember, in that year I spent five months in America. This after eighteen years in Bournemouth and one in Camberwell and one in Lewisham. We all knew quite a lot more than we did. 'Popscene' and Rollercoaster were not massive successes. But we kind of got a vision; we knew we were good. We knew where to go.

Where to go was home. Back to Blighty. To forget Balfe's transatlantic ambitions for the group and forge a new and very British image. In the end, of course, it was to pay rich dividends, but there was still some pain and disappointment to come. For one thing, Balfe was still unsure about production duties. The Lovell/Power partnership had dissolved and though Lovell had been working with the band on new material, Balfe was dubious. Also 'Popscene', from these sessions, had flopped. Furthermore, he was persisting in his refusal to commit to Street.

DAVID BALFE: It was all very complex at the time. We had always argued about producers. Stephen Street had had a go at 'Bang' and it hadn't been a great success and I wasn't bowled over by the production. Similarly 'Popscene' with Steve Lovell. I felt we could get better production. Well, we argued over a few names and I have seen this misrepresented subsequently. One of the names was XTC's Andy Partridge. This was very much at the band's suggestion. Although it

Sunday Tea With Alex

6/9/92

was a good idea and I liked it, it was definitely at the band's suggestion, or maybe Andy's. Anyway, they did four songs, I think, which were quite expensive although not ridiculously so. They were about to go abroad for a week's work or something and I said I had bad news and good news. 'The bad is I don't think what you've done to date really works. The good news is I think it could work with a lot more work.' They were very keen on these recordings and so they were really pissed off with me but when they returned they were the opposite. They didn't want to proceed and they didn't want to use those sessions. Since then, they've said that we forced him on them. But that's bands for you.

On paper, Andy Partridge was an inspired choice, whoever's choice it was. Partridge's roots lay in the art punk of his band XTC, a genuine English one-off forged in the quiet Wiltshire town of Swindon whose music combined new-wave brio and bug-eyed psychosis with a deep love of the English song tradition stretching right back through The Beatles and music hall to folk, plus a heady sense of psychedelia. Albums such as *Nonesuch* and *English Settlement* had been critical successes and the making of a compact but devoted cult that stretched from provincial England to Tokyo to US colleges. A string of hit singles in the late 70s and early 80s confirmed that the group had the popular touch too. It seemed like a marriage made in heaven.

GRAHAM COXON: I was a big XTC fan. I liked the idea of Andy Partridge producing us. It was the band's idea. Damon went to his house to work on his four-track and saw his painted soldiers. We did some stuff at The Church in Crouch End. The trouble was that it ended up sounding like Andy Partridge's music at that time. You might want to sound like The Eagles but not Don Henley, you know. We enjoyed working with him. It was fun . . . but he had this horrible way of saying 'Trust me' – and I don't trust people who say that. So there was a slightly nasty atmosphere between me and him sometimes. Balfe and Andy really liked what we'd done, which I couldn't understand.

DAMON ALBARN: We started to work with Andy Partridge but that went wrong very quickly. He had this weird habit of regularly saying, 'Don't make the mistakes that I made.' There was a very odd vibe. It's fairly well known that he's quite insecure. Maybe because he didn't write 'Making Plans For Nigel'. I don't think he really knows how to be a producer. For various reasons it didn't work but what I did get out of that was an eight-track that he sold to me which I still use. That was great.

Three songs were recorded in the eventually aborted sessions: 'Sunday Sunday', 'Coping' and 'Seven Days'. None have ever seen the light of day although the first two, re-recorded with Stephen Street, appeared on *Modern Life is Rubbish*. Some sources have suggested that Partridge's somewhat schoolmasterly demeanour may have irked the band and he himself acknowledged this when he spoke to XTC's biographer Chris Twomey about it some time later. In his view, the problems began 'when they picked up their instruments and started playing!' He adds, 'It wasn't totally successful. We didn't seem to hit it off. I think I am a bit dictatorial. I know what I like and I don't think they were delivering what I thought they were capable of. Maybe they thought I was pushing them a bit too hard. Maybe it was the "difficult second album" syndrome for them.'

So the band refused to continue and have consistently refused to allow the sessions to be released, even as B-sides. Andy Ross is still faintly baffled by the whole 'Andy Partridge episode', as he refers to it. 'My observation was that everyone was really up for it. We all thought XTC were great. We all met up in the Mixer and arranged to go into the studio and try these three or four tracks. A week later, nobody's talking to each other. They delivered a DAT which sounded great and still does. But they felt they were being pushed too much in an Andy Partridge direction rather than Blur. Balfy and I thought it was great but they weren't having it and record companies can only be so ogreish and they wanted nothing to do with it. So we said fair enough, we wouldn't even let them out as B-sides.'

Graham's personal problems and excessive drinking meant that though he was aware of the group's worsening situation, he feels now that he – and Dave and Alex – may not have felt the full pressure bearing down from Balfe and, above him, his paymasters at EMI. 'I knew we were in trouble but I still didn't know we were in danger of getting dropped. I didn't know it was that desperate a situation. But Balfe was not confident in us after "Popscene" and he was getting pressure from EMI. There was a mild state of crisis all the time, but I've only recently realised how bad it was. I probably wasn't showing any interest. Damon was getting most of the pressure. I don't know why he didn't tell us. Perhaps he didn't want to scare us. Perhaps he was protecting us. That was kind of nice of him but maybe not the best idea.'

On 1 October, with the Partridge sessions over and Blur's second album effectively stalled, Graham went out to the old Marquee on Wardour Street to see hotly tipped new Irish band The Cranberries. 'It was one of their first London shows when they were still too scared to face the audience. I bumped into Stephen Street there and he said, "Where's your album?" and I grumpily said, "Not started yet." He was really surprised and upset.'

STEPHEN STREET: We hadn't had any contact in ages but I knew things were going wrong. There'd been a little buzz about them and then they'd gone off to America and had this horrendous time. The period you can see on *Star Shaped*. They were in a bit of a state and Suede had overtaken them. I'd heard they were working with Andy Partridge and then I bumped into Graham at a Cranberries gig at the Marquee. I'm all 'How's it going?' and he was obviously very down and not forthcoming. I said, 'Chin up, you're a great band. It'll all work out.' I tried to give him a bit of a pep talk. When I got home I thought, Wouldn't it be nice to work with them again but they've gone their own way. Too bad. The following day, I get a phone call from Damon: 'Stephen, come and meet us.' Very direct. So the band then were very keen and they were on to Balfe to 'give Streety a try'. But Balfe's attitude was 'over my dead body'. He was very against me. If the band hadn't really stood up to him, they wouldn't have used me. But they did and we got on great again and we went back in to do what became *Modern Life is Rubbish* in the last quarter of 1992.

Chris Morrison confirms that 'David Balfe did not want Stephen Street involved. We had to fight tooth and nail to get him on board which meant convincing David Balfe over several meetings.'

Balfe states: 'I thought the Andy Partridge stuff was great and for reasons I couldn't understand they wouldn't have it. I wanted to get these tracks out and I got more annoyed with them than I'd ever get with a band now. We had a very major run-in about them wanting to go in with Stephen Street and, as always, if the artist wants something they get their way. You can't force them. You can only persuade.'

But Balfe's persuasion had failed. On 9 November 1992, as America got its first Democratic president in twelve years, another phase of Blur's hiccupping odyssey began when they resumed work with Stephen Street. Over the next month, they amassed seven tracks which all eventually appeared on *Modern Life is Rubbish*. Indeed, they represented the thematic spine of the record, at least as it was originally presented to Food.

'Coping' was a track they had attempted with Andy Partridge which had met with Food's approval. A catchy tune with a nagging, anachronistic synth line, Andy Ross thought it a potentially career-saving single on first hearing. 'Colin Zeal', a character study of the kind Damon was to become increasingly fond of, had been written in America while in the thrall of The Kinks and concerns the workaday life of an imaginary provincial Englishman. Graham, thwarted from drenching the track in Sonic Youth-style guitar noise, was allowed to play a Black and Decker drill quietly at the song's close. 'The trick with Graham,' reveals Damon, 'is to give him the illusion he's creating a racket.'

'Blue Jeans' concerns a Saturday afternoon shopping in Notting Hill and the gorgeous chord change to A with an F sharp bass on the Saturday of the first verse and repeated thereafter displays the group's increasingly adventurous nature. Alex recorded this song 'completely pissed' having spent the afternoon in the pub with the band's accountant Julian Hedley. 'Advert' is energetic and slyly reminiscent of Seymour. The crashing A/G chord riff originally introduced the song before the grafting on of the toytown piano intro. The siren noises are produced by the crowd-control megaphone that Damon had acquired on the band's first Japanese tour. The opening remark, 'Food processors are great,' was sampled by Damon from the Shopping Channel on the cable TV at Maison Rouge on to a Casio SK1 keyboard with built-in sampler. 'Pressure On Julian', while not often thought to be actually about Julian Cope, certainly uses the name because Damon knew that alluding to The Teardrop Explodes' singer 'drove David Balfe bananas'. The song has a long lineage, written in September 1991 and demoed at Matrix in January '92, and was played every night on the Rollercoaster tour. The line 'magical transit children' was spotted on a wall in St Pancras. 'Turn It Up', a reasonably catchy pop-rock song, is now disowned by Damon ('it's crap'), perhaps for those very reasons. Graham adds, 'When we wrote it we thought it was a perfectly good jangly pop song. But it turned out to be an MOR song. It didn't have any peculiarities so we were turned off by it.'

'Star Shaped' takes its name from a caption in Kurt Vonnegut's

Breakfast of Champions and refers to the characteristic shape of a supine figure, hence 'insensible'. Once mooted as a single, this terrific track marks a major advance in Damon's songwriting (though Andy Partridge had encouraged them to attempt a samba arrangement which they detested). The song's highlight, the wind ensemble segment at 1.38 – cor anglais, oboe, soprano sax – is played by former Julian Cope cohort Kate St John. Stephen Street adds finger cymbals at various points (1.34, 2.34, etc.). At the close, Graham contributes a note on a Moog synthesizer which increases in pitch and finally passes out of the human hearing range, hence the credit 'anti cat and dog Moog tone'. Though one of Blur's finest moments, the bass line to the song gave Alex more headaches than any other. In fact, he was struggling to get a good version on tape when David Balfe and Andy Ross dropped by to check on progress.

Bear in mind that at this juncture, Blur, for all their difficulties, had a crusading zeal for the music they were making. The American ordeal had, as Alex puts it, turned them into revolutionaries. The songs on *Modern Life is Rubbish* – off-kilter, clever and above all, 'British' – reflected a sensibility at odds with the mainstream of alternative rock but all the more exciting for that.

'The British music press had turned away from anything going on in Britain,' states Dave. 'Nothing in England counted and that really pissed us off. It's one thing to be called crap, but it's another to not even think you counted, not important enough. So we decided to make the record as English as possible; a record full of English references and English cultural icons. You get the fighting spirit when things turn against you. We'd started work on *Modern Life is Rubbish* and were very excited. We'd found a way of working and songwriting that worked, managing to do the other things, include the energy and lunacy, and it was working.'

'It's one of our best records,' asserts Graham. 'British music had turned farcical and we were reacting against that. We'd got a lot better at playing and were pushing ourselves musically. We didn't want to make leaden rock with blues scales and dreary lyrics like everyone else. We were quite weird at the time mentally. We were trying to make the records we really liked. You can hear on "Oily Water" I'd been listening to The Pretty Things – the *S.F. Sorrow* and *Parachute* albums – and a lot of other British psychedelia. And I was obsessed with Francoise Hardy and Nick Drake.'

Imagine then their horror at Balfe's reaction. He hated it. Absolutely hated it. Dave's recollections of the afternoon are vivid. 'We were really excited. We wanted to play them this one and play them that one and show them just where we were at with this new direction. And Balfe just turned round and said, "Personally, I think this is worse than suicide." He said it was bollocks. Art wank. Which from someone who's been in The Teardrop Explodes is the pot calling the kettle black. Essentially he said we had no hope of selling any records. We were staggered. I remember at the end of Balfe's session of slagging us off we finally got him to agree to at least let us finish the album. He said, "Well, I think you're making a big mistake and after this I'd say you're dropped, basically." This was effectively Balfe saying, "You are dropped at the end of this record."'

Andy Ross was to some extent caught in the middle. 'I think he was in despair,' says Graham, 'because by then he'd become a friend of mine.' But Ross shared Balfe's reservations, albeit to a milder degree. He felt the record as it stood was 'hermetically sealed, a house without any doors'.

'Andy, good bloke though he is, was very little help at this point,' says Dave. 'I'm sure Andy will say that he was responsible for rescuing us and settling all our differences and whatnot but to be honest he was pouring oil on the water. He was in fact getting us to accommodate Balfy, not the other way round.'

DAMON ALBARN: I've always got on well with Andy. I used to stay at his house. I got the taste for the London scene from Andy. We were definitely much closer to him than Balfe. But they were both wrong about this. Neither of them have proved that they have magic ears. Andy's musical knowledge is amazing and he's passionate but they got lucky with us. They told us we were doing the wrong thing with *Modern Life is Rubbish* when in fact we were predicting the way, in fact, creating the way, everything would go in British pop for the next three years.

Damon's artistic theory, as outlined on *Modern Life is Rubbish*, was that soon the public would sicken of the hand-me-down angst-ridden banalities of grunge, its ugly, shapeless music and slacker values of apathy and ennui.

DAVE ROWNTREE: Damon said, quite rightly, we were going to focus on Englishness and say very clearly we can make English music a force to be reckoned with. I distinctly remember him saying that within a couple of years the tide will turn and English music will be trendy again. Everyone will be on this wavelength. Balfe ridiculed him. 'Well, Damon, you can look in your crystal ball and predict the future but I have to look at the market as it stands at the moment.' Fucking cunt. He had no faith. But we were moving away from formulaic pop that he understood so we were bound to have some almighty clash with him at some point. And this was it.

Alex's memory of the afternoon is straightforward. 'It was nearly all done and Balfe and Ross came down and basically said, "What are you doing? No singles on here. This is shit." Later I got a letter – we all got letters, I think – saying it's all over, basically.'

Balfe and Ross left the studio and the band descended into stunned and despairing silence. Even for a group as high on self-belief as Blur, this was a sucker punch to their confidence and self-esteem. 'It started to cross our mind, – my God, what if we are mad and this is wrong?' says Dave. 'We were quite inexperienced and didn't know bullshit from the truth. It's more obvious to me now that when someone says, "There's a right and wrong way in the music business to do things and you're doing it the wrong way," then it's bullshit because there is no right and wrong way. But we didn't know that then and we wondered if Balfe might be right. Perhaps we'll fuck ourselves if we continue on this route. I mean, he had a proven track record. He'd been in a successful band. He'd taken Jesus Jones to Number 1 in the States. It was difficult to know who to trust. Damon had a very clear idea of what he wanted the record to sound like. Balfe had a very clear, different idea of what the band should be. Who do you trust?'

Stephen Street was similarly devastated by Balfe's reaction. 'When he left we all just crumpled. What do we do now? He'd diseased the whole thing. He'd said it was shit and washed his hands of it. "You'll sell to a few *NME* readers and that's it" was one of his parting shots.'

Gamely, the band soldiered on and the record was completed and delivered to Food in December 1992. They rejected it. Balfe felt the record was lacking commercial clout. 'It didn't have any hits on it. I knew they had to come back with something really big after the failure of "Popscene". They won't accept this but I had their best interests at heart . . . and my own, of course.'

Dave Anticipates Another Party

Balfe wanted Damon to come up with another song. Damon was angry but allowed the idea to percolate. At this time, Blur held a curious Christmas gig at the Hibernian Club on Fulham Broadway, 200 yards from Maison Rouge, on 16 December. The unorthodox bill consisted of a Salvation Army band and feted leading lights of the abortive Riot Grrl movement, Huggy Bear. Few punters who attended can have known the turmoil the group were in as they filed in to collect their free single, 'The Wassailing Song'. This single, a medieval carol that Graham and Damon had sung at Stanway Comprehensive, was recorded during a break in the *Modern Life* sessions. Its limited edition run of 500 means it is now their most sought-after rarity. All great fun, although Food thought the gig a mistake.

'It was a completely pointless gig which ended up costing them money,' judges Andy Ross. 'It's very symptomatic of where heads were at Christmas '92. Certain gigs have been benchmarks along the way and reflected aspects of their career and personality: the great one at the Reading Festival '93, the terrible one at the T&C, the pointless one at the Hibernian.' Soon after the gig, mired in depression, the band repaired to various parental homes for Christmas.

DAMON ALBARN: I went back to Colchester. It was a really horrible Christmas. Balfe had said write some more songs and that was on my mind. I went out on Christmas Eve and got really drunk and woke up really early on Christmas morning very hungover and went down into the kitchen and wrote 'For Tomorrow'. I woke my dad up. He came downstairs and wanted to know what the fuck I was doing up this early. That was a really important song for us. It was the beginning of us being a different kind of band.

Incidentally, during the same holiday, Damon also wrote 'One Born Every Minute', which he describes as 'The Kinks song Ray Davies never wrote' and insists will see the light of day at some point.

Back in London directly after New Year, the band and Balfe instantly recognised the potential of 'For Tomorrow', not least for the irresistible 'la la' chorus. 'Everybody, wherever they are in the world, knows what "la la" means,' explains Graham. When Food heard the song, its expansive pop mood so reminded them of ELO that they thought of hiring Jeff Lynne to produce it. Fortunately they didn't and Blur went into Maison Rouge with Stephen Street to lay down the song with The Duke String Quartet, whom Street had known since his engineering work with the Durutti Column, and backing singers Miriam Stockley and Mae McKenna, whom Street instructed to sing like the singers Thunderthighs on Mott The Hoople's classic 70s singles.

The results were breathtaking: a magnificent pop song that alternated regally between the stately verses – punctuated by Graham's staccato B flat barre chords – and the Tommy Steele chirpiness of the choruses. There's no doubt that this song, and indeed Damon's songwriting over the next few years, was heavily influenced by a curious record by the performer Allen Klein called *Well At Least It's British*, which Damon picked up in a junk shop. It contains a song, 'He's A 20th Century Englishman', whose title is echoed in 'For Tomorrow''s opening line. Balfe liked the song but was still angling for further additions.

DAVID BALFE: I said, 'That's great. Now can you do another one like that.' And they were very pissed off. Absolutely no fucking way. In the end I gave up. So we whacked it over to the American company who'd sold 100,000 copies of that first album – I don't think they beat that in the States till *Great Escape* – and they've sold a million Jesus Jones records and thought Blur would be the next moneyspinner. Later on it would be seen that SBK were a fairly shit label but at the time they were very successful. I think in fact they'd had the most successful first year ever of any label. SBK's response was to say exactly what I'd said – it needed more singles. The two main guys came over and sat down in my offices in Camden and said, 'There is no American hit on this record.'

CHRIS MORRISON: Blur delivered the record and I went to a meeting at EMI with David Balfe, Tris Penna the product manager and Tony Wadsworth, head of marketing then, the MD now. And Balfe drops this bombshell. 'The Americans don't like it and I agree with them.' Up until then the whole company had been excited. My jaw dropped. I'd never experienced anything like it. Balfe was undermining the group from within the label. Tris Penna quite rightly attacked him. I came out of that meeting and spoke to Damon and broke it to him that the Americans were very down on it and that Balfe would like you to do another track. He said, 'I've bloody done it.' I agreed but I said, 'If you're smart you'll do it and show willing rather than stamp your foot.' So he went into the studio over the weekend to do another song.

Demoed at the Roundhouse, Chalk Farm, under the sarcastic working title 'Americana' and recorded with Stephen Street in the last album session, 'Chemical World' is another thunderously good track that asserts the group's growing confidence and skill; a sonically powerful observation of city living full of seedy voyeurs and check-out girls at the end of their tether. Andy Ross describes 'For Tomorrow' and 'Chemical World' as 'a knight in shining armour and the seventh cavalry respectively'. SBK loved it and, incredibly, demanded even more in this vein. Indeed, they wanted the whole album re-recorded with Butch Vig, now of Garbage, then the premier grunge producer. As Graham states, 'That seemed a thankless task. So obvious and just what you'd expect from such a shit label. Butch Vig had produced his piece of history with *Nevermind*. He wasn't going to do it again.'

This time, all concerned – except Balfe who was fighting for more singles but acknowledges that the group were 'really pissed off' – said enough was enough. Blur's second album, named *Modern Life is Rubbish* after a piece of graffiti on the Bayswater Road near Marble Arch, was ready for release fifteen months after work on it had commenced. The nine most recent tracks had come from the sessions with Stephen Street over the past four months. 'Oily Water' and 'Resigned' dated right back to the October '91 sessions with John Smith at Matrix.

Two songs came from a session with Steve Lovell they'd undertaken in the wake of the Partridge false start, before resuming work with Street – 'Villa Rosie', a paean to an imaginary and fabulous gentlemen's drinking club, and 'Sunday Sunday'. The latter has taken on an irritating cast now and Graham has said he would be delighted never to play it again. Its significance lies in its acerbic observation of the minutiae of ordinary English life, in this case the Sabbath's tedious rituals (although it was written while watching from a hotel window a shopping mall scene in Minneapolis). It points the way very clearly to *Parklife* and the new Blur. Balfe hated it – 'When was the last time you heard a hit single that sped up in the middle?' – almost as much as he hated the album's two instrumentals 'Intermission' and 'Commercial Break' (John Smith demos that Street thought worthy of inclusion as they stood). The former, which they had begun their set with as 'The Intro' back in Seymour days, gives a flavour of that group's style; a drunken, dizzy, cake-walking piece of nonsense with a real undercurrent of menace. Both tracks give the impression of the music from *Postman Pat* gone horribly wrong.

The inclusion of 'For Tomorrow' and 'Chemical World' certainly made *Modern Life is Rubbish* a better album, which seems to vindicate Balfe's judgement. Stephen Street thinks so. 'In retrospect, it wasn't finished. Balfe was right. He was downright rude and upset me and the band a lot but ultimately they made it a better album.'

Andy Ross defends Food's intransigence by pointing out that, 'They were coming within an inch of being dropped by EMI. They were in the middle of a backlash and Suede were everywhere. Then they deliver this album that's less overtly commercial than the first album and at the time didn't contain "For Tomorrow" or "Chemical World". Balfy was adamant and he was right. He had my total agreement: they had to write some singles. Of course they were sensitive – they'd made their big statement and here's Balfe the philistine saying it's too arty. Chris Morrison got involved and was quite rightly defending his artist. There was an almighty row with Balfy. But Balfy was right. And it ruined their relationship.'

The band go along with this so far, although Graham asserts that, 'There were singles on it before. That's what Blur did; we made singles.' Alex and Damon are of the opinion that whether he was right or not, the manner in which he treated them – 'bawling us out while I was trying to do the bass part to "Star Shaped"' – was unforgivable.

DAVE ROWNTREE: For another band he might have been right. For us he was completely wrong. When he signed us he liked the free-wheeling lunacy he remembered from his Teardrop Explodes days. He liked the echo of Cope he saw in Damon. He saw us as young and impressionable enough to be his playthings on which he could try out his theories of the music biz and whom he could discard if things didn't work. We just weren't having that so there were always going to be major differences. So perhaps all this crystal ball business was just his final attempt to assert himself and to influence us. 'If they're not going to do what I say I'm not interested,' and maybe he rationalised that by saying what he thought we were doing was rubbish. Who knows? What I do know is that that was one of the last times we ever let either of them come down mid-session. Although they'll both deny this, a problem with Balfe and Andy is that they can't hear a song in progress and listen to it as a song in progress. They both tended to say, 'What's this fucking song with loads of stuff missing?' It takes a lot of years in studios to get that kind of skill. They didn't have it so we had to stop them coming down.

GRAHAM COXON: I've blocked a lot of this period out because it's so upsetting. But I remember he would shout at us, furious, like a headmaster in his office. I do remember being in his office like at primary school on the black plastic seat. He was a pig. He's quite frightening when he's angry and we were getting defensive and hating him more and more. We wanted to be The Smiths – well, we wanted to be ourselves and he'd accuse us of being contrary. I think he thought we were trying to be weird and difficult. Anyway, he was dreadfully unfair and a bully. He made us feel small and choked so that we couldn't be rational. He was destroying us. It took us a long time to get over the scarring of 1992. It was the worst year of my life on every level. It's etched in my mind. I moved into Andy's flat at the tail end. Walking to Camden from Archway every day, hoping someone would buy me a lager when I got there, making dog-end rollies. I know the violins are coming out but it felt like no one cared, and we were trying our best to please everybody. I'm glad it's over. It got better after that. It had to. It couldn't have got worse.

DAVID BALFE: We had real run-ins. Damon really proved to be far stronger than I thought. I think he discovered what he believed in in those fights. I was trying to mould them slightly, yes, in a pragmatic way. I should have understood that we'd have one bad meeting and we'd get on with something else but Damon would go off and have three weeks of angst. It's their career but it's just one of our projects. At the end of this period, I came out with a new-found respect for him but our relationship was damaged.

It was damaged beyond repair, as the coming months would prove. But for now, *Modern Life is Rubbish* was about to be launched on an unsuspecting world wearing flannel shorts and ripped denims. How would they react?

A final telling point. SBK eventually decided that the full-on dynamic production of 'Chemical World' done specifically with the US rock market in mind was not to their taste. When the album was eventually released in America seven months later, they used the band's original demo. They may have had the most successful opening year of any label in history but SBK's difficulty in discerning

Grez going for the Seattle Look

Smith
2/10/92

arse from elbow was to spell doom for the company within two years. No doubt Alex James raised a glass of Krug at the Groucho Club. For, though it was still only a dot on the horizon and seas were decidedly choppy, Blur's ship was coming in.

7 Soft Porn and Sport

G EORGE ORWELL ONCE REMARKED that the English intellectual will accept anyone's jingoism except the English's. He had a point. He wasn't thinking of pop music at the time – he was actually talking of the praise heaped on Irish republican playwright Sean O'Casey – but he might have been. Periodically, the whole of the pop media, never a place for the most coolly cogent discussions of politics, gets very red-faced about 'jingoism'. True, this was much more prevalent in the late 80s and early 90s pre post-feminism and the rise of the Lad. Nowadays, when odious fat DJs routinely slight women for entertainment, one might actually pine for a spot of good old sparkly-suited political correctness. Five years ago, though, the refectory sit-in and 'Maggie, Maggie, Maggie' mentality was still dominant in most music paper offices. Hence sporadic skirmishes over various *cause célèbres*.

In August 1992, while Blur were drowning in alcohol and rowing with David Balfe, even they must have noticed the brouhaha surrounding Morrissey's solo appearance at Madness's Madstock event at London's Finsbury Park. The former Smiths singer took to the stage to sing 'Glamorous Glue', draped in a Union Jack. From the front ranks of the audience – some of whom may have been twerps of a far-right persuasion – came a half-hearted bombardment of orange peel, litter and coins.

As art riots go, it was no Rite of Spring. Yet a furore ran through the offices of the weekly music papers. At the *NME* on the following Monday morning, production was halted and the cover was switched to feature a shot of the hapless Moz and his inflammatory garb. Great swathes of the paper were given over to fulminations about crypto-Nazism and 'flirting with Fascist imagery' (these words are used so often in the music press, it was suspected that the sub-editors had the phrase ready made up waiting to be 'cut and pasted').

Imagine the *Daily Mail* in full 'dole scrounger/single mum/illegal immigrant' apoplexy and you have the idea.

In truth, Morrissey had been a fool. Given his predilection for provocative titles like 'National Front Disco' and 'Bengali In Platforms' and the traditionally high percentage of skinheads in a Madness audience, he might have known that his actions would be subject to full public scrutiny. His explanations for such songs had always seemed oblique and unconvincing and he did seem to enjoy the kerfuffle.

But then why not? It is a cliché to talk of 'a free country' but none the less true for that. And freedom means the freedom to be a fool. If a black man such as Linford Christie can drape himself in a Union Jack and be (rightly) seen as a symbol of a vibrant, pluralist culture and honourable patriotism then why not a working-class, second-generation Irish Catholic? Perhaps it's indicative of how times change that Kula Shaker's infinitely more dubious discussions of Aryan myth and swastikas received much less attention when that scandal boiled over in the late 90s. As for Union Jacks, by the mid-90s, when one strove to contain the buxom Spice Girl Geri Halliwell or others were emblazoned upon Noel Gallagher's guitar, it was apparent that it had become depoliticised, neutered and returned to the place in pop iconography it had held in the 60s: a colourful, silly totem, like the Lambretta, the Mini Cooper or the mini skirt.

In 1993, though, Britpop was unheard of. The independent music sector was resolutely outside the mainstream. The notion of bands like Manic Street Preachers, Oasis, Radiohead or Blur being best-selling artists was laughable. And the indie culture still drew on ideas and accepted theory that bounced around the not entirely representative ideological climate of the student bar and the pages of the *NME*.

Thus, when Blur unveiled the first publicity materials for their new project in early April 1993 to coincide with the release of 'For Tomorrow' as a single, there was an almost predictable froth of outrage.

The picture looks innocuous enough now: the four band members are arranged in front of a white wall which bears the legend 'British Image 1'. They wear three-button mod-style jackets, Fred Perry shirts, jumpers, zip-up cardigans and Doc Martens boots and shoes. In the foreground stands a Great Dane. They look great. It's a hugely effective press shot. Within a year or so, most British groups would look like this and indeed the bulk of their audience. In spring '93, though, it had the music papers spluttering with outrage. The *NME* accused the band of, yes, 'flirting with Fascist imagery', although quite what they meant was unclear. As far as we know, the Spanish Falangists did not favour the Fred Perry. Neither was Mussolini ever spotted with his Great Dane.

We are being disingenuous. What they meant was that the group had chosen a very English proletarian style adopted at various times by mods, skins, rude boys and others. Blur intended it as a complete rejection of both the sloppy, untailored, frankly gruesome indie look as modelled by Ned's Atomic Dustbin and Carter USM and the ubiquitous slacker look of flannel or plaid shirt worn open over washed-out T-shirt and denims or fatigues. To talk of Fascism is nonsense and particularly unilluminating since it prevents a real discussion of what the style adopted means.

In his book *Subculture: The Meaning of Style*, the British sociologist Dick Hebdige posits the notion that the rude boy/boot boy style of the late 60s was a conscious attempt to reassert traditional values of masculinity and working-class pride by young men who had become deprived of traditional roles (breadwinner, family leader) by the collapse of their communities and the return of mass unemployment. The look was a very conscious rejection of the florid, effeminate, exotic look favoured by the hippies. These youths had been, of course, a fertile breeding ground for football violence, gang fights and, yes, racism. That was the dark side of the values of working-class vigour and subcultural style that Blur were drawing upon. But to accuse someone who wears a Fred Perry of being a Fascist is intellectually as sound as accusing someone who wears a replica football shirt of being a Fascist. It's an unthinking response; the same character flaw that Orwell talked of; our own version of what the Aussies call 'cultural cringe'; a knee-jerk embarrassment at our own traditions. Actually, there was much more of the mod than the skinhead about Blur's new look and that was easy to read. Grunge celebrated apathy, torpor and self-pity; this look – sharp, tailored, striking – spoke of hedonism, wit and energy.

Damon declared this new motivation explicitly in a rash of interviews given to promote the release of 'For Tomorrow'. 'When we were in America, England became this wonderful fantasy place. The album is a soundtrack for a fantasy London,' he told *NME*, talking specifically of 'a modern retard in an Essex new town . . . who's got cable TV and watches World Wrestling Federation'. Elsewhere in the same piece he relates the tribulations over the release of the forthcoming album. 'The record company said, "Why are you singing in such English accents? Why are you using brass bands? Why aren't you rocking out more?" . . . I remember going to speak to them and saying, "In six months' time you'll be signing bands who sound English."' To the charge that they had become an anti-grunge band, Damon had happily owned up, saying, 'People should smarten up and be a bit more energetic. They're listening to Black Sabbath again. And that irritates me.'

Of course, what they were listening to was about a tenth as good as the dynastic, fantastic Black Sabbath, but let it pass. We take his point. This whole diatribe was reproduced in the *Daily Mirror* under the marvellously crap headline 'Grunge Grudge'. Damon was quoted as saying, 'If punk was all about getting rid of hippies, we're about getting rid of grunge. People are walking round like hippies again with stooped shoulders, greasy hair and horrible clothes. There's a lot of great music being made in Britain and it's time kids stopped listening to American rubbish.'

DAMON ALBARN: 1992 had been a desperate year. It was a very emotional time too what with our experience in America and the rise of Suede and the bad feeling about Justine. Course, it wasn't made easier by Balfe, who was very negative. He was very cynical about what I was saying. Well, perhaps it was just because it was an emotional time but I had a gut feeling that things were going to change and that British music was going to change. I just knew it was going to happen. Our reasons were very different from some of the other bands who came along. Very complex and lateral. It wasn't just about Union Jacks and Fred Perrys.

DAVE ROWNTREE: I remember us walking round Lake Ontario and seeing all these Canadian flags outside people's houses. The British flag had been so tainted by the neo-Nazis in the 80s. Now apparently Doc Martens, which I'd been wearing since I was fourteen, were a Nazi symbol too. Only the very stupidest people got upset and the ones who wanted a fight with us and we took 'em on. Half the fun is winding up the right people. It was a load of wank. What we were saying was wank and what they were saying was wank. It was a lot of fun.

When 'For Tomorrow' was released on 19 April, it was clear that not everyone was going to get this radical shift in emphasis. While the smarter journalists were sympathetic, some were frankly baffled by this turn of events. One, writing in *Melody Maker*, told them to 'fuck off' and pointed out, wittily, that their name sounded like someone vomiting. Most, though, acknowledged, if mutedly, that Blur were trying something new and admirable, even if they weren't sure where it was all heading. Perhaps the most typical response came from the long-gone, unlamented *Indiecator* magazine which revealed, bemused, that the track 'sounded like The Kinks. Yes, you read that right. The Kinks. Has Damon lost his marbles or does he know something we don't?' To which the short answer was yes.

Not everything was new and improved about Blur, though. Some things never changed. After a party to promote a new record by ageing punk rockers The Buzzcocks – whom, ironically, one could detect traces of on *Modern Life is Rubbish* – Dave Rowntree became so drunk that he got involved in a fight with Buzzcocks' Tony Aber. The ever reliable Linda Duff reported the scrap at length, in colourful ringside reportage: 'The odds looked good for Blur as their tall, thin, 25-year-old (sic) drummer squared up to the spiky-haired 30-something Buzzcock . . . Traffic in London's Soho was brought to a standstill as the rebel stars slugged it out in the street . . . POW! Punk rocker Tony launched a barrage of blows on the Blur drummer's face. THUD! Dave fought back with an uppercut that Frank Bruno would be proud of . . .' etc. etc.

DAVE ROWNTREE: We'd been to some top gig in Soho and then all bundled off to the pub, Tarquin from Chapterhouse and all the journalists, and we got hammered and had some stupid scuffle with some bloke who turned out to be the bass player in The Buzzcocks. It started as a kind of joke and then got out of hand cos I was in sleepwalk mode those days. Linda Duff the following day did this big piece about how he'd called my mother's honour into question or some such and I, justifiably, had beaten him to the floor. Actually Miki from Lush broke it up. Far from it being manly fisticuffs it was a crap drunken brawl broken up by a girl. But people didn't mess with us after that. They thought we could handle ourselves.

On 10 May 1993, *Modern Life is Rubbish*, Blur's long-overdue second album, was finally released in the UK; internal collapse at SBK and a newly 'streamlined' alternative division consisting of one woman were to hold up the release in the US for seven months. The cover was another superb production from the Stylorouge studios, whose work was now visually synonymous with the group. For 'For Tomorrow' they had commissioned a scene of World War 2 fighter planes over English skies from a Yorkshire greeting card company and then blacked out the planes and repainted the sky hyper-realist style to give a sinister, unreal quality. For the album, they produced a lovingly nostalgic picture of a stream train, the Mallard, chugging through the English countryside; a 50s *Boy's Own* comic conceptualisation of an ideal England.

Reaction was, by and large, good, as more and more pundits came round to seeing Blur's point: that it was time for Britain to wake from its debilitating grunge hangover, put on 'Hunky Dory' or 'Waterloo Sunset' or 'Anarchy In The UK' and pop off down to the greasy spoon for chips, egg and a fried slice. This is a caricature, of course, but to an extent so was the record – a kaleidoscopic, encyclopaedic, slightly grotesque sight-seeing trip around an England that was a land of McJob opportunities, supermarkets, golf courses, commuter belts and high rises filled with characters from Martin Amis and Charles Dickens. *Modern Life is Rubbish* provided a slightly bitter twist on John Major's eulogy that month for the 'real' England of warm, flat beer, cricket and spinsters cycling to evensong.

Most reviews were warmly encouraging and made the obvious comparisons: The Kinks, The Who, Bowie, The Small Faces. Cleverer ones also pointed out the distinct colourations of Wire and The Teardrop Explodes while, cleverest of all, Tony Parsons spoke in his *Daily Telegraph* review – a delicious irony in itself – of Ford Escorts, fish fingers, football pools and Flanders And Swann.

To anyone who would listen – and there were more every day – Blur expounded their new-found love-hate relationship/total immersion in English mores. Damon claimed, 'This album doesn't celebrate England. A lot of it is triggered by things which are quite sinister such as the Americanisation of England . . . I'm talking about bubble culture; people feeling content in these huge domes that have one temperature and are filled with this lobotomised music. That's all happening here and a lot of feelings about it are on the album.' Alex proclaimed, 'Ours is the sort of Englishness a war wouldn't change. It's to do with a latitude and a history.'

They were at pains to point out two things. First, that there was no proto-Fascist sub-text to their work. The ultra-right BNP had recently had its first councillor, Derek Beacon, elected to a seat on the Isle of Dogs and people were getting edgy. Damon's comment that 'our culture is under siege' was a little strong for some. But he was referring to what he called the 'Coca-Colonisation of Britain' rather than the foreign immigration that fuelled the race hate of the bullies and morons of the extreme right. 'Besides,' he confided to The Stud Brothers in *Melody Maker*, 'there's even a disco track on our next album.' (No one at this point could have known what a momentous track that would be.) In the course of the same interview, the group vied to rail against Nirvana's accepted position as demagogues and rebels. 'What have they done?' asked Dave Rowntree. 'Turned soft American rock into slightly harder American rock. Big deal . . . does it mean they're dangerous? It doesn't mean shit!' In the same vein, Damon queried, 'What have these blokes got to say for themselves? "I'm fucked up." Fantastic.' Before closing, he had his now obligatory pop at Suede and Brett Anderson. 'Too obsessed with his own sexuality, or lack of it, to articulate anything about Britain.'

The other point they were keen to make concerned the album title. After considering *England v America* and *British Image 1*, they had plumped for the Bayswater Road graffito and were keen to assert that this was not a pejorative value judgement but a statement of fact about the recycled nature of the modern world. 'We're in a period of accelerated recycling of old culture,' commented Damon. 'By 1995, we'll be celebrating 1995 . . . everything that we see around us is rubbish. We're all living on the pinnacle of this huge rubbish tip. It's quite a simple statement really.' At times, they seemed to be in danger of overstating the case, however. 'I think it's the most profound statement from pop culture since "Anarchy In The UK". That's why I want to graffiti it everywhere.' Egged on by the roguish rock photographer Kevin Cummins, they did just this for an *NME* feature, which brought down yet again the wrath of the *Colchester Gazette*.

'GRAFFITI POP BAND RAPPED . . . Colchester pop band Blur were today told to clean up the seafront graffiti they sprayed to promote a record . . . Terry McKean, chairman of the Clacton and Tendring Hoteliers and Guest House Association, said, "They should be made to come back and repaint the whole building and the money should come from the album royalties."'

If only Mr McKean had known that Blur would have been lucky

to repaint a Wendy house out of their own pockets. They were still in dire penury, though Chris Morrison and Julian Hedley's prompt actions had secured their immediate survival. Alex puts the speed at which they recorded *Parklife* down to their straitened financial circumstances, as we shall see later. For now, *Modern Life is Rubbish* reached Number 15 in the album charts. Not great but creditable, particularly in an early 90s music industry fiscal climate which was completely different to now.

> **ALEX JAMES:** I don't think we got on *Top of the Pops* for any of the singles from *Modern Life is Rubbish*. I think we sold 20 or 30,000 copies initially, which isn't fantastic but no one was selling records then. Certainly no guitar bands. A gold record then was a very big deal. It's hard to imagine now. Old people were the only people selling records; that and very poppy things. Bands didn't sell albums. The Stone Roses had had a platinum record and that was the only indie thing that had sold in years.

But a corner had been turned. Sales of tickets were brisk for their early summer tour, which began at Leicester University on 26 May and on which they took additional musicians and keyboardist Cara Tivey out for the first time. Blur's defiant new stance – ruefully celebrating and questioning the 'real' nature of English culture while rejecting all that was 'rawk' and MTV – was apparent, to the chagrin of some, before they set foot on stage.

The stage set consisted of a surreal, gargantuan bedsit-cum-domestic lounge. Standard lamps, cooker, fridge; an ironing board as a keyboard stand and a huge settee as a drum riser. Pride of place, naturally, was given to the TV set. This was tuned to ITV and *News at Ten*, a wry comment on pop groups' normal 'intro' tapes of obscure funk or torrid orchestral music designed to show the audience how hip they are. It was a point lost on some, though. Journalist Johnny Dee overheard one irate punter grizzling, 'This isn't a gig ... I didn't pay six quid to watch Trevor fucking MacDonald.'

That it was indeed a gig was confirmed minutes later when the band took the stage and crashed through a maniacal 'Intermission', a nod to their Seymour days, and then into the bracing amphetamine charge of 'Popscene'. This was to become their standard opening gambit for some time and it worked extraordinarily well; visceral as hell but anything but standard rock fare. At some shows on this tour they showcased 'Girls And Boys', their 'disco track', and 'Parklife'. Receptions were generally ecstatic and critical assessments positive, apart from the odd murmur of dissent such as *The Times*' reference to their 'studied surliness'. Best of all for a band who had been accused of courting unpopularity, the tour was a sell-out and an extra gig at London's Astoria was added. There was even a show in Tallin, capital of Estonia, newly liberated former Soviet Baltic state.

In June, Food released 'Chemical World' as a single, thus fulfilling its manifest destiny, although it only reached Number 28 (curiously the same position as 'For Tomorrow'). This was not the altitude of chart placing David Balfe was looking for, although he too realised that there was a sense of a turning tide and a feeling that perhaps the group's hour was coming. 'I was still disappointed. There'd been a big drop down in sales from the previous album but funnily they seemed set up now in some way. The singles too were keeping their head above water though they only got to 28, both of them, and the next, "Sunday Sunday", only managed 26. Even then that wasn't great but it was OK. We were still very much a player. You'd be very third division now in the alternative rock world with three Top 20 singles.'

> **GRAHAM COXON:** Generally, it felt like things were getting better. 'For Tomorrow' had left us with that feeling. But there were still great pockets who weren't really understanding what we were doing. Basically, sheep with brains got it and sheep without brains didn't. It's funny seeing the 'Chemical World' video now. Beavis and Butthead said, 'Are these guys Australian? They look like they want to be pissed on.' That's funny but frustrating because if Beavis and Butthead didn't like you you were fucked. And there seemed to be so many videos to make. I loathed them. They take over your life and 'Chemical World' and 'For Tomorrow' were all location shoots in the country. So you do twelve-mile hikes and then you're expected to perform. And look reasonable.

If tabloid reports of the time are to be believed, the situation was not helped by a six-month 'booze ban' Food had placed on Graham following a doctor's orders. This does not seem to have run its course.

At the Great Xpectation show at Finsbury Park, headlined by The Cure, Damon and Graham dropped by to perform an acoustic

'For Tomorrow' – the highlight of the day for many. One show of the summer stands out in everyone's memory, though, and that's their appearance on the second stage at Reading. Held annually on August Bank Holiday weekend, Reading has none of Glastonbury's exotic, magical, new-age eco-warrior vibe and has traditionally been chiefly notable for the dull backstage area and affording an opportunity for the bikers of the Thames Valley to throw bottles of piss at Meatloaf. Vastly improved organisation and a more alternative clientele have seen it become progressively more palatable through the 90s, but the 1993 line-up was still characterised by dour, worthy, antagonistic American rock *à la* headliners Porno For Pyros and Rage Against The Machine, the articulacy of whose politics and outlook was shouted down by their formulaic industrial rock. Over in the blue corner, though – or rather the red, white and blue corner – were Blur.

> **CHRIS MORRISON:** It was a strange situation because although no single went above 25 in the chart, things felt like they were moving forward. Then they played the second stage, the big tent at Reading on the Saturday night, and I'd say there were 10,000 in there and 5,000 outside trying to get in. The The came on on the main stage and no one left. They were just brilliant. Damon came off and the mood was absolutely euphoric and the crowd had gone mad and he said, 'Maybe now the industry will pay attention.' I said, 'You don't need the industry. Those people out there are paying attention and they are the ones that count.'

> **STEPHEN STREET:** The real turning point for me was the night they played in the big tent at Reading. It was just awesome. The tent was packed and they were great. 'Bank Holiday' was in the set by then. A really telling point was the little gaps in 'Colin Zeal', the pauses before the '. . . and then he!' The whole crowd knew them; knew the timing of the song. It sent chills down the spine. For me, that's the best gig they've ever played. You knew they'd survive. More than survive.

Damon later confirmed that, 'It was amazing. The first time I was ever in control of my performance. It was a lovely feeling and I suddenly realised what we were.'

'We always seem to realise when it's a big deal and when it's important we get it right,' says Graham Coxon. 'Damon will always tell us stuff like that and we try to ignore it. Our crowd went far beyond the tent and we played really well with a lot of passion and proved something to ourselves. We knew as soon as we came off that something very good had happened.'

Over the summer, Blur had been sporadically demoing with John Smith at Matrix. One session produced the curious but attractive B-side 'Es Schmecht', bad German for 'it tastes good', and a tune that recalls Van Der Graaf Generator in the sax part and legendary German avant-gardists Can in Alex's bass line. In a typically Blur switch of emphasis, they also demoed, right after 'Es Schmecht', the new number 'Parklife', which had been proving popular on live dates. (Radio One DJ Mark Goodier gave a very early preview of the song that July, the best part of a year before it appeared on record.)

Ahead of live shows in the autumn – the Sugary Tea tour, named after the line in 'Chemical World' – it was decided to release 'Sunday Sunday' as a single. Though again not a substantial hit (Balfe's theory about hit singles not speeding up in the middle seems intact – although Alex points to Fatboy Slim's 'Rockafella Skank' as an exception), it served a neat conceptual purpose. For if anything, 'Sunday Sunday', with its acerbic observations of quotidian English life cloaked in heel-clicking Tommy Steele bonhomie and boozy brass arrangement, is thematically conjoined to *Parklife* rather than *Modern Life is Rubbish*. For the B-side, the band and a loose amalgam of friends repaired to Matrix one Sunday to record versions of the music-hall standards 'Daisy Bell' and 'Let's All Go Down The Strand' (a third song, 'For Old Times' Sake', was later wiped by Damon). The backing vocalists included Justine Frischmann. Damon was absorbed in music hall at the time and if the gesture seems a little overdone now, it serves to remind how the group, especially Damon, were thinking in mid-'93 and their obsession with native British idioms. Another practical reason for their recording was the then current craze for different formats of single releases. This meant more chance of getting a record in the chart but proved a constant drain on material to fill the extra CDs and B-sides. Yet another version of the single had the earliest Seymour demos included too. 'It was like the nuclear arms race,' says Andy Ross shrewdly. 'You didn't like it but you weren't going to stop while everyone else was doing it.'

The short but sweet Sugary Tea tour consolidated the group's rising prestige and self-confidence. The group were accompanied on

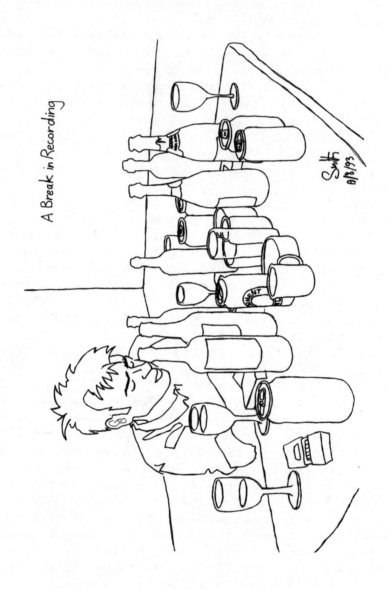

all fourteen dates by Salad, whose engaging quirkiness sadly never struck a chord with the public, and also held a series of question-and-answer sessions at local colleges, the outcome of which was every bit as awful as might be guessed: 'Do you take sugar in your tea?' 'Is this the death of intelligence?' etc. As soon as the Sugary Tea tour had ended, the group returned to the studios to begin work on their third album. Damon attributes this alacrity to the fact that, 'I was on a roll. Really confident, really passionate about what I was doing.' Alex is more prosaic.

> **ALEX JAMES:** We recorded *Parklife* so quickly after *Modern Life is Rubbish* because we were skint. Nigel Frieda who runs Matrix and Maison Rouge studios sort of took pity on us and used to give us 50 quid a day to keep us going and we had to go into the studio to get it. £12.50 each. One of the reasons we were so prolific was that we had to go there. All the money had gone in this management fiasco and £12.50 was at least a packet of fags and a few pints. This is absolutely true. On tour you get free food and a tenner a day PDs. When you're at home in a skint band, it's hand to mouth. Being in a band, you spend half your time eating in expensive restaurants and the rest being hungry at home.

Hunger or creative zeal, Blur began work on the album – whose working titles included *Soft Porn* and *Sport* – in earnest in the September of 1993. Filling the producer's chair brought everyone to the usual loggerheads. 'Balfe kept saying "I told you so" about *Modern Life is Rubbish*,' states Chris Morrison. ' "Look, I told you. It's done 40,000 in the UK. It's a commercial disaster." I tried to tell him that it didn't matter. It was a precursor; the smart people had bought into it then, but everyone was going to get it next time. But he was adamant that he didn't want Stephen Street to do it. Tristram Penna said he thought that *Modern Life is Rubbish* was good but felt the rhythm tracks could perhaps be bettered. Well, I could see his point but I thought it was stupid to ditch Stephen Street and lose that 80 per cent that was obviously right to take a chance on someone else. It was throwing the baby away with the bath water. So Tris and I took Stephen to lunch and Tris made his point that he felt the drum sound could use a little modernising, let's say. We convinced him to try that.'

Stephen Street was well aware of what was going on. 'Balfe didn't want me to do it but I got the impression he had basically washed his hands of the group by then. He'd been so critical that there was no future between him and the band. They couldn't relate to him at all. So when they said they wanted me for *Parklife*, that was it. At that point, he just sort of bowed out of the argument. One day Chris Morrison and Tris Penna took me for lunch and said, "We'd like you to do the album but this is the big one so, you know, do your best." They gave me this pep talk basically. I did feel like saying, "Get off my back. Am I doing something wrong here?" '

Street, then, was installed as producer. Among the first songs to be attempted were 'Parklife' itself and 'Girls And Boys'. 'Parklife' had been demoed in the summer and become part of the live set for a while. Generally, omens were good. 'They played it at the Astoria at the end of the autumn tour,' recalls Chris Morrison, 'and the audience went mental. Tony Wadsworth and I were there and we just turned to each other in amazement. Audiences notoriously don't like new stuff.' Stephen Street was present at the same gig and his attention was also caught. 'I liked the bass line and the spoken delivery which was unusual. I thought, There's some good stuff building up here.'

Perhaps mindful of his 'pep talk', programmed drums were used but they were too tight initially so Stephen got Dave back to 'just bash some really loose new drums in over the top to give it that character'. The other distinctive musical flourishes are Graham's sax playing and clipped intro guitar chords (an E sharp raised to the thirteenth fret to give heightened pitch and tension) and the bass line that had been written by Damon which, whether knowingly or not, contained a leap of an augmented fifth, known as the 'devil's interval' and actually banned by the Christian church in the middle ages for its demonic sound.

Originally, the cockney narration was delivered by Damon, but he felt that it was inauthentic and strained. He had contacted the actor Phil Daniels, a boyhood hero of his and Graham's via his appearance in *Meantime*, with a view to narrating over an instrumental Damon had written called 'The Debt Collector'. 'We were all really amazed when he turned up,' says Street, 'cos we were expecting this sharp cool mod from *Quadrophenia* and he had this long hair and straggly beard cos he was playing some tramp in the musical of *Carousel* at the Shaftesbury Theatre.'

Unfortunately, Damon hadn't actually finished the lyric to 'The Debt Collector'. 'Oh fuck it, I thought. He can do "Parklife" ', says

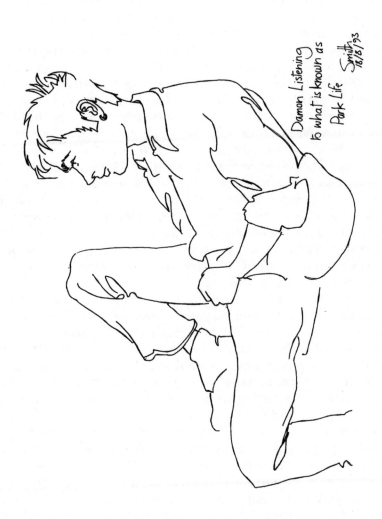

Damon Listening
to what is known as
Park Life   Smith
18/8/93

Damon. 'It was that random.' Daniels gave the narrator just the right tone of voluble idiocy and wit and a modern classic was born. The same batch of recordings (the whole album was put together in work sessions of two or three tracks) brought forth three further tracks included on the album. The appropriately punkish 'Jubilee' concerns a teenager born in the Silver Jubilee year of 1977 and hence sixteen when the song was written. 'Clover Over Dover', beginning with seagull sounds from Stephen Street's oft-used BBC *Sound Effects* disc, is arguably a better arrangement than it is a song and was originally attempted as a ska tune. 'It came out sounding like Nirvana meets Doctor Drugs,' comments Alex. 'Badhead' is more memorable, a gentle tune that Graham finds 'good for hangovers'. 'There's nothing abrasive there. Like Nick Drake is good for hangovers.' The mellotron featured on the bridge is taken from the Vintage Keys selection of antique keyboard sounds, something the band were tremendously keen on at the time. Also dating from this period is the likeable but inessential 'Bank Holiday', chiefly memorable for Graham's agile foot-pedal work, the heavy debt to punk and Damon's acutely observed lyric, 'Grandma's got new dentures to eat the crust on pizza.' A wickedly funny, admirably succinct observation on modern family leisure.

At this time, the band were in a very positive frame of mind, despite the fact that in many ways their situation was still precarious. 'They were enormously in debt to the record company,' confides Mike Smith, 'but they seemed supremely self-confident. In fact, there was a general growing sense of confidence and vibrancy in the whole music biz and it was in lots of ways generated by Blur and the kind of things they were trying to do and the scene they moved in in Camden. After years of this slacker culture and everyone wearing flannel shirts and jeans and taking their musical cues from the States, there was a lot of talk of the influence of British music. Beat music of the 60s and 70s punk. Everyone was listening to punk rock. Elastica were starting to come through, and a lot of lesser bands like Smashed and These Animal Men, the so-called new wave of new wave. People were starting to wear suits and borrow those sort of stylings from *Modern Life is Rubbish*. I remember the Manic Street Preachers saying it was the laziest fashion statement you could make; basically dressing like your dad. But at the time it did feel very much a statement going out in a suit to clubs.'

In terms of the respect of their peers, bands and critics, there was a real sense of Blur's stock being on the rise. 'A number of influential people had stopped laughing,' is how Dave puts it. 'People had started to see beyond all the gobby rubbish we could talk and see the artistic intentions in what we did. People like that in a group.'

The mood was already buoyant, then, when the time came to record a new number of Damon's that the band had already tried out live. 'Incredible as it may seem,' says Stephen Street, 'the normal operational procedure with tracks was that Blur would demo them and when Food and EMI had heard them they'd be given approval to go and record them, if they liked them. So already in that way we'd done "Bank Holiday", "Jubilee", "Parklife" and "Badhead", I think. Three or four. Then one day Damon brings in this little demo he'd done himself of this tune "Girls And Boys". Straightaway I said, "This is great." I knew we had to do this immediately.'

The song's subject matter – sexual hedonism on holiday – and its clear allegiance to disco meant Street and the band knew that 'it was definitely one for programmed drums.' 'It was sitting-around-with-a-book day for me,' remembers Dave. It was decided to set the song's tempo at the long-forgotten 120 bpm (beats per minute). At this point, dance tracks tended to be paced at the loping Happy Mondays beat of 100 bpm or the more frantic 130 bpm of house music. But 120 was the heartbeat of disco, of the brilliant life-affirming music of the Chic organisation and the irrepressible cheap and potent sounds of Abba, The Human League and the New Romantics. Central to this effect was Alex James's superb bass line, fizzing with wickedly anachronistic octave leaps and grace notes.

STEPHEN STREET: Alex got his Duran Duran obsession exorcised. We had such fun making it. Andy Ross phoned me to ask how things were going and I said, 'Great, and by the way, we have recorded this track you've got to hear called "Girls And Boys". It's fantastic.' He said, 'Why are you doing this? We haven't given you the authorisation to record this.' I told him, 'When you hear it, believe me, you'll understand.' I told Damon whilst we were doing it that this was his first Top 5 record. It was so different to anything else out there at the time. Everyone was very serious at the time and Suede were at the height of their powers. And here's this thing that had everything. It was catchy and original. And it was witty and humorous in a way Suede never were. That gave us real momentum and freedom to experiment elsewhere.'

Certainly, the instantly gratifying results from 'Girls And Boys' exerted a talismanic influence over the rest of the recording.

Initial *Parklife* sessions came to a halt in late September while the band undertook three months of live dates in Europe, America and Japan. Just prior to this, in the October, Damon and Street convened at Matrix to work on a song for the new Steven Berkoff movie, *Decadence*. Berkoff is a man who engenders strong feelings. 'Everyone loved Berkoff,' states Mike Smith, and certainly Damon admired him. Let us merely state that others adopt a different stance (see the hilarious parody of his work in the film *The Tall Guy* and his own self-inflicted destruction aided by Chris Morris in the satirical series *Brass eye*). Whatever we think of Berkoff, 'Theme From An Imaginary Film' is a delightful song which Berkoff, with typical caprice, insisted be removed from the soundtrack at a later date. 'Damon put his heart and soul into it,' reflects Mike Smith, 'and then Berkoff saw an early screening and didn't know it had been included on it and he pulled it which was incredibly insulting because it's brilliant.' Before leaving for America, the group continued to add enthusiastically to the stock of ideas for the forthcoming album. One track, tentatively called 'This Is A Low', was clearly something of an epic, an anthem of sorts. Instrumentally complete, it merely lacked a finished lyric from Damon. In fact, it would be the penultimate track to be completed and is worth discussing at some length in due course. Right now, it was off to the US of A with only slightly more enthusiasm than previously.

Left behind in Camden, David Balfe was having a minor crisis of faith. In part, this was due to the deterioration of his relationship with Blur. 'It isn't that we weren't speaking. As far as I remember we were still relatively friendly on one level; we'd still go out and have drinks and have a laugh backstage at gigs and all that kind of thing. But there was a great deal of angst. And a lot of things had been said between Damon and me. It all got quite brutal. Professionally, things had gone very cool. I'd backed off and passed them over to Andy. Our relationship had got to the stage where I couldn't get involved really so I was leaving it to them. Andy was and is a nicer guy than me. I felt he wasn't as prepared to be challenging or demanding, not as prepared to argue as much as I was. Andy's a far softer A&R man. I'm very hands-on and interfering. I'll tell you that that bass line's not working – though I always thought my contributions were positive – whereas Andy's more, "Hmm, sounds great." Andy was your best mate and kept your spirits up, which I now think might be the right way. The longer I'm in the business the more I believe in that approach.'

'It was good cop, bad cop,' states Andy Ross. 'Balfy was always the villain. Frankly, at the time, he had more bollocks.' But Balfe's disillusionment ran deeper than his differences with Blur. 'It was a very difficult time. Everyone had had very high hopes for that album [*Modern Life is Rubbish*] and for Food, it was the follow-up to a Jesus Jones record that had sold two million copies. We'd gone to Camden. We'd expanded. We'd gone from signing a band a year to feeling like we should sign two or three. Now we were in a bit of a trough and it got to me. It was very hard and depressing. We'd signed a few bands and weren't getting them away and I got fucked off with it. At Christmas time I told Andy I was getting pissed off. By then I'd already decided that I wanted to see if EMI would buy the company. The irony was, I had the tape of "Girls And Boys" by then and I loved it. It seemed once I'd given up fighting them, they did exactly what I'd been saying. This is the kind of record I'd said they should be making. "Put a fucking dance beat on it – it worked for you before." Which is the kind of crap thing we A&R men say. But I knew that was going to be a big hit. Honest.'

Returning from America, Blur immediately resumed the recording of an album that was developing a critical momentum. While still hardly being carried shoulder-high to the studio, they at least felt more encouraged and valued than previously, as Alex explains. 'We knew a momentum was building and some kind of artistic respect and we were on our way out of this slightly twatty, teeny thing we'd been part of. Gigs started selling and as soon as we started work on *Parklife* we knew it was a big record. You knew "Girls And Boys" was going to happen. We'd learned how to work studios, we had a producer we got on well with, and to an extent we knew how to handle our record company. It was all primed. If you can hit it big on your third album it's great because you know how it all works by then.'

The recording process was less arduous, too, since, as Dave puts it, 'We'd gained a degree of independence from Balfe and were dealing more directly with EMI. The mood changed then because they seemed more positive. They encouraged rather than bludgeoned us into submission.' The band and record company also took heart from their excellent showing in nearly every end-of-year music paper poll.

Appropriately, the first song to be recorded during the second phase of *Parklife* was 'Trouble In The Message Centre'. The lyric was written, as the *Parklife* CD booklet reveals, shortly after checking out of the Wellington Hotel, New York, on 7 December 1993. It contains several phrases taken from the touch buttons of the hotel's phone system – 'message centre', 'local and direct', 'room to room'. The line 'strike him softly away from the body' was written on a book of matches by the phone. The use in the CD booklet of the actual room receipt proved irritating for video director Kevin Godley. He was in discussion with Damon over the 'Girls And Boys' video at the time and his number is scribbled in a corner. He was bombarded with nuisance calls till he eventually changed it.

Neither Street nor Andy Ross is overly keen on this track, the former stating that it 'lacks melody' and the latter finding it 'a bit tinpot'. Neither is it mentioned in discussions of this band's finest work. Why? 'Trouble In The Message Centre' is not just a great track in itself – aggressive yet cerebral, coldly dynamic – but it shows the group's width and breadth of musical expertise, exploring the obscurer corners of English pop and in this case modelling the song on the great 80s Mancunian avant-garde rock band Magazine. Graham's short but effective arpeggiated solo at 2.09 is a highlight too.

'Tracy Jacks' is Damon's attempt to write a name song in the manner of The Kinks' (and later The Jam's) 'David Watts'. The titular hero is not a cross-dresser (this misunderstanding seems to stem from the proximity in the CD booklet of a Graham sketch of a balding man in floral-print frock addressing a golf ball); rather, this is a tale of slow breakdown in the seaside town of Walton on the Naze. Such towns were a fixation of Damon's. 'They fascinate me, all those dead seaside towns on the Essex coast. Walton on the Naze, Frinton-on-Sea. They have one guest house and it's boarded up. It's a couple of council estates, a few old houses and the bleak, bleak North Sea. They're half-places.'

Street adored the song, particularly Graham's vocal harmonies, and assumed it would be a single. It certainly has an array of attractive, evanescent moments: the rippling keyboard introduction, the ingenious military drumbeats in the bridge, the formal string arrangement by The Duke Quartet at the song's mid-point and end and Graham's ingenious seagull cry guitar parts, achieved with echo and feedback.

'London Loves' features a second-hand portable sequencer, the Yamaha QY 10, which Damon picked up for $100 on the States trip. A very hungover Dave Rowntree had helped him master it in his hotel room in San Francisco. 'It's a little machine with a keyboard, a drum machine, a sampler . . . I think it's even got a groupie in there,' remembers Dave. The fidgety rhythm of 'London Loves' was the first thing Damon tapped in, though the traffic report was added much later, taped from GLR radio station on the morning of mixing. Lyrically, the song reflects Damon's absorption in Martin Amis's 1989 novel *London Fields* and its repellent protagonist Keith Talent, darts enthusiast (another *Parklife* working title, as well as *Soft Porn* and *Sport*, was *Magic Arrows*, a darts commentator's term of approval). Musically, there were more hints of England's past glories.

> **GRAHAM COXON:** It wasn't so contrived that we'd say, 'Let's do a Bowie here or whatever.' We always think we're doing stuff nobody else is doing, though I don't know if that's true. 'Trouble In The Message Centre' is quite Magazine-y, that 'Shot By Both Sides' feel. For 'London Loves' I used the same effects box that Fripp would have used on 'Fashion' by David Bowie. My solo was modelled on that solo. I always liked that style and Streety liked it. Big fat notes going on for ever.

After recording the curios 'The Anniversary Waltz' and 'Magpie', which were soon to appear as B-sides, the group began work on *Parklife*'s two instrumentals, which would fulfil a similar role to that of 'Intermission' and 'Commercial Break' on *Modern Life is Rubbish*: disconcerting touches of weirdness in the midst of consummate pop craft. 'The Debt Collector', whose non-existent lyric would have been sung by Phil Daniels, is redolent of a Theatre Of The Absurd staging of *Steptoe and Son*; comic and vaguely macabre. Graham wanted the track, which was recorded live with no overdubs, to have a Tom Waits feel. His count in of 'one Mississippi, two Mississippi' is designed to set up the tune's waltz tempo, a favourite of the group ('The Anniversary Waltz' was originally called 'Why Is The Time Signature of 3/4 Obsolete In The Late Twentieth Century'). 'Lot 105' refers to the Hammond organ, central to the arrangement, which Damon picked up at an auction for £150. The band were particularly pleased with the cheesy in-built samba rhythm. Later, they would open the *Parklife* shows with this instrumental. When the album was sequenced, it was decided to end with 'Lot 105', twelve seconds after the close of 'This Is A Low', which was felt a little 'heavy' as a closing mood. The appearance of 'Lot 105', believes Graham, is akin 'to Barbara Windsor coming along to take you up the arse'.

Of the next two tracks laid down, one, 'People In Europe', was never intended for *Parklife*, being an affable but inessential bit of Eurodisco, compiled from various foreign phrases brainstormed by the band. 'Peter Panic', though, nearly made the cut, being a particular favourite of Stephen Street's. This Ziggy Stardustesque piece about a benevolent alien was constructed conceptually, according to Dave Rowntree, in that it was discussed in detail before a note was recorded.

When Damon first played 'To The End' at the piano, all in the Blur camp were convinced of its brilliance. An early Matrix demo features Justine Frischmann on the spoken French sections. 'The demo with John Smith sounded absolutely great,' asserts Stephen Street. 'But Food were still doubtful about me hence they got Stephen Hague in to do it. They wanted a big production number and figured he knew about that having done Pet Shop Boys and New Order. They thought it was the big hit and they didn't trust. Shame. I would have liked a go at that one but there you go.'

Hague and the band recorded the track at RAK studios during a three-day sabbatical from the main sessions with Street at Maison Rouge. However, as Street states, the band's original demo was so good that Hague kept most of it, including nearly all of Damon's original vocal. The strings were added not by the trusty Dukes but by the Audrey Riley string section. The drums are looped, the vibraphone is very real and the song's lovely meandering ambience may be down to its unexpectedly long five-bar line. Hague plays accordion, though it's barely audible in the finished mix. For the whispered 'Jusqu'a la fin' sections, various chanteuses were mooted, including Charlotte Gainsbourg, daughter of Serge, and Graham's favourite Francoise Hardy. A version with Hardy was eventually recorded at Abbey Road and released as a single in France, but for this version the band used Laetitia Sadier of the excellent Anglo-French experimental pop group Stereolab. Musically exceptional, 'To The End' is also notable as one of Damon Albarn's finest vocal performances to date (Alex is said to have cried when he heard the finished mix). Recorded while stoned, the lyric treads a line of anguished ambiguity. Is 'the end' the end of the affair or the end of some period of trial and uncertainty? It's never made explicit.

More apparent is the lyrical gist of 'Magic America', another tale of cross-cultural disappointments. A typical Barratt home dweller – called Bill Barratt to emphasise the point – fantasises about what America must be like. Magic America itself is the name of a porn channel based in Milan, another hint at the song's sarcastic take on the discrepancy between fantasy and reality.

Stephen Street viewed 'End Of A Century' as evidence that, 'Damon was really getting the art of songwriting really sorted . . . We were having fun with genres all the time. We'd discuss the vibe we wanted on each track. Got to have a bag to put it in. Let's be Bowie here. Let's have a Numan or Magazine vibe here or a New Romantic feel. I always thought of "End Of A Century" as having this stripped-down feel; one guitar in each speaker. A sort of Kinks feel.' Damon remembers the finished song as being almost identical to his original demo. 'If he wants to think that, I'll let him,' comments Graham ruefully. Other points of note: the brief, lyrical trombone solo at 1.36 is by Richard Edwards of The Kick Horns and the song's opening line concerns an infestation of ants Damon and Justine suffered in their Kensington flat. While much loved, when 'End Of A Century' was released as single, it was a mild flop. 'This was a single, "This Is A Low" wasn't. Maybe it should have been the other way round,' says Andy Ross.

The striking and dramatic backing track for 'This Is A Low' had lain in the vaults since the earliest *Parklife* sessions. Utilising a warm, purring Hammond, a drum track flipped, looped and run backwards with live drums overlaid and a cluster of mesmeric guitar parts, it excited everyone. But still Damon had failed to come up with a lyric before the Christmas break. All he had was a only a four-word phrase: 'There Is A Low.'

Damon spent the Christmas holiday with his parents at a cottage in Cornwall. At night, he played the backing track constantly on his Walkman as he walked on the Cornish cliffs, and various ideas and images – of coastlines and meteorology – began to percolate. But he was still no further to finishing the lyric and thus, to the dismay and consternation of Street and the others, he was adamant that the song could not be included on the album. Street stood his ground and insisted that Damon come up with a lyric by the next day, 4

February 1994, the penultimate day of recording and the day Damon was scheduled to enter hospital for a hernia operation. Sometime between midnight and 1 a.m. that night, Damon finally came up with the lyric. It was inspired by his Christmas present from Alex, a handkerchief purchased from Stanford's map and travel bookshop in Covent Garden displaying the poetically mysterious sea regions used on the BBC's shipping forecast. 'We always found the shipping forecast soothing,' explains Alex. 'We used to listen to it in America to remind us of home. Very good for hangovers or insomnia.' Damon began at one corner of the handkerchief – the Bay of Biscay – and worked his way round, choosing names as the mood struck him and as rhyme demanded. 'I'd had this line, "And then into the sea/Go pretty England and me", for some time. So I started at the Bay of Biscay, back for tea. Tea rhymes with me. Then 'hit traffic on the Dogger bank . . . so up the Thames to find a taxi rank.'

By the early hours, the lyric was complete.

Stephen Street recalls: 'He had to go to hospital for this hernia operation but I'd been quite hard on him and said, "You've got one night to finish the lyric and one morning to record it." So he dragged himself in and did it. He was in a lot of pain, I think. Then he went straight off to hospital and we mixed it immediately. He rang us up later very sedated and asked how it was going.'

The addition of the lyric turned an already superb musical piece into Blur's finest work to this date. Alex surmises that the lyric 'is about people taking smack' and Graham too thinks the song has a 'sinister, gouched-out quality'. Whatever, the song has a queer, elegiac, nocturnal atmosphere, drawing heavily on the incantatory power of the magical shipping forecast areas. And the fantastical and phantasmagoric imagery – 'The queen she'd gone round the bend/Jumped off Land's End', the traffic on the Dogger bank and the Thames taxi rank – is Edward Lear out of John Lennon; surreal, nursery rhymish and unsettling.

Parklife was complete but for one track, its oddest moment and one of its most charming. 'Far Out' was the first Blur composition to be credited to one member, Alex James, and reflected his love of astronomy. The song had actually been demoed the previous autumn at Maison Rouge in a version much nearer the song's obvious ancestor, Pink Floyd's 'Astronomy Domine', another trippy gazetteer of heavenly bodies.

ANDY ROSS: It's a bit of a non-song in some ways. Or at least that's the impression you get from the *Parklife* version, which is mildly spacey nonsense, but Alex wrote another version that was really quite rocking. They'd done a version at Maison Rouge and it was great. I'm not even sure if Damon was on that. It was a really good song. Uptempo but heavy and nothing like the 'Far Out' on the album. But I don't think Damon was too happy then about Alex getting credit for a song that didn't have that much to do with him and he applied a lot of pressure to not have it on the album. Certainly I was saying very strongly to Alex that this should be on and Alex didn't want to stand up for himself. So I made my opinions known and got outvoted. I understand why Damon was feeling a bit fragile around then but I don't think he was right.

However, a new version was attempted, weaker but still quixotically likeable, featuring loopy organ chords and Dave on congas. Short of a proper ending, Street simply lopped off the song midway through the bridge section and put the vocal track through an echo filter so that Alex's voice would die away on the word 'sun', getting duller and more distant as it went. All this was done in one day, 18 February 1994, two weeks after the completion of 'This Is A Low'. *Parklife* was finished and, though no one knew it, Blur had engendered a seismic shift in the terrain of British pop in the 90s. Dave Balfe's needle never flickered though.

'From what I remember of my conversations with Balfe,' states Chris Morrison, 'he was adamant that *Parklife* was a mistake. "This is a mistake", he said to me quite clearly. "We shouldn't be doing it." He wanted them to make a Jesus Jones record. I, of course, aligned myself with the band. I tried to point out that they had made a Blur record, not a David Balfe record. I tried to convince him that he ought to at least let them make their own mistake, not his. That's the artists' prerogative. You can't deny them that.'

DAVID BALFE: *Parklife* was Damon's vision and realised between the band and Stephen Street, who made a great team. We'd had the big fight and Damon had won. He had the authority. He'd surprised me by how strong he was. But there's many different ways albums can get made. I forced them into it by being, well, wrong, I suppose you'd say. I don't mind giving you the quotes that will make me look stupid. I quite liked 'Parklife' as a song. When I first heard the demo without Phil Daniels, I said that the chorus was brilliant but it was such a shit verse. Dum der dum dum. I thought it was fairly tedious and the talking verses were not hit single material as far as I was concerned.

The band, however, had a missionary zeal about their new venture. 'I remember going out driving around London with Damon and we were listening to "Girls And Boys" and he was very pleased with it,' recalls Mike Smith. 'He was particularly delighted with Alex's bass part. Everyone was quietly very excited. "Girls And Boys" was obviously a big record. But it was only when you sat and listened to the whole album in its entirety that you realised it was incredible, very special. It ran together seamlessly like great albums do. You sat there waiting for the duff track and it never came. Still, though, no one had the faintest idea whether it would work. It was a great record but it was still a great record by a guitar band. Guitar bands didn't sell and this one had had a more chequered history than most.'

8 Early Imperial

'ALL VERY SUCCESSFUL POP groups go through an imperial phase,' Neil Tennant of the Pet Shop Boys once astutely observed. He refers to the period where they can do no wrong. Like fabulous potentates, they are feted and worshipped wherever they go. It's a choice observation for another reason too: empires fail and change and dwindle. Emperors succumb to the lures of excess; they suffer the perils of fame. Blur grew to hate their imperial dynasty like a boy emperor grows to hate his imprisonment at court once the attraction of his toys and his playground has worn off. To even say it was fun while it lasted is doubtful, since some members of the group endured their worst times since 1992's harrowing American tour. As historians, though, we can date Blur's accession to emperors very specifically to the first week of March 1994, the release of Blur's eighth single, 'Girls And Boys'.

The media clamoured about the record like the most breathless fan. Most of the pretence at cool indifference had evaporated. A year later than the smarter social commentators, even the more cloth-eared were wising up to the shortcomings of grunge and the attraction of something sharper, more flavoursome and home grown. Everyone fell for its simply irrepressible mixture of robotic New Romantic disco and cleverly ambiguous observational tone. The song did clearly concern 'following the herd down to Greece', but the lyric, full of memorable touches like 'avoiding all work, cos there's none available', kept the tone nicely neutral, avoiding the pitfall of sneering at the ordinary person which even the best English songwriters, including Albarn, are sometimes prey to. Damon confirmed in the NME that he had written the song after a Majorcan holiday and that it wasn't 'a dig at those 18–30 people, more a celebration. That soft porn thing runs through the whole album.'

The gently parodic nature of the track, though, was helped by both Stylorouge's superb 70s Durex condom packaging and Godley and Creme's lurid video. 'Great video but we could have done it down the Trocadero for five grand,' jokes Mike Smith ruefully. David Balfe hated it, according to Chris Morrison. 'He thought it was horribly *Sun*, horribly page-three. He thought it was real lowest common denominator stuff. He couldn't see that it was tongue in cheek. I tried to persuade him that it would work on two levels for different audiences; the intelligent ones will get the joke and the others will think, Oh, look, it's just like my holiday in Greece.' The record also gained the group a substantial gay following, who twigged the coded references to anal sex in the song's chorus. Damon was delighted. ' "Girls And Boys" is every bit as rude as Frankie's "Relax" but it got played on the radio. Ha!'

While the *Newcastle Journal* compared it, in either a brilliant *aperçu* or a moment of insanity, to The Gang Of Four, most spotted the kinship with the New Romantics ('It's the sound of now, i.e. the sound of 1982,' trilled wry teen weekly *Smash Hits*). Some of the dumber critics mentioned the New Wave of New Wave for no other reason than it was a current fad and because Elastica, the group led by Justine Frischmann, were the only decent group associated with that movement. Blur treated such comparisons with scorn and rightly so. With a typically grandiose flourish, they claimed to have invented the genre anyway with 'Popscene', a record which they seriously considered reissuing to cash in on the entirely media-contrived NWONW craze.

Balfe's low opinion of the 'Girls And Boys' video (though he was greatly enthusiastic about the song) reflected his ongoing disenchantment with the music business. By now, he had decided to quit and sell Food to the parent label EMI. 'Andy wanted to carry on, which was fair enough. I said, "I can set this up so it doesn't all have to change." I said I wouldn't do it if they wouldn't commit to keeping Food on as a going concern because I didn't want to drop him in it and he was fine with that. And EMI agreed. The weird thing is you can't consult the band in a matter like this. It entails very complex negotiations which took the best part of three months, January through April, three very focused months of work on it. It might not happen in the end, after all, and as soon as you tell the band they become players. But once the deal was signed, Andy and I heard they were having a meeting in a Camden restaurant with Chris so we ran round there and told them.'

The Gordian knot of record company financial dealings wouldn't unduly concern us here but for the fact that David Balfe's sale of Food to EMI does have a very definitive cultural impact. It directly inspired a Number 1 single, after all. For Blur, Balfe's ostensible retirement was a kind of victory. As they saw it, he was admitting that he'd been wrong about them all those years.

ALEX JAMES: We delivered *Parklife* and at the same time he basically sold his share to EMI and bought a big house in the country. We knew 'Girls And Boys' was good and I remember Balfy saying, almost as if he was making the best of a bad job, 'Well, I suppose "Parklife" could be a single.' 'Parklife' was obviously a single! The first time Damon played it to me, I was certain: 'Damon, this is it, man, this is great.' It was one of the most complete things I'd ever heard. It was all there in the demo. Usually all that there is is just an acoustic guitar and a vocal melody, not even any words often, but that was pretty complete. So we delivered the album and then Balfe sold Food, who thought at best we'd do 60,000 or so. Ha – unlucky.

'Balfe had practically retired whilst we were making *Parklife*,' reveals Graham. 'He'd faded very much in the background. Why did he do that? I wonder. Did he think he was past it or that music was past it? Knowing Balfy, I think he probably thought music was wrong. He certainly Pontius Pilated us.' Mike Smith also attributes Balfe's abrogation of power to his loss of appetite for the game. 'He felt guitar music was over; that was the big reason why he called it a day. His experimentation into that sort of music hadn't gone well. He didn't see that a huge renaissance was just around the corner.'

Chris Morrison, offering a touch of psychology, feels that the burgeoning success of Blur and the mood of triumph around the newly delivered *Parklife* had shaken Balfe's faith in the certitude of his own judgement. 'He certainly sold the company prematurely. A profit's a profit, though, and he chose to get out of the business and he didn't know at that stage whether he'd ever go back. His vision of what Blur should be and what Blur are are very different things. But he was a very shaping force. Damon's anger with him over *Modern Life Is Rubbish* worked in that out of it came two great extra tracks and, ultimately, *Parklife*.'

Balfe is gracious in what might be seen as defeat. He is affably rueful about what looks, with hindsight, to have been very bad business timing. 'If I'd sold the company a year later, after the success of *Parklife*, I would have made a lot more money out of the sale than I did. Luckily I sold it in April '94 so I at least still got a royalty on it. I've never been sure how to feel about that. Of course, I'd have been happier with several hundred thousand pounds more in the bank but every extra copy of *Parklife* sold would have made me look more of a fool and made even more stupid the mistake I'd made even while it was making me money. Philosophically, I think what happened is a good thing. In the end, I made a lot of money from believing in Blur but not as much money as I would have made if I'd believed in them more. That's how it should be.'

Parklife was in the can, 'Girls And Boys', already attracting major radio play, was poised to hit the shops, and a sea change in the group's fortunes was mustering below the horizon. On a more personal level, a dramatic change was underfoot. Blur were Olympian boozers. As Andy Ross states, they were 'principally a beer rather than a drugs band', though he repeats 'principally' with a wry smile. The fact that Blur could normally be found rolling around on the carpet of any lig or showbiz party by closing time was a standard music business joke. Dave Rowntree's drinking was an especial source of mirth within the group. Alex's favourite anecdote concerns Dave being out on the town in Prague and, blind drunk, trying to direct a taxi driver to his hotel. 'He was banging his hotel key on the glass divider and being very abusive, shouting, "Just fucking take me here," and the cabby was refusing and it was getting ugly and in the end the taxi driver dropped him off at the police station. I ended up getting this phone call from the police station saying, "We've got this nutter of a drummer in here." It turned out that he'd been waving his hotel key from Berlin the night before. No wonder the taxi driver wouldn't take him.'

But behind the parade of drunken high jinks, Dave's drinking had for some time given cause for concern, not least to Rowntree himself. He had begun as an amiable peace punk who liked his pint of Guinness, but his drinking was becoming more punishing and its effect on him more destructive. Having recently married his Canadian girlfriend Paola and moved to a home in Hampstead, his bibulous lifestyle was looking increasingly untenable.

DAVE ROWNTREE: I wasn't a very good drunk. I'd wound up fighting drunk and covered in blood and vomit once too often. My drinking would make me miserable which would make me drink and it was all just feeding off itself. I was so depressed and miserable I was thinking I'd rather not be in a band than be like this. So I decided it had to stop. My first day of not drinking, or first work day, anyway, was the on-line edit for 'Girls And Boys'. I went to Alcoholics Anonymous. It was a very hard thing to do. It was the classic AA cure. They don't actually encourage religion, though a lot of people get religion because the technique is to get you to admit that you have no control over it and that to cure yourself you'll have to rely on something else that they call a higher power, which can be the comradeship and support of the group, or for some it's religion or for some it's meditation. For some people it's cocaine maybe! Believe me, if I could have cured myself, I would have done it already. I had a really bad time for a long time. I had very bad shakes and horrible stuff pouring out of me. It was a time of real emotional seesawing. It was pretty dreadful. It was two years before I was remotely confident about myself. I never felt I could just go back and have a drink, not for a couple of years. There have been many times since but you just don't do it.

As they now willingly concede, the other group members could have been more supportive. It's fairly easy, though, to understand why they weren't. Dave's admission that his drinking was a problem and had to end struck at the very heart of the values the group had nurtured since Seymour. 'I didn't really get any help from people in the band. They found it quite a threat, my not drinking, because they were all drinking. Until then, I'd always been the most drunk person in the band at any event and they could take heart from the fact that they would never be as bad as me. Then suddenly the safety net of Dave was gone. So, no, they didn't help at all. They were quite keen for me to start again so they got drunk and I started avoiding them when they were drunk and it wasn't a pleasant time at all.'

GRAHAM COXON: We thought he was boring. We didn't see the problem. When we'd come home from a tour, we might not see as much of him and perhaps he was carrying on in the same vein. He realised that he couldn't have what he wanted in life from then on and have booze. And he was getting really useless at drinking. He was obviously not enjoying it and putting himself through agonising mental strain and torture. We thought he was a boring old sod. But that was us being scared that he was looking down on us like we were infants with our stupid nights out boozing. We were frightened really that he might think we were silly. But he never did. He carried on being social and he still does.

'I miss things like going down the pub,' he told a reporter at the time. 'Do I miss the oblivion? I can't say I do because I never remembered anything. One of the reasons for me giving up drinking was a lot to do with waking up with a hangover every day for three years.'

'In the end they just got used to it,' says Dave today, sober for five years. 'Maybe my calming down did calm them down a bit; Damon and Alex, anyway, to some extent, if not Graham. After a couple of years I think it got people to think about being drunk in slightly different ways. People started rather hoping Graham would go the same way though I think he's much better now.'

What Graham means by the things Dave wanted in life could be life itself. Alex states that Andy Ross is of the opinion Dave Rowntree would have died within a few years had he continued drinking. Andy is more circumspect than this publicly but will be drawn thus far: 'Suffice to say, it was medically disadvantageous for him to carry on.'

It was perhaps as well that Dave got firmly on the wagon when he did, given that the booze would now begin to flow like water and the champagne corks would pop wherever they went. As is ever the case, the group were to move directly from famine to feast without passing 'nicely full, thank you'. Buoyed on massive radio play and a tide of critical adulation, 'Girls And Boys' entered the chart at Number 5. 'At that point,' says Alex, smiling, 'it was realised that we knew best. Andy [Ross] thought the single would do well and the album but he had no notion that it would become the ridiculous thing it was. "Girls And Boys" went in at 5 which no one had done for years. Now everyone does because the charts are so mad but then singles had chart careers. You still went up. That's a major change. So "Girls And Boys" was a big hit.'

The immediate success of 'Girls And Boys' was 'very satisfying' for Dave. 'And it seemed to hang around for months. It was the hit of the summer, the big holiday record. More importantly, it was the first time we'd ever got the recognition we felt we deserved. And we'd been proved right with Balfe. It was very satisfying. You'd

walk into a shop and it would be playing on the radio, then you'd
go into the shop next door and it would be playing in there as well.'
A huge, proper hit single was the greatest fillip the group could have
had. They'd enjoyed a more temperate climate for most of the past
year but this was cold arithmetic proof that the group were on the
up.

Crowning all this, Blur's third album, *Parklife*, was released on
25 April 1994 to almost universal acclaim. Looking back over the
reviews, one is struck by the evenness of the tenor and the zeal of
the converted. The decidedly unexcitable trade paper *Music Week*
(who can forget their inflammatory 'stabilise our volatile charts'
rallying cry to the nation's youth?) declared it was the pop album of
1994, a year admittedly only four months old. Robert Sandall,
august critic of *The Sunday Times*, eulogised it, as did many, as a
return to the highest standards of vintage British pop; the names of
XTC, Madness, The Kinks and The Jam were pressed into service
yet again. *Q*'s reviewer delivered a lengthy, quite brilliant essay
which teased out the various elements of the group's art. Andrew
Harrison in *Select* concluded his review with an insightful para-
graph: 'What bubbles up from this fascinating soup of urban stupid-
ity, cultural cringe, satire and celebration is more than just Blur's
best album. In drawing together pretty much everything worth
talking about in Britain '94, Blur have elected themselves panellists
on Britpop's very own *Question Time*.' In the newish lads' mag
Loaded, itself a prime 90s cultural catalyst, James Brown delivered
himself of a wonderfully lyrical if not entirely sound resumé of the
album. '*Parklife* mines that time of British life between adolescence
and the dole when warm summer evenings are spent lazing round in
municipal parks, lolling on bikes, destroying park benches, snogging
boy and girlfriends, drinking cider and getting that last game of
soccer before the lure of the pub ruins your health and ambition for
ever.'

Only the daily broadsheets got it spectacularly wrong in the
manner only the higher-minded critic can manage. Both *The Times*
and the *Independent* missed the point entirely and seemed unaware
that the raffish collage of bric-a-brac and English heritage was both
deliberate and necessary. And an honourable mention must go to
the sadly anonymous reviewer of the *Lancashire Evening Post* who,
with the bold wrong-headedness of the Decca A&R man who told
The Beatles, 'Groups of guitars are on the way out', described

Parklife as, 'The awful hit single "Girls And Boys" and 16 other jaunty tracks . . . a major disappointment.'

> **ANDY ROSS:** When *Modern Life is Rubbish* came out Blur were officially uncool. They got no front covers for that release which is quite a snub given how well the first album had done. Those papers have 50 covers a year and yet they couldn't find space for them. Commercially there was a muted response to the album but they somehow started to win friends again and the fans liked it. The Reading gig had been an obvious turning point. The good thing about backlashes is when you do turn a corner, there's a sense of elation. At that moment we knew it was back on course and bigger than ever. The press twigged it. You sensed them thinking, Oh, shit, we all fucked up here. Around that autumn, the press began saying, 'What a great band.' In the meantime, they had steamed into the next album. By the time *Parklife* came out they couldn't fail; it was a classic case of overcompensation universally. *Parklife* would have got great reviews without hearing a note, rather like the third Oasis album. We were absolutely set up; it was a catapult effect. As for Food, we were aware that it could do quite well. But I have to say, not that well. Balfy certainly didn't think so because he sold the company before it came out. Balfy got out, saying the songs were still indie and the album wasn't going to do very well.

While Ross is right in saying that the press did come to fawn on Blur as methodically as they once scorned them, there's more to it than that. *Parklife* is one of the most complete albums of the pop and rock era. Moreover, it caught the whiff of change like no other. 'Zeitgeist', like its pals 'seminal', 'literally' and 'reactionary', is one of those words that is almost never used correctly either in the papers or in the pub. But this time, it was spot on. Zeitgeist refers to the 'spirit of the times' and *Parklife* was both a reflection of and a progenitor of a new cultural mood. With a tragic but striking synchronicity, Kurt Cobain had killed himself in the week that 'Girls And Boys' had gatecrashed the Top 5. American grunge rock was far from dead but the death of its one true talent was to mark the closure of its chapter of dominance in the UK. Slowly, the tides of flannel and plaid receded to be replaced by the Harrington, the three-button vented bum-freezer jacket, the Ben Sherman button down, the Adidas gazelle and the Tachini top. Blur even attempted to put a name on this new style – 'mod-ual', their blend of mod and casual, the floppy fringed, designer sports gear look of the football terrace style guru circa 1984. As well as Martin Amis and music hall, Damon was starting to mention his passion for Chelsea FC in his interviews, in which he and Alex in particular warmed to their theme of cultural renewal. 'Pop has been devalued by slacker,' Alex railed in *The Face*, 'but we stuck to our beliefs all the time and that's why we were devalued. Gangs were unfashionable; being into clothes wasn't considered hip. It all got far too serious. Blur are a band for the hoovering classes. We're the Nanette Newman of pop.' 'Slacker culture says nothing to us about our lives,' continued Damon, 'but I believe America will reject slacker culture. They're going to see it as useless and unproductive. They're going to need bands that smile and take the piss and have a bit of a cavort, something that isn't all aggression and neurosis.'

As the decade ends, the birds, booze and football culture that *Parklife* presaged and indeed partly ushered in now seems formulaic and tired. Blur were always more ambiguous and intelligent than to simply advocate the Neanderthal line of thinking by which we arrive at *FHM* and Chris Moyles, and the group have noticeably turned away from this lads' mag culture. The few still peddling it look increasingly sad and old-fashioned. But then it seemed refreshing and different; a vigorous, cheeky and peppy rejection of slackers' ear-picking sullenness.

'*Parklife* changed the perceptions of the UK music industry,' says Andy Ross. 'There was the status quo which included Status Quo and the indie sector and *Parklife* moved the goalposts almost without us knowing. It didn't just sell a shedload of records, it invited a lot of people back to music as a hobby. A lot of 30-year-olds decided they liked music again.'

Accepted wisdom has it that *Parklife* is where Britpop begins. This isn't true, of course. Musically, *Modern Life is Rubbish* can lay claim to being the first 'Britpop' album and the term itself had first been used a whole year earlier in a lengthy polemical article in *Select* calling for a new British perspective in pop culture. But it would be anal and snobbish to pretend anything other than the fact that *Parklife* was Britpop's defining moment, the point at which a coterie crusade became the accepted cultural milieu. When *Select* had run its ground-breaking piece, even to talk of celebrating Tommy Cooper, *The Likely Lads*, Wire, northern soul, bacon butties, football, black cabs, The Fall and amphetamine sulphate was cause for mockery or accusations of Fascism. With *Parklife*, the baseball caps and sloppy joes went right back in the wardrobe and the Ice T and Alice In Chains records straight to the back of the pile. It was amazing how many people had actually loved *Ogden's Nut Gone Flake* and *Pink Flag* all along.

'It would be great,' muses Dave, 'if we could say that we'd had a meeting where we'd decided to change the face of pop culture. Let's just check the minutes: yes, Graham was in the chair and we passed a motion deciding to make the definitive British pop record of the decade.'

GRAHAM COXON: We made *Parklife* just like any other record. We approached it in exactly the same way but it was done without the hassle. We worked from scrappy demos of Damon's as usual. I remember doing 'Girls And Boys' and thinking it was a bizarre direction to go in: if everything had been like that I'd have been very unsure but it was funny because it started a friendly battle between me and Alex. He wanted to be funky and I wanted to be completely honky. So I was deliberately going against his rhythms. I suppose it was an early attempt at merging rock and techno that foreshadows some of the stuff we're doing now. I'm wary of implying that *Parklife* was completely thought through, though. We've always done a lot of our thinking about things after the event, when we've made the record. That's when you know what you've done. I've never enjoyed intellectualising about music anyway. I've never read any Martin Amis. That kind of talk can get you into trouble or make you seem foolish. It's got Damon into a bit of trouble over the years. People have said he was dilettante or a Nazi.

Parklife's status as cultural touchstone for the coming years was further aided by another piece of striking design by Stylorouge. The cover featured two greyhounds cornering a dog-track bend at full speed. Clear, colourful and buzzing with energy, it packed the same punch as the 30s Italian futurists like Balla and Marinetti had intended. But, more than this, it strongly identified the group with greyhound racing – a robustly English, faintly nostalgic, slightly seedy, proletarian pastime – via Paul Postle's back cover photo of the band trackside and the stylised tracklisting reminiscent of a dog-track race card.

At Andy Ross's suggestion, this motif recurred in the band's choice of launch party, which was held at Walthamstow Greyhound

◀ Damon, aged 4, in Arthurian knight gear . . .

. . . and in civvies
▼

▼ Real Lives, l-r: Paul Stevens, Damon, Graham

◄ Graham, aged 14,
in classic seventies
school photo . . .

. . . and aged 17 ▶

Dave Rowntree: a very
ginger production

Alex, aged 11, at home

Postcards from the edge; Blur, London, 1995 (Kim Tonelli)

Live on the seaside tour, ▶
1995 (Ed Sirrs)

Blor? Blundie? Recreating *Parallel Lines* cover for *NME* (Kevin Cummins)

Damon and Justine, Blur party, 1997 (Andy Phillips)

Blur, 1999 (Paul Postle)

Racing Stadium, east London, on the night after the album went out to the shops. Coaches were laid on from the West End to ferry rafts of industry liggers, hosts of now forgotten indie groups and the odd genuine celebrity (e.g. Eddie Izzard) to the track. The highlight of the night was to be the tenth race, the *Parklife* stakes, sponsored by the group. The winner would receive a trophy and a special presentation CD box of the album worth £100. After nine previous races which had gone smoothly, the *Parklife* stakes took a very Blur turn. One dog became caught in the traps and couldn't run. The hare became derailed. One dog stumbled and the others turned on it savagely. 'Didn't they bite its head off?' asks Dave Rowntree now. 'I know that all the people at the track were saying it was unprecedented. No one had ever seen anything like it in the history of dog racing.' The race was declared null and void but the revels were a great success. After the dogs, everyone repaired to a party at Charlie Chan's restaurant and club, where one of the most energetic dancers was the fleet-footed David Balfe, who enjoyed himself immensely. 'Although we'd had major differences, we still got on fairly cordially. I went to the launch and had a great time. Put it this way, we were getting on sufficiently exuberantly for Damon to dash across to me on the dance floor and stick his tongue in my mouth. Over the next few months as they became massive and a media frenzy overtook them, I became the evil man who'd tried to thwart them in the past. Fair enough. There has to be a bad guy for the good guys to overcome in any good story.'

On the Sunday evening after the launch, *Parklife* entered the UK album chart at Number 1, an extraordinary feat made positively Herculean by the fact that it actually outsold Pink Floyd's *Division Bell* by roughly three to one and ousted it from the top of the chart. The success had a bitter-sweet resonance given Blur's abiding respect for Pink Floyd's former leader, Syd Barrett, now a childlike recluse cared for by a supportive family after acid had lain waste his personality. *Parklife* was to remain on the UK chart for an astonishing 90 weeks. And for most of that time, British pop's dominant style would be one stemming directly from *Parklife*.

Off the back of *Parklife* and 'Girls And Boys' – the single had been a hit in various far-flung territories including Top 5 in Israel and Lithuania – the group took to the road for a sixteen-date tour through the early summer where they bounded on to their distinctive stage set to the strains of the theme to *The Italian Job*. This tour culminated in their appearance at Glastonbury in late June, sandwiched between the ascendant Radiohead and the soothing, somnambulant rock drones of Spiritualised. At the bottom of the bill, five places beneath Blur, were a new Mancunian outfit signed to Creation called Oasis. The band had been struggling nonentities until singer Liam Gallagher's brother Noel – a former roadie for Inspiral Carpets – had instituted a creative putsch and given the group a shot in the arm via his impressive songwriting. Though apocryphally signed after Creation boss Alan McGee saw them hijack a gig by another of his bands, McGee had in fact been watching them for some months. Their new single, 'Shakermaker', was an undistinguished trudge through the melody of The New Seekers' 'I'd Like To Teach The World To Sing', but most saw some promise buried beneath the surly demeanour. Indeed, they were soon to release both the single 'Live Forever' and the album *Definitely Maybe*, records which would alert the pop world to a truly feral, native talent and instigate a rivalry-cum-feud that would engulf the country.

Blur, of course, were blissfully unaware of this as they gave a well-received performance – 'This is just one and a half minutes of us doing what we do,' is how Damon obliquely introduced a rabid 'Bank Holiday' – but for most the festival was overshadowed by the growing spectre of organised crime that had led to five shootings. Less eventful, happily, was Blur's appearance at Scotland's Hamilton Park on 31 July as part of the T In The Park festival.

Just prior to the festival season, Blur released the heart-breaking John Barry-inflected ballad 'To The End' as a single. It was by no means a universally approved gambit. There was a feeling that Steven Hague's production was not the epic creation it should have been and, partly because of unrealistic expectation, there was considerable disappointment when the record stalled at Number 16, despite the presence on the B-side of the Pet Shop Boys' thumping, hedonistic remix of 'Girls And Boys'. None the less, a mood of triumph continued unabated as the parent album continued to sell in droves. Ironically, the group were guests of honour at a rock film festival at the South Bank, where their 1992 tour movie *Star Shaped* was shown, a vomit- and blood-spattered voyage into alcoholic mayhem and misery.

Recognition also came from another (fairly) august source. The Mercury Music Prize had been launched in 1993 in an attempt to create a rock version of the Booker Prize. A cheque for £25,000 and a small but noticeable amount of kudos was attached to the prize, voted for by a panel of establishment bigwigs which had so far honoured Primal Scream's indie-dance template *Screamadelica* and Suede's debut album. The shortlist for the 1994 award: Blur, Shara Nelson, Paul Weller, Michael Nyman, M People, Ian McNabb, The Prodigy, Pulp, Therapy and Take That. Blur immediately became the bookmakers' favourites with odds of 2–1 on them taking the prize.

The fact that Blur did not win the prize is the clearest indication yet that, though admirably intentioned, the prize is something of a nonsense. *Parklife* is not just an aesthetically great record but viewed objectively it is one of the records, alongside albums by Goldie, Radiohead, Fatboy Slim and The Spice Girls, that have set the tone of British pop in the 90s. Yet none of them have won the Mercury Music Prize. Roni Size and Reprazent, though, have. The most ludicrous omission is *Parklife* itself. The problem is an ethic of musical correctness; a need to keep the prize interesting and an overweening desire for moral rectitude and hipper-than-thou credentials. The prize could simply not be awarded to another group of young white males with guitars. Hence it was given to amiable if anonymous multi-racial M People for their collection of well-made beige pop-soul, a politically acceptable decision which said nothing about the musical climate of the day. Even Jon Savage, arguably Britain's finest and most perceptive pop writer, chose to read the decision as a victory for the ordinary lad and girl over the effete metropolitan indie industry. An interesting point, but wrong. Ordinary lads and girls from the north will be whistling the choruses of 'Parklife' and 'Girls And Boys' when no one can remember a single note of *Elegant Slumming*; come to think of it, can anyone now? Interestingly, a Mercury judge remarked later that *Parklife* did not win because it was too laddish.

Giving the prize to Michael Nyman's soundtrack to Jane Campion's feted movie *The Piano* would have made more sense; that had, at least, touched hundreds of people outside the traditional classical music audience and soundtracked a thousand dinner parties. It was a genuine phenomenon that turned Nyman from coterie delight to global star. But the classical selection, of course, can never win, since the panel is drawn primarily from the pop wing of the industry. The prize's desperation to be even-handed is its undoing.

An interesting comparison can be made to the scandal that sur-
rounded the publication of literary scholar Harold Bloom's *The
Western Canon*, which unashamedly placed DWEMs (Dead White
European Males) firmly at the heart of literary development.

One final point. At least they didn't give it to the lugubrious Paul
Weller – that really would have been intolerable. Blur, meanwhile,
nursing their hangovers, jetted off to the States the following morning. The lessons of 1992 had been learned, though. With a Number
1 album to their name, the band were this time playing only nine
major metropolitan shows and flying between cities. 'It costs a little
more but at least we keep our sanity,' explained Damon.

On their return, Blur had the exciting prospect of their two biggest
shows to date – a couple of major arena appearances consolidating
the upsurge in their fortunes. Supported by deadpan Yorkshire
ironists and fellow chroniclers of Albion, Pulp, they performed a
rousing set at Birmingham's Aston Villa Leisure Centre. Two days
later, they were to play Alexandra Palace in London, the highlight
of their career thus far. If any of Blur had chosen to dip into the
current edition of rock monthly *Vox* while driving down the M40,
their eye might well have been caught by remarks made by Oasis's
voluble, perplexing and often berkish lead singer Liam Gallagher. In
the piece, he shared with us his highly distinctive philosophy. 'Being
a lad is what I'm all about. Define lad? I don't define anything. I'm
just me and I know I'm a lad. I can tell you who isn't a lad – anyone
from fucking Blur.' Later Liam, incorrigibly Wildean as ever, added,
'We showed that fucking twat from Blur how to pogo,' while
jumping up and down and rattling some railings. This seems to have
been the first crackle of animosity between the two bands though
Damon, as will be seen, dates the commencement of hostilities rather
later.

'Ally Pally' had the air of a benevolent imperial rally about it,
and the choice of venue was significant, as Mike Smith points out.
'The Stone Roses still represented the acme of what an indie band
could achieve so there was an echo of their big Ally Pally gig five
years before in Blur's show there. It was a huge success. A fabulous
line-up that fitted the times just right. Supergrass and Pulp both
played with such a flourish. There was a huge party backstage.
Alex's mum and dad were there and then everybody went on to the

club Smashing which had taken over from Syndrome as the London music scene's after-hours club.'

Now installed as press darlings, notices for Alexandra Palace were drooling in their enthusiasm, though the *Independent* was still clinging to its 'vastly over-rated cod cockney mod-pop' line. 'A genial raucous celebration of a career rescued from the dumper' was one shrewd assessment. But more than just a triumphant arena show by Blur, the evening constituted a tribal gathering of sorts. In retrospect, it may well have been the high-water mark of Britpop in terms of fervour and optimism if not sheer popularity. There were mega-units still to be shipped by Blur, Pulp, Oasis, The Spice Girls and other manifestations of the Britpop boom, but it was never healthier than this creatively. In the week that Blur played to a capacity crowd at Ally Pally – they could have sold out the huge venue five or six times over – they received gold discs for 100,000 sales of *Parklife*. Immediately after, they released *Parklife*'s title track as the third single, featuring of course the spivvy barrow-boy persona of Phil Daniels. It reached Number 10 and it was hard to escape Daniels' luvvaduck tones in the pubs and shopping centres of Britain that autumn. It was a performance that in truth rapidly lost what charm it had and, worse, eventually caricatured the group as a jellied eels grotesque *à la* Dick Van Dyke and Tommy Steele, when in fact what they were about ran deeper and murkier. Still, there is no denying the effervescent sense of fun in 'Parklife''s lurid, silly video featuring, among other things, Graham Coxon as a portly, moustachioed everyman neighbour. They were enjoying themselves hugely, or so it seemed.

Alongside Blur's success ran the burgeoning career of Elastica, the group formed by Damon's partner Justine Frischmann. Their first release had been the limited edition 'Stutter' in November 1993 but it was in late '94 that they began to really emerge into the popular consciousness, largely due to the Top 20 hits 'Line Up' and 'Connection', brittle, astringent new-wave tunes steeped in the heritage of The Buzzcocks and Wire. Elastica's success, Blur's purple patch, the associated rise of Supergrass, Sleeper, Pulp and their ilk – English music was going through its most fertile period for a decade.

MIKE SMITH: It was a very boozy hedonistic time. Everyone was dressing up and pretending to be mods and punks and there was this feeling of, Isn't London great? Pulp and Elastica and Supergrass were starting to go overground. As we went into '95 Damon and Justine were increasingly going to be seen as the premier couple of pop. Alex was actually becoming the Soho bohemian, now in a position where he could actually do it. They were beginning to enjoy being pop stars. Also, Oasis were developing. I saw them first in Manchester at the Canal Cafe during the In The City event the previous September. I tried to sign them but, amongst other things, they wanted a huge amount of money. Then in the spring, 'Supersonic' came out. Andy Ross hated them. He thought they were just another sixth-form rock band. Right at the start, Blur too thought they were just another band and took the piss out of me for trying to sign them. Later, though, Damon went to the launch for *Definitely Maybe* at the Mars Bar on Endell Street. Any rivalry was very matey at this point, certainly on Blur's part, but then they were on top of things. They ruled the roost and they liked the idea of there being a huge scene that became Britpop.

'It was a euphoric time,' confirms Blur manager Chris Morrison. 'During this period they walked on water. There is a period when a successful band can do no wrong. You can make dreadful mistakes and get away with it. It was great; it was very exciting. One of the best things about being a manager is seeing success through the eyes of new artists. That initial thrill. "I'm a pop star. People want to hear my music. I can travel the world playing for them." If you can't enjoy it then, you will never enjoy it. Because it can get tedious later.'

In truth, the first faint stirrings of tedium were already there. Behind the much-eulogised blue eyes of the nation's favourite 'Baudelaire-reading terrace hooligan', Damon Albarn was experiencing inner turmoil, to be discussed in more detail in the next chapter. But as they took *Parklife* to the arenas of the UK, Scandinavia and Europe towards the end of 1994, Graham Coxon was also beginning to lose his appetite for some elements of pop stardom, a life he had dreamt of and now found himself thrust into with dizzying speed.

GRAHAM COXON: It was wild initially, ticking off another ambition, another dream, every day, it seemed. Realising things you'd nurtured for years. But I started to lose the ability to take it seriously. I started to feel detached from what we were doing. We'd become very much a pop group and I was beginning to feel uncomfortable with that. That big arena tour at the end of '94 was disturbing. The noise as we went on stage – kids screaming – was unbelievable. The sound of scream-ing is pretty frightening plus it ruins the soundcheck. It felt like a freak show. I'd be trying to make them hate us. I think Damon was loving it and getting his needs met. But you see little kids being crushed and it's not nice. It was freaking me out. By this time I personally was becoming quieter and less comfortable with rows and chaos in my life than when I was twenty. Now, I don't like any noise at all. If you're of a nervous disposition like I am, it's all very startling. We were leaving shows and getting our hair pulled as we tried to board the bus and I'm thinking, 'This shouldn't be happening to us. This is someone else's thing.' It wasn't me. It was before the coming of the boy band and I think they were making the best of what was available, the little bastards. Reasonable-looking lads making reasonably poppy music. Even then, I kind of thought, I don't really wanna do this any more.

But even entertaining such thoughts seemed faintly churlish. The dynasty, it seemed, had hardly begun, although their final release of the year, 'End Of A Century', felt perfunctory and only made it to Number 19. December, however, brought one of the most interest-ing and unusual ventures. Graham and Damon's former music teacher Nigel Hildreth had now taken up a post at Colchester Sixth Form College. He was involved in a biannual expedition to raise money for an orphanage in India and to that end was attempting to raise funds.

NIGEL HILDRETH: I think I jokingly said to someone, 'Well, some of my ex-students are doing rather well' – *Parklife* was everywhere – and the idea began to form in my mind. I spoke to Keith Albarn, Damon's dad, and asked whether he thought they might come back and make an appearance, sign some autographs or something. He put me on to the agent and eventually I got to speak to Damon. He didn't want to turn up and sign autographs though. He said, 'Why don't we come and play along with some of your students? Why not do an acoustic gig? No PAs – play with an orchestra. You can get them to arrange some of our numbers.' Well, we did all that. But it was literally the day before the gig that I told the students, 'You'll be playing on stage with Blur tomorrow.'

The gig was a great success and it is illuminating that Nigel Hildreth believes one of the reasons Damon was so keen to play the concert, aside from the obvious charitable cause, was the attractive intimacy of the setting – the band and a seventeen-piece orchestra in a gym – after the impersonal arenas they'd been visiting in a mind-numbing round. 'They seemed uncomfortable with the big arenas they were now playing.'

Tickets went on sale on the day of the gig, 16 December. By the 5 p.m. show time the gym was filled with an audience of 500; less than a tenth of the size of the one that had seen them at Alexandra Palace and an infinitesimal fraction of the number that had watched Damon present *Top of the Pops* the previous evening. The set comprised 'Tracy Jacks', 'End Of A Century', 'Parklife', 'To The End' and 'The Debt Collector'. The venture raised £3000 for the orphanage (the student expedition set off that weekend) and some of the tracks would have been released were it not for the poor sound quality of the recordings. However, posterity was served in that student Simon Exton's arrangement of 'Parklife' helped gain him an A level Music pass.

The year ended with Blur 'there or thereabouts', to borrow a phrase from the footballing lexicon Damon was becoming more familiar with daily, in all the end-of-year critics' and readers' polls. They were often sandwiched uncomfortably between Suede and Oasis, a poignant juxtaposition. Still, even with stiff competition from their rivals offerings, *Dog Man Star* and *Definitely Maybe* – both superlative albums – *Parklife* held cheery, yobbish dominion everywhere, to the delight of most and the consternation of some.

Blur's reign as grand viziers of the Britpop boom was to extend far into the coming year. Indeed, the most orgiastic triumphs were still ahead. But running concurrent with them would be the group's growing unhappiness as the internal workings of the band ratcheted tighter than an overwound watch. The last days of empire were just around the corner. The excess, the madness, the tears; all the gory fun of Robert Graves' *I Claudius*. If they could have made a horse their tour manager, they would have done so in the glorious bloody heyday of 1995.

9 Late Imperial

Though Blur had spent most of 1994 as boy emperors of the newly revived British pop scene, their symbolic coronation came in Alexandra Palace in the second week of February 1995, ironically the scene of their grandest concert to date the previous year. They were crowned before a jury of their peers, before the voracious lenses and flashguns of the press and the gripping and grinning Politburo of corporate rock, all tanned and aerobicised, Bossed and Calvinned.

The Britannia Music Awards, or Brits, as most know them, has a chequered history. For most of their breezy, glitzy existence no one knew or cared about them. It was a glorified trade bash, where product managers would feel up their secretaries on the coach home after five buckshee bottles of Nottage Hill. It was perhaps more glamorous than the Fishmongers' Presentation at the Southport Floral Hall or the Federation of Master Butchers' Dinner Dance, but roughly as meaningful to the outside world. Then, it was decided that the 1989 awards would be televised and, thanks to one of the greatest debacles in the history of live television, the event staggered and pratfell its way into the nation's consciousness. For two agonising yet mordantly comic hours, lanky Fleetwood Mac rock drummer Mick Fleetwood and tiny, pneumatic, topless model turned minor pop star Samantha Fox – a pairing of excruciating incompatibility – presided with rictus grins and desperation over a farrago of technical catastrophes and inexplicable, unfunny routines. For days, people talked of little else at pub and bus-stop. Though in itself a travesty, the 1989 Brit Awards put the event on the map and by the time Blur were nominated for a clutch of awards in 1995, the ceremony had become a faintly cheesy but diverting fixture on the pop calendar.

Though barely perceptible cracks were beginning to appear in the band's ceaselessly smiling, winking, cheeky-chappie aspect, their

Brits 'gongathon' still had a huge, ecstatic resonance. It was confirmation that the group could probably get no bigger.

Dave Rowntree diagnoses that. 'Graham definitely had begun to feel disillusionment the earliest but we all loved that first flush of success. It was like being let loose in Toys R Us. Even so, there was a fairly slow, steady build. It wasn't until the Brits that things really went ballistic. In fact, I've never really felt much like a pop star apart from that one night. It was absolutely fantastic, I have to say. I remember someone who obviously knew the score telling me that "when we'd won the last one" there'd be a press conference. Last one? I didn't know we'd won any. So we'd won more than one then! Come the ceremony, I was almost in a daze. They just kept reading our name out.'

That meant that the band were continually trooping back and forth to the podium, and on one of these journeys Dave's curious makeshift facial adornment became apparent. The godlike but silly Prince (TAFKAP, Artist, Kevin, Squiggle, whatever) had picked up his award with the word 'Slave' painted on his cheek, a mute protest against his record company's refusal to release his new material. Dave, in solidarity, had hastily felt-tipped the word 'Dave' on his cheek. 'We have a lot in common,' he explained. 'EMI won't release my solo album either.'

Blur's tally of four awards – Best Band, Best Single ('Girls And Boys'), Best Album and Best Video ('Parklife') – has never been equalled. Indeed, Mike Smith contends 'No one had ever done it before and probably it will never happen again because there's no audience input any more. Their video award was voted for by punters.'

At an adjoining table sat Oasis, clearly miffed by Blur's success but remaining civil . . . just. 'I seem to remember us chatting across the tables,' says Dave. 'It was fairly good-natured though I think winning four did piss Liam off. But the media slanging match hadn't started in earnest then. I've never been on unfriendly terms with any of them anyway. All that passed me by. I am so not interested in any of it.'

It's easy to forget, in the wake of the public letting of bad blood that was to follow, how supportive Blur always were of the Mancunian newcomers. In several articles over the past year, they had affirmed their kinship to Oasis – admittedly at the expense of Suede – and now to cap it all, Damon actually announced from the stage that Oasis should be up there sharing the Best Band Award with them. 'Oasis were not a threat,' is Mike Smith's viewpoint, 'and Blur genuinely wanted to encourage this British pop renaissance. They felt anyone with a guitar was on the same side.'

Graham, though, describes the Saturnalian evening as 'not good fun at all.' He explains, 'I was sitting right next to Liam who was just being provocative and was trying to intimidate all night. Every time we came back from the stage with another one, he'd glare at me and say, "You fucking look me in the eye and tell me you deserve that award." Then he'd make to hit you. I suppose that's his distinctive sense of humour. Well, it was a weird enough night without him fucking going on and on. But I got to kiss Cyndi Lauper, which is very good or bad, I dunno, depending on your perspective. You've got to kiss a few famous people in life.'

Alex says with a twinkle, 'Graham was well chuffed by it all. I knew we were going to win four anyway. It was a great night. I met Keith Allen properly for the first time and ended up in one of those gangster late-night crack places.' Allen was an *éminence grise* in the British cultural scene. Originally a loud and abrasive alternative comedian, he had become a loud and abrasive TV presenter and finally loud and abrasive generally for a living with a nice sideline in straight acting in everything from costume drama (*Middlemarch*) to cult Brit film (*Shallow Grave*). Bizarrely, he had also written the lyric to New Order's 1990 World Cup anthem, 'World In Motion', and still fancied himself as a pop Svengali. In the coming year, Alex's friendship with Allen and with controversial young British artist Damien Hirst – former Goldsmiths pal whose Saatchi-sponsored animal carcass installations had brought fame and opprobrium – would make him both highly visible and much despised, even from within the band.

As the year progressed, each of Blur's personal relationships was to reflect or impinge upon the weird corkscrew parabola of the group's success. Alex would briefly part from Justine Andrew; Dave's new marriage would provide a haven from the insanity of the group's halcyon days; Graham's blooming relationship with Jo from Huggy Bear would colour his outlook on the group's new status as globe-straddling corporate pop colossus.

For now, though, Damon Albarn and Justine Frischmann were the premier couple of British music. It was Britpop as scripted by a particularly hammy Hollywood scriptwriter. By day, he is the handsome, troubled, tousled intellectual superstar with the common touch loved by moppets and indie kinds alike; she is the androgynous, sexy punk poetess of cross-gender appeal with 'the voice of a grumpy angel'. By night, they cuddle up with their veggie risotto and Rioja in shabby, bohemian High Street Kensington, casually knocking off icily hip yet hummable hit singles.

Damon described himself and Justine as 'the Hugh Grant and Liz Hurley of Britpop . . . everywhere we go we're watched. It's invasive but interesting.' This, however, was soon to pall. Coverage of the twosome's activities was relentless and the same few mildly private nuggets were endlessly warmed over in celebrity pieces from *Tatler* to the *Daily Star*. Their untidy flat with its cats, books and records, Damon's low sex drive, the pictures of naked couples pasted to their loo wall, their celebrated role reversal and the image of Damon at the sink in marigolds while Justine reclines in bed with chocolates and Andre Gide. And the occasional off-the-cuff reference to the tribulations of making a relationship work with both of them in successful rock bands.

'Damon's away six months of the year at the moment and I just can't expect him to get into his single bed every night with a cup of cocoa,' commented Justine. 'It just doesn't work like that . . . Sometimes I find out things that piss me off and I go on about it for a day but if I had a problem with it I wouldn't be with him. I've never been possessive. I just don't understand people who go to pieces when they find out their boyfriend's snogged someone. Is he leaving you? No, well, why do you care? . . . We have an excellent time. Even though we're all going out with people we still end up running around hotel rooms at 4 a.m. and having a wild time.'

DAMON ALBARN: Elastica were doing very well and we were just everywhere. So you have these two people right in the public eye constantly. We'd become the big showbiz couple. And the long-term effect it had on our relationship . . . well, it fucked everybody up eventually so truthfully the effect it had wasn't great. The truth is not very pleasant, I'm afraid, and most of it's not for public consumption. Despite all the trouble and pain that gets caused because of the lifestyle, despite all the absences, I was in a relationship with someone I thought I could spend the rest of my life with. I was that stupid and naive. It makes me laugh in a nasty way to think I could be that idealistic and optimistic about something as potentially damaging as fame and stardom and the rest.

The symbolic apotheosis of this came on the Wednesday following the Brit Awards when Elastica and Blur both appeared on *Top of the Pops*, which new producer Ric Blaxill had made over as a showcase for indie music in general and Britpop in particular. As Mike Smith recollects, 'That night sort of symbolised the peak that both bands, that everyone, was at really. Elastica were playing 'Waking Up' and Damon was playing keyboards on it under his Dan Abnormal pseudonym [the anagram of Damon Albarn he'd contributed to the Elastica album as]. Then he dashed across to the other stage to do this fantastic totally punk version of 'Jubilee' with Blur. We didn't know it then but that probably was as good as it got.'

It was the highest of the high life. There was nowhere else to go but down. Damon stood on the terraces at Chelsea one day and drank at the Chelsea Arts Club with Laurie Lee the next. He wrote articles for the *Modern Review* on the rise of yob culture, of which he was an ambiguous avatar. Visible, voluble, glamorous, they were playing up to their new role as the country's leading pop group; the Simply Reds and U2s might sell more but there was no sense of urgent cool, no 'zeitgeist' about them.

Of course, this was the nocturnal Blur. By day they were working fastidiously on the follow-up to *Parklife* and thus the most eagerly awaited British pop record in years. The group had always been enormously prolific and hugely industrious. They had never been ones for hiatus and recharging periods lazing on beaches ('That's a relatively recent development,' jokes Dave today). In fact, they had been back in the studio with Stephen Street the morning after the Brit Awards.

STEPHEN STREET: There was such a euphoria over *Parklife*. It took on a life of its own, independent of all of us. Six, seven, eight months later it was still in the Top 10. Even when they didn't win the Mercury Prize, it doubled its sales overnight. It was a bit like the Robbie Williams phenomenon in 1998. You find yourself wondering, Who on earth is still buying this? I got a call one day very soon after *Parklife* saying, 'Are you ready to do the next one?' *Great Escape* always felt like a strange album in the sense that they were still doing loads of publicity for *Parklife*. That album hadn't died at all and was still riding high. Other groups would have waited for that album to run its course and that may have been the sensible thing to do with hindsight but Damon in particular is so prolific that they wanted to get on. They were good sessions but you could feel the pressure beginning to tell. Imagine going off and winning four Brits and coming straight back into the studio next morning. That kind of thing sometimes made it difficult. It was hard to forget *Parklife* and concentrate on the job in hand. Fortunately by then we'd arrived at a very comfortable working routine. I'd instilled in them the idea that you don't have to be in a boozed-up frenzy all the time to make records. That's a myth. They'd come in reasonably early, mid-morning, and then work till ten at night. Then we'd go off and unwind and have a pint. It was very professional and workmanlike. I always tried to make each one feel special. When Graham began he wouldn't even play the guitar in front of me in the control room. He'd sit in the corridor. Alex usually wouldn't have arrived at a bass line when we arrived so we would sit there, he and I, and try things out. I'd try and give each one my undivided attention when they needed it. It was a good working partnership and a good friendship and we'd go out for drinks afterwards. Though I'd got on well with The Smiths I'd never socialised with them. Perhaps it was the Manchester–London divide. I felt much closer to Blur.

So as Blur worked by day on their projected final section of the 'life' trilogy – three records that would encapsulate their sardonic resumé of British life at the end of the century – by night they still moved in the swirling heady orbit of *Parklife*. They were everywhere; practically everywhere. The leathery, embarrassing Peter Stringfellow barred them from his ghastly eponymous club saying, 'I found them to be the most obnoxious little shits I have had in my club in a long while.' Bearing in mind the old Arab proverb, 'My enemy's enemy is my friend', we must warm to Blur here.

ALEX JAMES: And it just got more and more ridiculous. The next thing we knew it's quadruple platinum which isn't *What's the Story (Morning Glory)* but it means if you get on a bus, someone on the bus has got your record. Things became very strange very quickly. On that first tour people were shouting Jesus at Damon. Suddenly I'm hanging out with my favourite supermodel, going to the Groucho Club, cocaine everywhere all the time. It's brilliant. Graham was already starting to go a bit weird but generally it was fantastic. There's nothing to beat that first rush of success when everyone thinks you're the future and all the other bands are going, 'Shit, how did they do that?' Part of Graham's difficulty with it all was to do with his girlfriend at the time. Commercial success didn't sit very well with her outlook. I thought it was ridiculously funny and if you could have it all, you might as well.

I made a point of drinking two bottles of champagne a day for eighteen months. England only imports something like 100,000 bottles a year so I reckon I drank 1 per cent of England's total champagne import. You work out early on that if you demand stuff you get it. And you get a reputation for liking certain things. Damon gets beads, Dave gets aeroplane books, I get champagne. Pretty soon, the record company makes sure there's always champagne. Only drawback is it gives you bad breath. All the acid in it.'

Sharing in this champagne lifestyle with Alex was Mike Smith who, having originally been a professional associate who became a close friend, was now hoping to renew his business links with the group. The publishing deal with MCA he had signed them to was coming up for renewal and he was determined to woo them to his new employer, EMI Music. 'Negotiations went right down to the wire. I don't think they realised what they'd got at MCA otherwise they'd never have let them go. They thought Blur were a fashion, a fad. You should never lose an act. But the deal kept getting very dodgy. Chris Morrison told us three times we'd got them and then we hadn't. That might have been a negotiating tool. If so, it worked. But we got them in the end and it was great to be working with them again legitimately.'

From his vantage point of close proximity to the group – often as close as the bottom of a glass – Smith saw the way the various Blur members took to their new lives. 'Damon had a relatively sensible existence. He and Justine had moved up the road from Kensington to Westbourne Park Road. They had a lovely house and were very happy together at the start of 1995. But Justine was then away touring all year and Damon was alone a lot and getting invited to everything. If you wanted a pop star at your party, he was there. Alex had got heavily into the arts scene in London because he now lived in Soho. After years of blagging into the second-rate members' clubs like Blacks, now suddenly all doors are open. Groucho's became his thing, his second home. He thought he'd walked into a film. He was having a surreal existence. Damien Hirst and Keith Allen were his partners in crime. They were so much a part of what he loved and he threw himself into it. It did put an enormous strain on his relationship with Justine, who moved out eventually for a time. So he carried on this debauched life in his one-bedroom flat in Endell Street; an absolute shithole.'

As well as Keith Allen and Damien Hirst, Alex was at this point also inseparable from Russell Barrett, former member of Chapterhouse, the long-forgotten shoe-gazers. Smith describes him as, 'Extremely bright. A philosophy graduate. Immersed in Soho so Alex and he became drinking partners. There was very bad, very stupid behaviour constantly. Alex would walk into parties and simply wave in a very vague and general sense to everyone so that he was sure to greet the people who knew him. All the time this is going on, they're making *The Great Escape* by day. Lunacy. Everyone drinking very heavily except, of course, Dave. Graham was by now going out with Jo from Huggy Bear who didn't see eye to eye at all with lively antics and laddish behaviour. *Loaded* magazine had just started and that laddishness really seemed to fit the time. Those kind of attitudes were prevalent. Graham's relationship with the band became very strained because of this. But all the time the record's being made and everyone's very very excited. It seemed really groundbreaking.'

If we don't count the extraordinary impromptu warm-up gig they played in Camden's Dublin Castle to a noisy throng of invited guests and beery 'lads', one of whom threw a glass at the stage, then the first public airing of the new album and the prelude to a summer of high, rare madness was the group's Mile End Stadium performance of Saturday 17 June 1995. Over 27,000 people made their way to the East End in a dispiriting drizzle to watch Blur and their handpicked bill of supporting talent. A rum roster it was too: psychedelic Scouse noise-pop from Boo Radleys, old favourites The Cardiacs, venerable electro ironists Sparks, the legendary Wire (ex-charges of Mike Collins), affable roguish pop craftsmen Dodgy and The Shanakies, the hand of friendship extended to Eddie Deedigan and band from all those years before. The nature of the bill served to confirm that there was still something of Seymour in the nation's favourite pop group, as did the noteworthy if clichéd stage set (plastic hamburgers seemed to be rather hammering home a dated point) and Damon's curious entrance in a rubber old man mask.

Damon may be right when he talks of it being the first gig where indie kids and football lads rubbed shoulders but there was also a deflating associated feeling that the group were becoming public property of the worst sort. Of course, this is elitism – the wheedling cry of the student bar opinion leader who sees his favourite group actually becoming popular. But the group shared the ill-defined

sense of unease. Symptomatically, Wire were booed off by the 'lads', who bayed 'En-ger-land' at every opportunity. To an extent, Damon had asked for it with his literate lager lout persona but the joke was wearing thinner and thinner. 'I wish we'd been booed off,' remarks Dave ruefully.

Though hand-picked, the bill was not exactly what the group wanted. Several first choices were unavailable and some were, frankly, suspicious. 'We probably wanted Ash,' says Graham when asked for names. 'We always want Ash.'

'It was roughly the same time as Oasis did Maine Road and the crowd felt very like an Oasis crowd to me,' remarks Mike Smith. 'Very laddish. Mile End is effectively the precursor to *Great Escape*. It was a big triumph really. Weather was bloody awful but the atmosphere was fantastic. It was memorable as the only time Alex did 'Far Out' on stage and as the first time they'd played 'Country House'. The entire audience went mad for it and that set *The Great Escape* up as an album.'

Damon later revealed, 'We weren't going to put "Country House" out, but we got totally carried away by how well it went down at Mile End. With hindsight it was probably a foolish thing to do – it led to a lot of things a lot of people could've done without, and could've really screwed us up badly. But the crowd loved it.'

Dave remembers the show as 'petrifying'. 'We were really sticking our necks out, I felt. It was a bit of an over-the-top gesture, make or break. For the first two songs I was literally shaking with fear. It rained, didn't it. But it didn't dampen the spirits. I was dry anyway.'

Graham found the day – ostensibly a victory rally – somewhat underwhelming. 'I found it dull. Drizzly and dull. It was the pinnacle of our bizarre period, evidence of our slow mental warping. Damon came on as an old man. Big hamburgers on stage. A bit pretentious really. Particularly since we took it all back and started to really like America.' Graham claims to have been satisfied with his performance, 'but not with what I wore – some horrible blue towelling thing like an old darts player.'

Predictably, Phil Daniels turned up for his now mandatory 'Park-life' cameo, an old warhorse by now among the first fruits of *The Great Escape*, such as 'Globe Alone', 'Stereotypes' and 'Charmless Man'. At the end of the month, they performed substantially the same set when they appeared at Milton Keynes Bowl as guests of REM, helicoptered in for a performance that the organisers had wanted curtailed at an hour but that the band insisted on being 80 minutes. Such was the confidence with having an album that would ultimately spend 90 weeks on the chart and sell almost a million and a half copies.

The Great Escape was finished by the time the group played these major summer outings, but a difficult choice remained about which would be the first single and the crucial flagship track for this crucial post-breakthrough album. Within Blur's camp, lively debate raged. 'I felt it would be good to lead off with "Stereotypes",' says Mike Smith, 'because it sounded like a fantastic radical move forward and pointed to the darker, edgier stuff on *Great Escape* like "Yuko And Hiro" and "He Thought Of Cars". I thought it was a less cosy choice. "Country House" is a great pop record. Stephen Street was hugely proud of it because in its own way, it's very sophisticated. There's four different melodies in there. Lyrically, it's great. As witty as any he'd come up with but musically it harked back to *Parklife*. That's probably why people loved it. Andy wanted it as the single. He thought it was so obvious that this is what the kids want. We sat outside the Black Horse in Bloomsbury and discussed it. Graham wanted "Stereotypes" but the rest had come round to "Country House".'

'Country House' was, of course, destined to become one of the most famous/infamous singles of the decade, indeed of the British pop era, almost entirely for reasons that had nothing to do with the quality or otherwise of the song. In fact, most of the stories associated with this adequately jaunty tune lie outside the piece itself. It had its genesis in Blur's strife-torn, convoluted history.

ANDY ROSS: Well, it's about Dave Balfe, obviously. No one would deny that. It still rankled with Damon that Balfe earned money from Blur but that is the nature of pop. He'd ostensibly retired on the back of them, though to be fair before *Parklife* came out, but none the less he did reap rewards from that album and that pissed Damon off a bit so this was his dig. I think Balfe was quite flattered so if it was supposed to wind him up it backfired. Ironic, really, because that song could have helped Damon buy a couple of houses in the country, which he hasn't done. It was great fun. The only annoying thing is that they haven't written a song about me. Or maybe they have and I don't know.

DAVID BALFE: The first I knew about it was when I wandered into Food's office one day as I often did and saw this pile of demos and this one tape marked 'Country House'. Now there was me out in my country house I'd bought after selling the company and I did think, that's a coincidence. So I said, 'What's all this about then?' and Andy looked slightly embarrassed and I realised it was about me! I thought it was OK. Not one of their best. I take it that half of it is about me. I'm the professional cynic whose heart's not in it and who left the rat race. But I don't think I'm the guy in the second verse who couldn't drink, who I assume is their manager. At the time I was drinking and smoking a lot and the only pills I took were not for your heart. If you're going to have a song written about you, it may as well be Number 1. When I come to sell that house I will certainly advertise it as 'As featured in the Number 1 Hit "Country House"' and I hope it gets a better price for its part in pop history. It's fun and flattering and my son will enjoy it when he's 35.

By virtue of its tremendous response at Mile End and the undoubted geniality of its rollicking nature, 'Country House' became the designated first single from *The Great Escape*. The only matter for discussion now was the release date. As is the case with any major band, Blur's marketing strategists looked at other forthcoming releases to try and optimise 'Country House''s potential impact. In this case, this obviously meant looking towards Oasis, who were at a very similar stage with their second album *What's the Story (Morning Glory)*.

As the world now knows, what eventually happened was that the Blur and Oasis singles ended up being released on the same day, thus sparking the most publicised confrontation in the history of British music. How this happened, though, has always been obscured by claim and counter-claim, allegation and denial. With the dust now settled, things are a little clearer.

ANDY ROSS: We did change 'Country House' to come out at the same time as Oasis. We tried to deny it at the time but it was the circumstances that forced us into it. Throughout the year Tony Wadsworth at Parlophone, who's quite matey with Marcus Russell, the Oasis manager, were keeping each other posted on how the albums were coming along on the tacit understanding that it would be stupid for one to come out in the same week or following week from the other. So we had our album provisionally scheduled for a certain date and to our knowledge the Oasis album was to be two or three weeks later.

That was all fine and it meant that our single would come out two or three weeks before, which seemed common sense to us. But we made the mistake of thinking that Alan [McGee] and Creation worked on the same level of logic to us. It turns out they had a different idea altogether. They had their single set up for six or seven weeks before the album. So instead of 'Roll With It' coming out two or three weeks after 'Country House', we found out 'Roll With It' was due to come out the week before.

Blur immediately reconsidered their schedule. It was clearly counterproductive for both groups to bring out singles at what was effectively the same time. However, Creation seemed wedded to their schedule and were not minded to change it.

At another meeting on licensed premises, this time outside a pub behind EMI's famous Manchester Square building, Blur's council of war comprising Chris Morrison, Damon and Andy Ross discussed their options. 'We were a bit nonplussed,' says Andy Ross, 'because it had never occurred to us we'd get this single clash. So we thought, Do we put it back for two weeks to make more of a gap? But, you know what it was like at the time. Oasis were very cocky and very much on the up and we knew that if we put our single forward or back they'd say we'd bottled it and they scared us off and quite frankly I wouldn't have blamed them.'

Grasping the nettle, Damon suggested the most forthright solution. 'In the end, I just said, "Fuck it, let's go head to head. If they want a kind of confrontation, let's do it properly."' Glasses were charged and raised. It was decided that Blur would shift the release of 'Country House' to 14 August, the same day as Oasis's 'Roll With It'.

Under normal circumstances, this would have added something of a frisson of excitement to the chart rundown of that week. Given the dire state of the British pop charts and the decline of the single as the bulwark of the industry, both were obvious candidates to enter the chart at Number 1. So a straight contest was now set up that had echoes of past rivalries (Beatles and Stones, T. Rex and Slade, etc.) but on a much more competitive level.

But the contest had a whole extra dimension. Originally joky sparring between two groups known for their loose tongues, the atmosphere had become decidedly sour. This dates specifically back to the previous April when Oasis had reached Number 1 with 'Some

Might Say' and thrown a party at the Mars Bar in Soho to celebrate. Damon went along. 'As I went in Liam was at the door and he came over to me, right in my face, going, "Number fucking one, mate." Good luck to them, you know, they'd got the first Number 1, but there was something weird about this naked ambition in his eyes.' Later in the evening, a dalliance between Damon and Liam's girl-friend was to bring down the wrath of the Oasis camp. 'The rivalry was all OK at the start. Quite enjoyable really. It was the first time in years that bands has been talked about in this way; that pop had been this important. But after that night it all got very nasty.'

If you visit the press office of EMI/Parlophone's offices in Brook Green, London, you'll notice something significant about the Blur archive. There are a couple of box files each for the years 1990, '91 and '92. A logarithmic expansion occurs in '93 and there is a large cardboard box full; two of them by '94 and so on and so on. No great surprise here: as the group gets more successful, they attract more publicity.

But there is an obvious aberration. One month in 1995 – August, to be precise – has *eight* bound volumes devoted to it; irrefutable testimony to the collective madness that swept the country that late summer. Everyone of a certain generation can tell you what they were doing the evening that Blur beat Oasis to the top of the singles chart.

The reasons for the deluge of publicity, the national fixation with this pop feud, are easy to find. Both groups talked a good fight. Oasis regularly taunted Blur for being 'wankers' or 'not lads' and even 'southern puffs'. Embarrassingly, Noel Gallagher frothed, 'Blur are middle-class wankers trying to play hardball with a bunch of working-class heroes. There can only be one winner.' They regularly made reference to Chas And Dave and 'chimney sweep music'. Blur sneered back a little and Damon joked about 'Status Quoasis', a reference to the unsubtle pub-rock strain in Oasis's music. It was playground stuff but it had a certain amusement value, particularly in the slow-moving summer.

'It was the height of the silly season, let's face it,' admits Dave Rowntree, 'but it was great fun. Journalists were being told to write about it. A. N. Wilson wrote about it. What the fuck was going on? We should have won an award for marketing genius. We should take consultancy posts with major advertising companies. Not since

The Beatles and Stones, blah blah blah ... but they didn't do anything like this. No one had done it before. If you're gonna sell records with gimmicks they've got to be fucking good gimmicks and this was. I bumped into Liam in a toilet, mysteriously enough, at the height of it all, and I said to him, "This is all bollocks, isn't it?" He said, "Yeah, of course, but it sells records, doesn't it?" '

Bollocks, indubitably, but there was another reason why the nation took up cudgels so swiftly. As Alex James has pointed out, 'Everyone could project something of themselves, some prejudice, into the debate. It was class war and regional differences and all that stuff.'

The *Evening Standard* ran a piece on the class ramifications of the contest. *The Times*, the *Financial Times* and the *Daily Telegraph*, august breakfast reading of the pinstriped classes, all ran leaders on the issue. Pat Kane, as is customary at such times, delivered himself of a breathtakingly dull socio-political analysis in the *Guardian*. CNN carried it in their broadcasts. The *Oslo Times* put the story on their front page. Tabloids ran splurges about Mandy and Richard Vivien-Thomas, who were filing for divorce over their divided loyalties. A million unfunny cartoons were born. Damien Hirst, now the country's most high-profile artist and friends with Alex for the second time, was enlisted to make his first ever pop video. The result was a moderately tiresome 'post-modern' bucolic romp modelled on the puerile Benny Hill routines of the 1970s. It features, inevitably, Keith Allen as the song's protagonist plus the band in various daft outfits and situations and what the rash of men's magazines would term a 'bevy of beauties' – notably Sarah Stockbridge and Jo Guest, giggling, pouting and exposing cleavages to the camera. 'At the time,' reflects Dave, 'I thought it could be quite interesting because Damien Hirst delights in pissing off the same people we do but in the end I don't think he had any ideas. I think he was just interested in working in another media. Really, it's the video Alex would have made.'

It would all have been rather forgettable but for the further couple of inches' extra torque it added to the rack Graham Coxon felt he was on.

On the Wednesday before the chart was issued, Damon Albarn hosted a TV special, *Britpop Now*, a showcase for the likes of Sleeper, Pulp, Elastica, Supergrass and the new Blur single, from which Oasis had pointedly absented themselves. All week, the papers and the nation talked of little else: Creation had had obscure barcode difficulties, EMI had shipped about 300,000 copies of the Blur single by Wednesday, the records were neck and neck in terms of airplay, though the midweek sales put Blur ahead by about ten sales to every nine of Oasis.

At 7 p.m. on Sunday evening, most of the country not lounging poolside on the Continent was ensconced by a radio. The Blur camp were geographically scattered. Chris Morrison was on holiday with his family in a remote Scottish cottage where his mobile phone was inoperative and thus had spent the week making pilgrimages to the isolated payphone with pockets of change to ring EMI's biggest wigs for updates and at night driving to the highest point of a deserted moor to check on Elastica's progress on their US tour. Damon had just returned from Mauritius where he'd been visiting his father who was lecturing there. His recollections reflect the growing blackness of the group's mood.

DAMON ALBARN: It was a horrible day, no pleasure at all. I'd gone to Mauritius to get away from it. When I got back, it was like a bloody election. The music had become immaterial. On the day, I was playing football in Regent's Park and Graham, really pissed, turned up at half-time with Andy Ross and then the day just got more and more unpleasant.

More congenially, Dave Rowntree was flying his light aircraft back from a holiday in the South of France. 'I was coming home with my wife. We were flying back for the party. I was asking the air-traffic controllers for the chart on the way back in. Control Tower at Elstree Aerodrome told me as I came in to land. I wasn't enormously surprised. Damon threatened pretty much everyone with the sack if we lost. All the management, everyone at EMI.'

In the end, Andy Ross puts Blur's victory down to that curse of the modern single, formats. 'It's that boring. We did two CDs and a cassette, I think, and they had two CDs and a seven-inch single. Our cassette outsold their seven-inch something ludicrous like twenty to one. If it had been the other way round they would have gone to Number 1. All a bit daft really.' None the less, 280,000 sales later, Alex wore an Oasis T-shirt for Blur's triumphant *Top of the Pops* appearance, explaining, 'It was a magnanimous gesture. I think they are a great band and this is the defining moment of Britpop. It's not Blur versus Oasis. It's Blur and Oasis versus the world.'

It's a great irony that the ultimate slug-out between Britpop's two definitive bands should have been fought between two of their worst songs. In the canon of either band, 'Country House' and 'Roll With It' do not rank highly. 'Roll With It' is, simply, a carthorse dragging behind it a cargo of awful formulaic 'boogie' best suited to a Status Quo B-side circa 1978. 'Country House' is vastly better but still no great shakes. Its best feature, the muted 'Blow me out, I am so sad' refrain, is buried beneath The Kick Horns' turgid oompahing and the clod-hopping time signature. Graham and Alex have a go with some sprightly embellishments but the result is one of Blur's weakest moments – though this is still a bone of contention in the camp. Andy Ross will 'grudgingly admit that Oasis have a few good tunes but "Roll With It" isn't one. I think "Country House", on the other hand, is a good song. The peak of that British bombastic oompah period of Damon's. I think it was very much a Kinks record and any criticism you level at "Country House" could be levelled at Ray Davies. It's a music hall record but a very good one. It certainly caught the imagination of people at the time.'

GRAHAM COXON: I grew to loathe it. It started out really well with that nice middle eight but turned into this oompah thing. If you take all the brass out it's not half as bad. But it came out with these huge, very obvious, horribly catchy garish brass hooks all over the place. It was too much. It seemed insincere and cynical. Like a great big trailer filled with money on the back of a fat man's car.

But it was, as The Beatles famously said, 'toppermost of the poppermost'. That night, the band and their entourage gathered at the Soho House club to celebrate their domination of British pop. It was a curious evening. Drink flowed freely and backs were slapped but there was an undercurrent of anxiety. Just to spell this out, the evening finished with Graham, blind drunk and in foul, lachrymose temper, attempting to throw himself out of the window. 'I listened to the chart countdown in the Soho House with a bunch of EMI people. I was really trying to hold in my feelings about the situation. But I drank a lot and spilled wine all over people. I was a bit of an arsehole but the mood was so self-congratulatory. Everyone was telling me that I ought to be happy. In the end I tried to jump out of the window.' As pop star revels go, then, it was interesting.

Damon had felt that undertow for nearly a year now, plucking at his heels even while he swam in champagne, to really stretch that metaphor. With a cruel irony, he'd started to feel anxious, depressed and insomniacal just as 'Girls And Boys' was garnering its first attention (the Pet Shop Boys had offered to remix it) and the group were beginning to emerge from their years of hardship.

> **DAMON ALBARN:** All the hard work of *Modern Life is Rubbish* is paying off. I'm on the verge of becoming a pop star and then I started having these massive panic attacks. Very frightening things. I went home to Colchester and late one night I walked back up to my old school and had this awful panicky experience which was probably to do with all those frustrating pride-battering experiences at school and after. I couldn't go back home after that. Suddenly, for no reason, right on the verge of everything I'd ever wanted to achieve, this was happening to me. That was the start of nearly two years of pressure and anxiety. It felt completely out of my control. I couldn't sleep and I seemed to spend all my time in this really heart-thumping agitated state. I remember doing 'To The End' on *Top of the Pops* and lying at the side of the studio really convinced that I was going to pass out right there on *Top of the Pops* in front of millions. A really hard time. I thought I was going to die.

At the time Damon dabbled occasionally in cocaine; regularly though not excessively, certainly not by the standards of the music industry where its recreational use is practically institutional. 'He was partial, as they say, on the run up to "Girls And Boys",' is one observer's viewpoint, 'but then he went through a slightly mad period.' Soon after the attacks started he went to see Justine Frischmann's doctor. 'It was a terrible move. I think she was very bitter about her own life and very moral and was projecting some of this on to me. She asked if I'd ever taken coke and when I said, "Yeah, but not much," she seized on this and said I had to stop taking it. Well, I did stop and that was probably a good thing but the fact is my problems had clearly nothing to do with drugs, nothing whatsoever. They were mental, internal problems. Every day I was frantic; no clarity in my thoughts and running on sheer adrenalin. Every step used to fill me with dread. I had a massive panic attack before the Alexandra Palace show and at the Brits I thought I was going to die. I never took pills to counteract this but I did drink excessively. She should have given me tranquillisers really but I'm glad she didn't.'

Stoically, Damon tried to keep these traumas hidden and continue with the group's hectic schedule. 'I tried to just get on with things. I don't tell people what I want generally. I wasn't good at that. I'm much better now. I just got on with it. Justine was having her own problems and wasn't very supportive so it was doubly hell. It was a horrible time that resulted in me drinking to excess and not being able to discern who was interested in me and why. I didn't know why girls were interested in me. I became promiscuous and didn't want to do it but thought I might as well just for the experience. That's dangerous thinking.'

Various matters, from his family's history of depression to Kurt Cobain's suicide, weighed heavy upon him. In the end he did achieve some measure of relief by, seemingly, sheer exercise of the will. 'The only depressions I've had, I've managed to sort out. I'm a great believer in sorting yourself out. You don't have to run to a doctor immediately. After trying numerous remedies from acupuncture to back specialists, I sorted it out myself. Panic attacks are very much a modern condition. People don't talk about them but they should. They're terrible things to endure on your own.'

Publicly, though, Blur's world was as slick, glossy and lustrous as the rather disappointing sleeve of *The Great Escape*, released on 11 September. The frontispiece was a pointless take on a travel brochure of watersports beneath an azure sky, the rear a witty pastiche of an Apple Macintosh advertisement. Quite what all this said about the record, an obsessively detailed, coruscating collection of brittle, bleak character studies, was not clear. The title referred more to the modern obsession with 'getting out of it' than the celebrated POW movie, although the band would acknowledge the loan by having The Kick Horns open forthcoming concerts with the movie's jaunty theme.

'Stereotypes' had been mooted as a single for reasons that were immediately apparent: an angular, modernist thrash introduced by the faintly sickly organ tones of the Proteus keyboard module. Lyrically, it was another despatch from saucy suburbia spooled out from the one initial line Damon had had for several months: 'Wife swapping is your future.' 'Best Days'' wonky, porchfront primitive guitar part illustrates Graham's love of the lo-fi and points the way clear to 'Country Sad Ballad Man', albeit in much dressier manner. The formally elegant piano obbligato at 3.14 is clearly an intentional echo of George Martin's superb contribution to The Beatles' 'In My Life'.

'Charmless Man' is a sticky one. The title's a clear allusion to 'This Charming Man' by The Smiths, whose cultural import Blur sought to emulate, but the song is almost a caricature of the writing style that reached its logical conclusion on *The Great Escape* and which Damon now balks at. He has near disowned the lyric, which is sure-footed but hollow. 'What the fuck was I thinking of when I wrote that? What the fuck was I thinking of generally? It was a very odd, very dark and confused time. I think in hindsight, when people realise it was not a happy period, the songs start to make sense.' It is another character study, though of whom we can't be sure. Ronnie Kray, an ageing gangster grotesquely feted by the more idiotic celebrities, later sent the group a bouquet of flowers for mentioning his name in the lyric.

'Dan Abnormal' is superficially a character study but the song is at least partly autobiographical. Good rather than great, the song has nice touches, such as the four-chord passage during the chorus, but is marred by the faintly gimmicky 'la la'-ing. The repeated 'TV' is a musical quote from the song 'Ex-Lion Tamer' on Wire's *Pink Flag* debut. Stephen Street confesses that he 'was never a huge fan of this one.'

'Entertain Me', 'Mr Robinson's Quango' and 'Fade Away' were, along with 'Country House', the very first tracks that Damon had delivered in demo form to Street. The producer took them on his New Year skiing holiday to listen to. The first is the album's most programmed track, a metronomic drum loop overlaid with snare embellishments from Dave. The track's most interesting feature is Alex's serpentine bass line. 'He's completely fantastic,' reports Street, 'but he'll sit next to me in the control room and fire off all these different bass lines. You've got to say, "That bit there."' The result, said Damon, was Alex's best bass line in years, even given his enthusiasm for his contribution to 'Girls And Boys'.

'Fade Away' had a working title of 'Rico' in honour of The Specials' trumpeter whose distinctive tone is clearly echoed in the brass parts. In fact, the whole track has touches of the Coventry band: Dave's snare rolls, the cakewalking piano, Graham's Morricone-inflected descending run at 2.43. 'Mr Robinson's Quango', the tale of a cross-dressing politician, had been premiered at Aston Villa Leisure Centre the previous autumn. Crowded with detail, it proved the most difficult track to mix. The promise of the fabulous intro, which returns as the song's instrumental bridge, is not delivered by the faintly ordinary verses and plodding brass parts. Still, there's Graham's fabulous guitar phrase (0.50 and various points from then on) which unspools like a slinky going downstairs.

'It Could Be You' began life as 'Dear Ray', a piano ballad extemporised in a break in rehearsals for Damon's duet with Ray Davies of The Kinks when the two performed 'Waterloo Sunset' on a TV show earlier in the year. With the addition of some nicely awkward guitar phrases and goofy vocal utterances, the song took on the shape of an XTC number and was known for some time as 'the XTC one'. Much later it became 'It Could Be You', the title taken from the newly instigated National Lottery's breezy, arithmetically dubious slogan (at fourteen million to one, your chances of winning are smaller than your chances of dying in a rickshaw accident before you can claim your prize). The opening line 'Ch . . . Ch . . . Churchill got his lucky number' refers to the controversial purchase 'for the nation' of the war leader's personal papers with several million pounds of Lottery money.

'Ernold Same' is very much a companion piece to 'Parklife', with Daniels' ebullient wastrel replaced by a tedious commuter drone played by popular left-wing politician and reptile-enthusiast Ken Livingstone (Street's suggestion; 'someone credible with a monotonous voice'). The traffic noise, originally an indoor swimming pool from Street's oft-used BBC *Sound Effects* disc, was captured by hanging a mike out of the window and picking up the ambience of the Goldhawk Road. The song returns, accelerated and *sans* all but banjo and keyboard, at the album's close after 'Yuko And Hiro'.

The punkish 'Globe Alone' was recorded almost live with Damon leaping around the studio with a hand-held mike and could almost date back to Seymour in its theatrical lunacy. 'Top Man' is a curate's egg, excellent in parts, such as the dry wit of 'He's never cheap or cheerful/He's Hugo and he's boss', Graham's slithering guitar fills and the sampled 'oh's. Elsewhere the detail gets self-defeating. Some brave soul should have vetoed the 'Open sesame' insert and the cheesy Arab keyboard fill.

Passing over the already discussed 'Country House' leaves three tracks which are the best things the album contains. 'He Thought

Of Cars' has been suggested by the eminent Blur scholar David Cavanagh as '*The Great Escape*'s 'This Is A Low'. While taking his point, 'He Thought Of Cars' is of a quite different tone; more despairing and less romantic, more sterile and abstract in its vision of a nightmare future out of Heathcote Williams' *Autogeddon* and J. G. Ballard's *Crash*. The arrangement is freakishly diverse: epic mellotrons are offset by stirring melodies (1.15) themselves undermined by their phrasing on quacking synthesisers. Here, the teeming details are piled on to haunting, original effect, the absence of drums during the verses and the heavily compressed 'mushy' sound adding to the queer, ambiguous mood.

'Yuko And Hiro' was originally known as 'Japanese Workers' and is, ostensibly, the very typical though none the less touching story of a young Nissan salaryman who never sees his beloved girlfriend because of the company's claims on his time. Novelistic at first glance or hearing, it is, of course, poignantly autobiographical. Indeed, it was perhaps the first time Damon had opened his heart about his own relationship. For Yuko And Hiro are Damon And Justine; distant, pressured, kept apart by the rapacious demands of the job.

There's nothing gimmicky or dishonest about this device. Quite the opposite. It pursues its theme with great tenderness and skill, viz. we are more alike than we are different. Pop star and company worker are still at the iron whim of the corporation or, less dramatically, still subject to life's grinding daily trials. When rock stars ask us to 'feel their pain' it is usually in terms that say nothing to us about our lives, to paraphrase The Smiths. 'Yuko And Hiro' is a world away from such self-absorbed angst. Like Elvis Costello's 'Shipbuilding' and Jim Webb's 'Wichita Lineman', it strikes deep because it is rooted in the things we all share: work and love, home and homesickness. A daringly different love song, it deserves more plaudits than it has received.

The album's centrepiece and the song that made the most forceful first impression had the most chequered and difficult history. 'The Universal' had been around since the *Parklife* sessions, when it had been demoed in its original incarnation as a cod-reggae calypso. 'It sounded like a Lilt advert,' opines Graham. Andy Ross, Stephen Street and Alex James loved the song, but Damon's confidence in the song had been dented. 'Justine had such a downer on it. In fact, she had such a downer on the whole album. She detested "The

Universal" and I thought this was a musical criticism when in fact I think given what was going on with her, she was actually saying something about our relationship. I really should have been smarter and truer to what I felt.' Damon's reluctance was fortunately worn down by the lobbying of Ross, Street and James.

In the song, it is early in the next millennium and the populace is placated by a prescription drug called The Universal which is clearly modelled on Prozac. Vacantly happy, the nation drinks its way around karaoke bars singing the praises of their chemical saviour. The dark and hopeless mood of the narrative is juxtaposed with the surging emotional climaxes of the tune; a superb arrangement by The Duke String Quartet scattered by horn interjections straight out of Burt Bacharach's songbook. In the early stages of the recording, the rhythm still gave problems. The reggae tempo had been wisely dropped but nothing adequate had been found in its place, as Stephen Street recalls. 'Perhaps because it had once been this weird cod-reggae thing, we couldn't get the rhythm right. I don't know whose idea it was but we arrived at that big off-beat which seems to push the song along. It's a very odd time signature.' Dave's off-beat, bolstered by Graham's chordal slashes and pizzicato from the basses, gives the song one of its most distinctive features – a crookedly elegant beat. The vocal performance is one of Damon's best ever. Dave Cavanagh, present in the studio, reports that he was anxious about getting it right and announced, 'Right, I'm off to make a fool of myself and do my saddo, would-be Scott Walker.' The final vocal was, as is usually the case, 'comped' or compiled by Street from several attempts. After Damon had been encouraged through yet another draining take, he said, 'I bet you showed a bit more respect to Morrissey.' It was all worth it in the end. If *The Great Escape* did represent the furthest the band could go in their quest for minutely detailed, encyclopaedic pop classics and sardonic social commentary, 'The Universal' was a fitting close to this chapter.

In view of the distinct cooling in critical ardour to come, it's interesting if unedifying to recall the gushing torrent of hyperbole that greeted the release of *The Great Escape*. It was received as if it were an amalgamation of *King Lear*, *Pet Sounds*, *Citizen Kane*, Beethoven's Ninth Symphony and the roof of the Sistine Chapel. 'Rammed with an edgy beauty that is beyond contemporary beauty,' said the *NME* enthusiastically if incomprehensibly.

And it wasn't just the constantly and dutifully excitable music weeklies, either. 'A truly great pop record,' clarioned *The Times*. 'Painstakingly crafted and brilliantly played ... it is the most truthful mirror modern pop has yet held up to 90s Britain,' said the *Observer*. The *Independent On Sunday* called it 'The benchmark against which all other British pop bands must be measured'. 'Will put them, *en passant*, amongst true pop greats,' read one review. It ended with, 'Oasis, do your worst.'

Funnily enough, they were about to.

10 Abdication

T HE IDIOTIC REMARK HAS a long and distinguished lineage in pop history. In the mid-60s, John Lennon boasted that The Beatles were bigger than Christ and incurred the wrath of the admittedly cretinous religious right. In the 70s, David Bowie, emotionally ice-bound by Class A pharmaceuticals, claimed Britain needed a Fascist dictator and Eric Clapton made a drunken anti-immigration rant that angered enough people to set the Rock Against Racism movement in motion. Elvis Costello is alleged to have called Ray Charles a 'blind, ignorant nigger' during a bar-room altercation with Steven Stills and Bonnie Bramlett and found America's rock establishment turned squarely against him for a while. Nearer our own time, Happy Mondays' breezy homophobia and Crispian Mills of Kula Shaker's fascination for the occultist elements of Aryan philosophy have both fired the hair-trigger sensibilities of the rock press.

In some ways, then, Noel Gallagher was merely upholding this tradition when in conversation with journalist Miranda Sawyer during an interview for the *Observer* on 18 September 1995, he expressed his hope that two members of Blur would die of AIDS. Having already delivered himself of one unsound opinion quoted earlier in the piece – that The Beach Boys were 'fucking hippy Californian surf bollocks' – he was later questioned on the subject of the Blur/Oasis rivalry. Sawyer wondered whether it might be time to let bygones be bygones and become friends. Evidently not. 'The guitarist I've got a lot of time for. The drummer I've never met. I hear he's a nice guy. The bass player and the singer – I hope the pair of them catch fucking AIDS and die because I fucking hate them two.' This was, it's said, one of many unpleasant references to Blur in the original article, most of which had been excised as potentially libellous.

Being insecure egomaniacs, rock musicians are perpetually slagging off their peers. It goes with the territory, much as it does with boxers and politicians. What lifted or rather lowered Gallagher's remarks outside the routine bad-mouthing and handbags-at-ten-paces was the sheer nastiness of it. Clearly the failure of 'Roll With It', added to the events at the 'Some Might Say' party, had cut deep. There was some mild outrage in the press. AIDS charities like the London Lighthouse and The Terrence Higgins Trust were appalled though, interestingly and rather shamefully, there was little outright condemnation from the constituency of rock journalists, most of whom were too desperate to be in Oasis's gang to upset the big lads in charge.

Within the Blur camp, the response was mixed. Wisely, the group members said little. Press officer Karen Johnson declared that though the remarks were 'grossly insensitive', Blur 'would not rise to the bait'. The group seemed bemused by the unnecessary mean-spiritedness of the attack. 'It was such a weird, unpleasant comment,' says Damon Albarn. 'What was going through his mind to say that? How could he say that, knowing what he knows? It changed the whole tone of the supposed rivalry. I've never spoken to him since.'

'Up till then it had all been quite piss-takey and friendly,' says Mike Smith. 'That certainly ended any kind of friendly rivalry. It was taken on board very seriously. Andy Ross was incensed. It was a ridiculous thing to say. I suppose Noel's remark says something about how he perceived them. What was gobsmacking was how thoroughly unrepentant he seemed. "I didn't mean to offend, know what I mean, but, hey, I hope you die of AIDS."' The sharpest comment came from the enraged Andy Ross. 'This is supposed to be the clever one talking.'

If Noel Gallagher's remarks had been taken as merely indicative of his own mind-set, it wouldn't have mattered. But by endlessly harping on about the regional differences between Blur and Oasis, by banging on in the tiresome and *de rigueur* Mancunian fashion about their geographic roots (anyone would think Mancunians came from Renaissance Florence or imperial Angkor Wat rather than a rather dirty, crime-infested conurbation), it reflected badly on every working-class northerner. It fed every metropolitan prejudice – fantasy, in the case of several bourgeois music journalists – about northern men; namely, that they are aggressive, cocky, ignorant, unthinking, loutish. It's the AIDS reference that really leers out.

'AIDS' , 'gay boy', 'puff', 'queer' . . . the characteristic insults of the dimmest oik in the playground.

Which Noel Gallagher most certainly isn't. Admittedly, at the time of writing, Oasis are in a creative slump. Now that the preposterous hype and the slavishly sycophantic reviews for their third album *Be Here Now* have receded into memory, it's widely acknowledged that it was their poorest work to date; leaden labour-club rock in the main plagiarised from the by now sucked-dry sources of The Beatles, The Sex Pistols and glam-rock. Noel Gallagher acknowledges this and by the time you read these words, they may well have returned with terrific new material. It's certainly to be hoped so.

For Oasis are simply one of the greatest bands to emerge in British rock for decades. Their combination of sheer adrenalised energy with punkish abrasive surliness and epic romanticism is, at its best, irresistible. 'Wonderwall', 'Live Forever', 'Slide Away', 'Don't Look Back In Anger'; populist rock doesn't get much better than this. A certain fall-off in quality was perhaps inevitable. Noel Gallagher blames it on overindulgence and he may well be right. But it was certainly also to do with the band becoming surrounded by fawning yes-men; not, it should be stressed, Alan McGee, but lesser figures in their entourage and the media basking in their reflected glory and leeching on their talent.

As Andy Ross sees it, 'My main role in the Blur set-up is being a guaranteed non-sycophant. Someone who'll tell them that something's crap or that one of their tunes is not as good as everyone else is telling them. It must be terrible to be in Oasis where everyone just tells you that everything you ever do or say is fantastic. Blur have recorded two or three hundred songs. They can't all be great. They don't need me to tell them how to write and stuff but my principal function is to disagree once in a while and it doesn't happen that often.'

The Oasis yes-men were to hold sway for the coming months and institute a Stalinist rewriting of history in the wake of Oasis's forthcoming album, *What's the Story (Morning Glory)*. For now, Blur were too busy to dwell on the matter. A Beatles-style performance on the roof of the HMV store in London's Oxford Street on 15 September stopped traffic for its twenty-minute duration and drew thousands of onlookers. This brief show was recorded by the same film crew that had produced *Star Shaped* for a projected *Great*

Escape documentary. Significantly, the video, full of too-candid footage, was never released, being described by Damon as 'too odd'. Almost immediately after the rooftop gig, they paid a short visit to the US to promote *The Great Escape*, their first release for new label Virgin, whom they joined in June at the instigation of vice-president Kaz Utsunomaya on departure from the hated SBK.

Back in England though, the first public signs of internal strain were beginning to show. Stephen Street acknowledges that artistically and commercially, the group were buoyant, 'but the band didn't take well to the success. There were a succession of slight breakdowns at that time, although whilst making *The Great Escape* they seemed very happy. If they had problems I wasn't aware of them. I was never aware of Damon's apparent problems with coke. I never saw him do anything like that in the studio so it was news to me. In the studio there was always wine and beer but nothing stronger. I think the problems probably started later when it was time for making videos and publicising the record and touring. They went off to America on yet another attempt to crack that market as "Girls And Boys" had been an underground hit. I have to say I wasn't party to any major difficulties but at this stage I suppose management would have been the ones to see if anything were going wrong.'

CHRIS MORRISON: You become a success and then you don't get the chance to enjoy it because you're kept so busy. It's the way of the game; if you don't jump on it and push the success you may never get it again so it's a lot of work. Adrenalin carries you through the workload to an extent. But it's endless. Ten interviews a day with ten different journalists asking you the same question. Different bits of promotion here and there. Soundchecks. Record companies in other territories expecting you to do photo calls at 9.00. And drink or whatever doesn't improve it. For an hour and a half it's fun. Graham became rapidly disillusioned. His motivation really isn't money. Managers do joke about artists, admittedly. Artists tell you that all that matters is their artistic credibility while in the next breath they're asking you for £250,000 for a house. Everybody enjoys money but other things are important. Certain things have never excited Blur very much and are just part of the job. You have to be very resilient and Graham started to be worn down.

Over several pints of lager in his (still) beloved Good Mixer, Graham told journalist Keith Cameron of his ambivalence towards their 'victory' in the chart war with Oasis. 'I got the phone call and thought, that's really nice ... Then it got to Sunday night and I found myself getting uneasy and acting a bit weird.' He went on to candidly express that 'my life is a mass of confusion ... and I feel like I'm letting Damon down in a lot of ways'.

He expressed his unease with and alienation from two elements of Blur's current lifestyle. First, he gave his take on the 'new laddism': 'If he [Damon] wants to go on about football and page three girls that means we all get associated with it ... I hate football and I hate anything associated with page three girls.' He railed against the most obvious symbol of this as far as the group were concerned – Damien Hirst's embarrassing video for 'Country House'.

'I hated it. Videos in general I feel completely awful about ... but I regret the "Country House" video. I'd even go so far as to regret "Country House" as a single ... I like the song but the association with it has become something else. It's become page three and Benny Hill and I don't think I had the sense to complain about it which is my fault. I didn't realise what dirty minds Keith Allen and Damien Hirst had. They're from an area which I don't want to associate with any more.'

This led directly to him declaring his contempt for aspects of the pop star life. 'The Mixer ain't The Groucho ... Why do you have to go to some exclusive, celebrity-ridden place to have a good time? I don't want to be snorting coke and drinking champagne with them cunts. I wanna be talking with my friends.'

It didn't take Holmesian deductive powers to work out that Alex, his flamboyant lifestyle and his choice of drinking partners were the chief targets of Graham's disdain. The two inseparable Goldsmiths chums had, sadly, become polarised at the furthest corners of the band. Graham was involved with a staunchly feminist member of an uncompromising uncommercial indie group who by day worked in a left-wing bookshop and immersed herself in obscure American hardcore music. Alex was living the life he had always lusted after: a feted pop star thrust into a bachelor life not entirely willingly but enjoying it to the full. A diary he wrote for the *Idler* magazine ends with an account of the conclusion to one evening's revels: 'Have some horrible fizzy beer and go outside to be sick. Someone follows me and asks for my autograph. Have a few beers and talk utter gobshite with Steve Mackey, my favourite bassist, and stumble home with the girls. Put the Kylie Minogue on and get the phone book out. Phone everyone. "Morning schmorning!" we scream down people's answerphones. Play the entire Oasis album down Albarn's, and much worse probably. Pink gin, white Russian and ruby red Margaux. You only live once. Get drunk, be a tart, enjoy yourself. The end.'

ALEX JAMES: Perhaps I did take to it the most enthusiastically. Dave had stopped drinking and he'd just got married and moved to Hampstead and settled down for a quiet life. Damon was with Justine. And my girlfriend Justine . . . well, she couldn't bear what I'd become. I was like, 'Whoarr! I am gorgeous!' I'd become impossible to live with; arrogant, greedy, selfish. So she moved out and suddenly I'm on my own living in the West End in the coolest band in the world with loads of money with an expensive champagne habit. I'd moved out of my parents' house to share with Justine when we fell in love so I'd never really lived on my own before. Like Damon really. Up until now, he'd never had success and money and been living alone. He moved out of his bedsit in Greenwich to Justine's place. Fuck knows what Damon was getting up to in Notting Hill. Don't forget, at this point Damon was the most famous person in the country. He couldn't really go out anywhere without getting lots of major-league hassle whereas the rest of us were only recognised by people who liked the band, which is really brilliant. I do love my anonymity really.

He may have been more anonymous than Damon, but at that time Alex was one of Soho's most high-profile boulevardiers. 'I'd always wanted to be an idiot genius Soho alcoholic. I thought it was a good way to spend my twenties. Mike Smith was doing it with me. We both had that attitude. Graham and I had always got on well but he objected to my lifestyle. I thought, If your band is cool you can go to all these shit stinko places and sit next to Prince and be ridiculous and blow raspberries cos you've had your champagne. I thought you might as well get in there and see what's going on. Let's have it all, you know. I was just becoming good friends with Keith and Damien at this point. They felt like kindred spirits. They seemed very clever; they seemed to know more than everyone else. And they weren't bothered about things. They could see the vapidity and fickleness of it all, as we all could. Success is a fickle street to live on but that's no reason to curl up and stay in your room. Yes, it's ridiculous and it's bollocks. It won't last so chop 'em out. So the Mars Bar in Endell Street became the major hang. Plus I was living above Freuds.

I was living above a cocktail bar and I was in the Mars Bar so often they gave me the keys. It was like Dante's Inferno.'

Although initially relations were cordial, and indeed Damon had been a habitué of the Groucho with Allen and Hirst too, all but Alex soon turned their back on it with a vengeance. 'Graham and Damon really hated Keith and Damien. I don't know why really. Well, obviously, at the time, Graham's got this very right-on feminist girlfriend. If I had to analyse his feelings I'd say he was torn between wanting to make art and the demands of the business. I think he was tormented by the fact that "Country House" wasn't our best record but it had sold more than anything else. That was what he was famous for but not what he was proud of.'

'Country House''s reputation had been further retrospectively sullied as Hirst's video gained more and more currency. Stephen Street believes it is this that contributes most to the low esteem the record is held in today. '"Country House" was fine till they made that awful video. It is just terrible and it cheapened the record so much. I cringed when I saw it. I couldn't believe how crass it was.' Andy Ross declares that, 'Graham was going through a bit of a PC period. The image of a scantily clad Jo Guest running around pursued by a pig was a bit at odds with that.'

GRAHAM COXON: I ended up being a milkman in it. If I'd have done what I was supposed to have done I'd have to have had a lobotomy by now. I was supposed to do all sorts of nasty things – getting bottoms in my face and chasing girls. There's some unintentionally funny bits where I'm not chasing them. 'Come on, Graham, chase them!' and I'm running in the opposite direction. It was so stupid. Alex thought it was great. Damon thought it was cheeky. It's all the *Guardian*'s fault for saying that football was OK. So Damon got into being a lad. Apparently, you could kick someone's head in as long as you could write an essay about it. You had to go on about tits but if you knew why you were doing it that somehow makes you less of a pig. It was all an excuse to act horrendously, I thought. Of course, Alex was loving Damien Hirst and Keith Allen. It made me very unhappy. I felt like a real stick in the mud or a monk or something. I was scared people thought I didn't like girls. I do. But I don't think you have to be rude about them. So I wasn't a proper bloke.

Damon and Alex, on the other hand, were conspicuously blokey; the former enthusiastic in his support for Chelsea, the latter linked in the tabloids with the Danish supermodel and 'world's most beautiful woman' Helena Christiansen, whom he was said to have stolen from the late Michael Hutchence. He later denied any intimate relations but said she 'was very nice though'.

An arena tour was scheduled for the year's end, taking in the country's biggest venues such as the Birmingham NEC, Manchester G-Mex and London's Wembley Arena. Ahead of this, though, the group lined up a series of shows in eight of Britain's sleepiest seaside towns, including Gorleston, Cleethorpes, Clacton, Eastbourne and Dunoon in Scotland. It was an idiosyncratic and charming idea – the band would take their music to the dilapidated seaside towns that held such a grip on Damon's imagination, while warming up for their larger dates which had now swelled to fourteen, with the addition of an extra Christmas date at Wembley.

The local press had a predictable field day. Blur were pictured looking windswept and faintly nauseous. There were interviews with local butchers and aldermen, bemused at the fuss. Delirious teenagers were pictured kissing their posters and showing off hastily constructed banners. Sober columnists mused in the 'you can't hear the words, it's all nonsense . . .' vein. Best, as in worst, of all these was a ludicrous, bitter diatribe from Tom Morton in the *Scotsman*, who declared, with Shavian wit, 'Britpop is rubbish,' and went on to eulogise several undistinguished bands of Caledonian origin. He ended, barely believably, by comparing Blur unfavourably to the rotten Irish comedy outfit Saw Doctors. Most of the local inhabitants were better disposed to the band than this. At Great Yarmouth, the band's tour bus was covered in lipstick after a pilgrimage from excitable teenage girls (one assumes). Nine hundred fans caused a Beatlemania–proportioned commotion in Clacton. The ticketless wept in the streets while touts charged 90 quid for a £10 ticket and the *Colchester Gazette* reported that many fans had dared to come dressed in 'Oasis-style check shirts'. It was all rumbustious good fun, with but one small cloud forming in the corner of the sky.

Midway though Blur's bijou coastal tour, Oasis released their second album, *What's the Story (Morning Glory)*. The reviews were decidedly mixed. Many critics felt that the record was pompous and uninspired and had a vague lassitude when compared to the urchin vim of their debut. Others mocked Noel Gallagher's lyrics as gibberish. Never the group's strong suit, they seemed especially vacant here, and more than one reviewer asked how exactly one might move 'slowly down the hall faster than a cannonball'. A reasonable question. However, for the most part the reviews were wrong. While some tracks – the opener, for instance – were unremarkable, 'Wonderwall', 'Look Back In Anger' and 'Champagne Supernova' had the unmistakable imprint of classics about them. As Stephen Street recollects, 'I felt miffed later when the tide turned but you could understand it. As soon as I heard "Wonderwall" I could tell it was a huge record. I thought, Fuck it, it's their year now.'

His premonition was right. By the end of the first week, it had sold 350,000 copies, making it the fastest-selling album since Michael Jackson's *Bad*. In America, it sold a quarter of a million in that first week; went to Number 1 in Sweden. Gamely, Karen Johnson, Blur's press officer, fought her corner, pointing to *The Great Escape*'s sales of half a million in its first month, but there was no doubting that Oasis had stolen Blur's thunder. They continued to bad-mouth Blur in almost every interview, calling them 'soft southern students' and 'lightweights'. While Noel had been forced into making an apologetic statement in the press for his AIDS remarks about Damon and Alex – 'whilst not a fan of their music, I wish them both a long and healthy life' – his brother bragged in print about having been 'double rude' to Justine Frischmann at a function and recounted how, waggish as ever, he had shouted to her, 'Go on, get your tits out, you slag.'

None of this seemed to matter to the weekly music press, who performed a shameless volte-face. Oasis were kings of the world, rude and robust northern warriors keeping alive the torch of rock's great spirit, while Blur were art-school dilettantes. *The Great Escape* was not that great after all (if they could have airbrushed their reviews out of existence with a Stalinist sweep, they surely would have). Furthermore, *What's The Story (Morning Glory)* was a bona fide classic. Who had said that it was second-rate and formulaic? Not me, guv. It was 'sorted' and 'well sound', etc., etc.

ANDY ROSS: I feel very strongly about all this though I must stress that it's a personal opinion. *The Great Escape* is my favourite Blur album. They've done *Parklife* and everyone loves them. Then along comes Oasis and everyone loves them suddenly because they're working-class lads and Blur, apparently, are middle-class wankers. Blur recorded this album on a high as opposed to the turbulence of the last record. It's brimming with confidence to use that cliché. It's almost like they're showing off how they could create a fifteen-song album. November, it's their second *Q* album of the year. Now, a great album doesn't become a crap album overnight but it became a scapegoat for 'Country House'. *Great Escape* got great reviews whereas the Oasis album got very lukewarm reviews. But it somehow became politically incorrect to like Blur and almost part of the job description of a music journalist to like Oasis. Revisionist history says that *Great Escape* was an inferior follow-up to *Parklife*. I think it's as good and in many respects better. I find *Modern Life is Rubbish* fairly hermetically sealed. *The Great Escape* isn't a rock opera, but it is a very diverse bunch of excellent songs. There's nothing wrong with it at all. *Leisure* gets a similar misrepresentation. The fact is, Blur haven't made a weak album.

In the course of a pointless vindictive interview with the *NME*, Alex was goaded into exasperatedly pointing out that pop music is an industrial process, that being in a band is a job albeit a terrifically glamorous and exciting one, and that '*NME* readers are such pompous cunts, aren't they? They think that what they think about music is so important but there's no point in deconstructing any-thing. At the end of the day, talking about music is like wanking about rain. The truth is, there's nothing unusual about what we do. I hate all that "He's a genius, he was just born with it" crap. Playing a guitar is about as mysterious as using a typewriter. It's the same thing only you have your hands the other way up . . . Talent, genius, BOLLOCKS! There's no such thing as talent, no such thing as genius. Some people just want it more, which is twice as important as being good at it. That's what Damon's got – DRIVE! And Oasis. Noel really f---ing wants to be the daddio and you won't ever be that unless you really want to be. Musicians just like to overcompli-cate what they do. When we're in the studio, I can't see anything mysterious going on.'

He finished on a note of poetic insight. 'Bands have always been about far more than music. But we're not judgemental about stuff like that. I don't want to tell people how to live their lives. I did to start with but people don't want that, people don't want a revolu-tion, people don't want to lay down their tools and stop working . . . They just want something to whistle in the dark.'

As Blur's arena tour rumbled through Europe, the Oasis/Blur feud continued to dominate the agenda of the increasingly glib and chattering broadsheets. On the streets, too, it appeared that this very

British spat exercised the popular imagination. 'I was aware of this backlash from people,' remembers Damon. 'It began to get really nasty. There was a time when everyone in the country had got whipped up in it. I'd go down the street and people would sing "Roll With It" at me. There was an atmosphere akin to football violence. People would open their windows and put Oasis on really loud as I walked past. Grown people. I was even abroad with Alex in this tiny isolated railway station in France and a guy shouted, "Where's Liam?" '

Let's not forget the mildly fun aspect of the whole silly business. As Dave Rowntree says, 'It still gives me a little twinge of joy, perhaps because it affected me least. It was a fantastic bit of bollocks. Matt Lucas on the seaside tour would even whip 'em up a bit. "Who's cheering for Blur?" "Who's for Oasis?" The police told Oasis to cancel one of their shows which clashed with one of ours in Bournemouth. They were strong-armed into it, I think. I'm sure they didn't want to. I remember once hearing our crew talking about how if it went ahead they were going to project a huge Blur logo on to the side of our venue. We said, "No, you're not. You're not going to do anything. You're going to set up and then tear down and go to the next town. Just do your fucking job." But even though we'd won the singles battle – and what a dreadful battle to lose – they were really on the up. They were all drugs and fighting and spitting and we were these old men.'

Graham admits that, 'I think it might have upset Damon a bit that I would happily talk to Liam and Noel and that they thought I was all right. It was all such a silly business anyway. I'd love to talk to them about it. Oasis are OK, Blur are OK. Now Kula Shaker, that's the fucking problem.'

When Blur had performed on the roof of Oxford Street HMV in the autumn, Damon had prefaced 'The Universal' by saying, 'You'll all be singing this at Christmas,' a reference to the intention to release it as a single at the year's end and the confidence that surrounded this gambit. 'The Universal' was duly released in mid-November and, by their own standards, underperformed badly. Even helped by one of the group's best videos to date, an eerie Stanley Kubrick homage echoing *A Clockwork Orange* and *2001: A Space Odyssey*, it could only reach Number 5 and was overshadowed by the clamour around Oasis. As Alex succinctly puts it, 'After being the people's hero, Damon's the people's prick for a short period. After "Wonderwall", basically, he was a loser, very publicly. It was a silly business to get into but it did take it on to a higher level. When the 90s are looked back on that bollocks will be remembered.'

As the pantechnicons rolled day and night from placid, over-looked English coastal resorts to soulless aircraft hangars to the theatres and rock clubs of Europe and the US, the rank tang of tension in the air became more apparent to those at close quarters. The tour bus rocked with arguments as Graham fought for his beloved hardcore music and Gravity Records. 'I wasn't obsessed. I still loved my Beatles and my Simon And Garfunkel. But I wanted to push The Kinks back into their faces.'

CHRIS MORRISON: You could see the strain. When we were in the bus doing the seaside tour soon after being Number 1, Damon said to me, 'I don't know if we can get much bigger in Britain.' I said, 'You go through this period when you walk on water but sooner or later you'll plateau. And then there'll be peaks and troughs.' That was prophetic. And they did plateau, although they didn't trough. But Oasis's success did overshadow theirs and made it look like we were less successful than we were. *The Great Escape* sold as well as *Parklife* all told and broke new territories which set us up for the *Blur* album. But Graham wasn't happy right then. We were in Paris and his girlfriend was with him and it took me an hour and half to persuade him to come down and make a video. Sometimes people don't tell you they're not having a good time. They let you know in different ways. They were hardly talking to each other. There was a touring schedule arranged for a whole year and I think if we'd fulfilled it the band would have broken up. Damon came into a meeting saying that they wanted to cut all this short at Easter and make another record.

That record was to prove a watershed in the group's development. For now, though, there were still the capacious British arena shows to fulfil. Each night, Graham's confusion and angst over what he was doing would surface more and more bitterly. 'When the Number 1s came the truth and the worth of the dream had gone for me. It didn't mean anything any more. I know it sounds like me being a contrary little bugger but that's what had happened to me. I was listening to music that never got anywhere near the charts, let alone Number 1. I was so confused about this. I wanted to play music I liked. I didn't see why that was so wrong of me. I was venting my anger on stage at those arena shows. They must have seemed really strange, me abusing my guitar trying to turn "Country House" into thrash metal and playing it too fast to get it over with and jumping around maniacally. I had such mixed feelings about our success.'

The Wembley gigs were further proof of the group's uneasy 'elevation' to the status of teen heart-throbs. They had been a gruelling six months on the road and by the time they rolled into the capital for the Arena shows (Wembley Stadium had been mooted at one point but Damon said it was for 'wankers'), the band were tired, emotionally fraught and riven with internal splits. The major fault-line was later to be perceived as running largely along the Graham/ Alex axis – 'the dour muso and the flighty popinjay' as journalist Danny Eccleston neatly put it.

'Alex had become the devil for a while,' acknowledges Graham today. 'It's nothing bad between me and Alex. It's just to do with sense of humour. We're very similar – similarly antagonistic. If he wants to try and be in The Average White Band then I'm going to be in The Gang Of Four. I'm cutting against him all the time, because he's like a sexy musician and I feel shy and clumsy. So I try and fuck up his funk. It's basically teenage jealousy.'

'Alex was the personification of a pop star,' opines Mike Smith. 'He was outwardly living the life to the full. His place was a shithole but every other pop star excess was there: the drink, the drugs, the girls. Graham was spending all his time with Jo from Huggy Bear who had no interest in this whatsoever and would tell him that these people are evil, they are bad people. He meanwhile is musically getting into hardcore and American underground. It was the first tour they'd done in a while. Beautiful girls followed them every-where and a plentiful supply of every rock star accoutrement. Alex had made some lewd suggestion to one of Jo from Huggy Bear's mates and that had been the last straw; Graham was ready to kill him. Dave had retreated from the group. I got the feeling from Graham and Dave that they were not enjoying this band.'

DAVE ROWNTREE: We'd gone from being unable to get arrested to pop stars overnight. There were fans and photographers everywhere. We'd trod the same circuit as Take That for a while and got to know them and suddenly the kids were waiting for us. I found that very hard to deal with. You'd come on stage to this Take That style screaming to the point where you were deafened for the first song. No one had ever screamed at us before. It's bizarre and once the novelty has worn off, not very pleasant. You'd say hello to a fan and they'd hand you an orange. It didn't seem an appropriate response. We'd happily thought we'd got this far and subverted the system but we hadn't. We'd just become another bit of tabloid teeny fodder. We hadn't achieved anything except acquired a load of baggage that Graham found quite offensive and no one was interested in except Alex.

Indeed, Alex's favourite joke of the period ran, 'What's 40 yards long, has no pubes and goes "Aaaaaaah!"? The front row of a Blur concert.' However, we should be wary of getting too po-faced and judgemental here. Alex was merely enjoying the fruits of his labours. He was, after all, a pop star, not a Bosnian aid worker. By and large, people who can't stomach the pop of the flashbulb or the attentions of Chris Evans should avoid music as a career.

That said, we can sympathise too with Graham's dilemma. A devoted and expert musician and student of music, he felt he had been reduced to wacky pop moppet, as Dave Rowntree recalls. 'Graham had put in a lot of hard work building a reputation as the thinking man's guitarist and he was now seen as just a pretty face who doesn't write the songs but plays a bit of guitar. It made him very upset. Graham was visibly getting unhappier and unhappier and that exacerbated all the drinking and the tension. He was storming off stage, not turning up to rehearsals, fighting on the bus. I think my not drinking helped us, simply because I could talk to Graham. Maybe we both get drunk in the same way. I could see where he was in his head. I could hold him with one hand and Damon or Alex with the other hand. Keep them at arm's length.'

The rancorous and weary mood at the end of 1995 and the beginning of 1996 was caught luridly in a piece by journalist Adrian Deevoy in Q early in the New Year. Its blurb ran 'Are Blur really going to the dogs? Behind all the adoring screams, we hear internal bickering, the tell-tale snii-ii-i-iff! of mediacentric decadence and a hollow champagne clink. Adrian Deevoy finds them on the verge of a nervous break-up.'

During the interview, Graham was inebriated, irritable and punching those around him. In a curious aside, he said that what might split the band up would be death. 'Or if we made another *Parklife*. I don't think we could carry on if one of us left . . . unless it was Alex.' The whole band were flu-ridden and surviving on whopping doses of medication. (Alex, typically, put the new flu strain down to the fact that the Chinese pen their ducks and pigs together. Graham replied, 'Shut up, you bollocker'.) Damon confessed that he worried about the other members all the time. 'Graham has a character change when he's drunk. I knew Graham before he smoked and drank. He is the sweetest bloke alive and he is the most gifted guitarist of his generation. No one can fucking touch him and for that I'm prepared to put up with all his lunacy.'

It was Damon's answer to Deevoy's questions about cocaine that became quickly notorious, though. 'Everyone is taking drugs apart from Graham and me. We are virtually the only exceptions in the entire scene. He drinks too much; I drink a lot but not as much as him and I smoke a bit of dope, but that's it. There's a fucking blizzard of cocaine in London at the moment and I hate it. It's stupid. Everyone becomes so blasé, thinking they're so ironic and witty and wandering around with this stupid fucking cokey confidence. Wankers. I mean, I did it but I can't say I was a cocaine addict. And I can't say whether that was what triggered the weird experience last year.'

Not surprisingly, when the piece appeared, it caused fury within the group and their entourage and not just for the haughty implication that alcohol and dope were superior drugs despite their potential for making people in the former case violent and in the latter boring.

'Damon had talked of using cocaine in the past,' remarks Dave Rowntree. 'He wrote a very thoughtful piece on it for the *NME* but the tabloids got hold of it and it's "My Cocaine Hell" by Damon Albarn. Up till then I thought you could control things. You can't. The tabloids are all-powerful so the best you can do is stay away from them. But there's a blizzard of cocaine and I hate it? Hate it when it's gone, maybe. Christ, he got some fucking shit over that. And a lot of it was a lot less than good-natured. He basically fired off with this 360 spray of bullets that implied "I'm the only one in the whole music industry that isn't addicted to cocaine." Everyone's mum read it! Everyone we worked with had an awful lot of explaining to do to their mums! And customs officers! Damon was eating humble pie for a while after that.'

Even Alex, normally the blithest of spirits, wasn't very comfortable with the *Q* piece. 'After Oasis became the coolest band in the world we became the uncoolest. It had to look as if it was totally

The Daddy

Smith
25/8/94.

falling apart for us. Which wasn't the case at all. And if you have someone on the road with you for a couple of days it's an emotional rollercoaster and you can concentrate on the highs or the lows. And I think they wanted it to look as if the wheels had fallen off which they hadn't.'

The wheels may not have fallen off but the steering had certainly gone. Moreover, they had driven into a cul-de-sac. For all its strengths – and they are manifold – *The Great Escape* marked the logical conclusion of a particular style: a hermetic, studied, almost clinically brilliant pop portfolio replete with clever but emotionally distant portraits and vignettes. Graham had lost interest in this first and now states, 'I think *The Great Escape* is our most difficult record to listen to. It's so fucking doom-laden, it's ridiculous. I listened to it recently. It's super-super-mad. A mad cow disease record. *Parklife* sounds chirpy to me. It's obsessive pop music. On our part, not just Damon's part. They're our pop albums, and maybe it's just my attitude to pop, but I find them really difficult to listen to. They're good, I guess, but there's an element of all our four personalities very, very awkwardly sewn together.'

Sewn very, very awkwardly together is precisely what Blur were by February 1996. On an appearance on *TFI Friday*, Damon made disparaging references to Alex and the group's fall from public grace. For an appearance on a prime-time Italian TV show, Graham was house-buying and was replaced by a cardboard cut-out. Alex missed the plane and his place was taken by Smoggy, the group's Black Country-born head of security. Though still comfortably a Top 10 pop band ('Stereotypes', the next single, reached Number 7), the group were clearly at the end of their tether. 'Graham wasn't turning up for stuff,' recalls Mike Smith, 'so Andy would go round shouting through his letterbox. That was the lowest ebb probably. He was so unhappy. Everyone drinking constantly. It's a miracle no one died.'

Damon Albarn had himself by now tired of what had become the group's perceived *oeuvre*. 'I can sit at my piano and write brilliant observational pop songs all day long but you've got to move on.' He acknowledges Graham's fascination with the more lo-fi, underground and extreme ends of the musical spectrum. 'I think he was coming round himself,' says Graham. 'He'd started listening to the folky side of Beck and Pavement and The Beastie Boys, which he'd always hated. He'd always said hip-hop had "no tunes."' '

STEPHEN STREET: I went for a drive with Damon and we talked through what kind of record we could make. He wanted to change things and I could see his point. I said, 'Let's strip everything down, let's not use strings and brass.' I think Damon was pleased that I liked the idea. Damon had tried to involve Graham I think but Graham had turned his back on the band. I had to go and talk him into it. So I went to a pub in Camden to meet Graham and we had an interesting conversation. He was really anti-Alex, who he thought was being a complete arsehole with Keith Allen and Damien Hirst, and wouldn't be in the same room as him. I hadn't realised how down on the band and Britpop in general he was. I was very worried they'd break up. Alex loves Graham but he'd become the devil. I reported back and said, 'I've done what I can but you'll have to tread very carefully.'

GRAHAM COXON: I actually don't remember this meeting. But it's true that by the end of that massive tour I was sick of the industry and everything; the nine to five, the being Graham from Blur for the rest of my life. It had become a job and I didn't like my job. That's not nice for people to hear but it's true. There are people in groups who don't like the music they do. I didn't dislike it all. It was just getting too jolly and too much into this music hall thing which I don't feel any connection to at all. I'd bottle it up and have mad outbursts on tour. I was getting into hip-hop and clothes-wise getting scruffy and baggy. During *The Great Escape* I brought some Pavement records in and they were instantly dismissed by everyone. I thought they were great. Alex is very contrary. He knows how to wind me up. I'd have some drinks and fly off the handle and say I wanted to be in a death-metal hardcore hip-hop group. Perhaps I was being mardy but I wanted to know why I couldn't play the music I liked. I was very pissed off. I had this great big shout at Damon. It seemed to me at that moment that if you didn't have the same opinion as Damon everyone thought you were zero and Damon thought you were mad. So I had this great big shout on the bus and it all went funny after that and we didn't talk. That was the low spot. I was ready to pack it in. We had a serious chat about the group and I remember Dave saying something about us needing to 'work this band' and that seemed so foreign. It's not my duty, I thought. I had to do something to apologise . . . to inspire . . . to say my piece. So I wrote Damon a letter just before we recorded *Blur*. I said I wanted to scare people again. He's probably still got it. I hope he has anyway.

DAMON ALBARN: Everyone's losing it. Graham's miserable. I'm miserable. Dave's doing his own thing. Alex . . . well, he was loving it although it did fuck him up a bit. Graham particularly hated having the little girl fans. Up to the making of *Parklife* it was a good period, really, all considered. But after that – right up until I discovered Iceland – it was a living hell. I like some of *The Great Escape* but can't listen to most of it. Justine had such a downer on it. She hated 'The Universal'. I was getting all the same stuff as Graham from his girlfriend in Huggy Bear. Justine thought what she was doing with Elastica was much more worthy and cool. I've always acknowledged that Justine was a great editor of my work. But . . . there was a lot going on. Elastica's vibe was not healthy.

Not healthy and destined to get much worse. Meanwhile, according to one close source, Graham was 'being driven slowly berserk' by his girlfriend Jo. Elsewhere, though, Blur's relationships seemed to be having a healing and stabilising effect. Justine Andrew had returned to Alex. Dave was settled in Hampstead with his wife. Justine Frischmann was, at least, back in the country, having returned from the touring schedule that had meant she and Damon had spent three weeks together of the previous year. One bright spot in this troubled period was the inclusion of Damon Albarn's curio 'Closet Romantic' and Blur's 'Sing' on the phenomenally successful *Trainspotting* movie soundtrack.

Over the previous Christmas, Dave Rowntree confesses they'd been on the verge of updating their CVs.'It didn't look like Graham could work with Damon and Damon didn't want to continue if Graham wasn't in the band and I was thinking, Fucking hell, if it carries on like this I don't want anything to do with it anyway. Our rehearsals were like you read about the last days of The Who – all screaming and throwing things. Things came to a head and the unexpected benefit was that the workload suddenly decreased. Everyone was busy all the time before. That could have been half the trouble. Six days of every week we spent working with each other. We needed time to ourselves.'

'We just needed a rest from the treadmill of tours and interviews and TV studios,' diagnoses Graham. 'We needed to spend some time living our own little lives.' Also, as he happily relates, 'The letter worked. Letters are good. You can say a lot without being embarrassed because you're not there when they read it. It was still embarrassing after admitting lots of stuff to then meet up and play together. But he was scared too. I didn't know how enthusiastic I'd be. But the new songs were inspiring.'

Out, then, of this period of doubt and chaos came *Blur*: complex, primitive, utterly different from its very beginnings. Rather than work from Damon's demos in the studio, the band jammed without any conceived structures. 'We just played together for two weeks in a way we hadn't done since 1991,' says Dave, who points out some other initial strategies. 'We wanted to purify the sound, to not have anything there not played by us. We reasoned that if we made small changes at the input end, we could effect large changes in the output.'

Added to this came salvation in the form of a most unlikely source: 40,000 square miles of lava, icefield and tundra just south of the Arctic circle. In Iceland's otherworldly beauty and solitude (and raucously accepting nightlife), Damon found everything that London at the fag-end of Britpop couldn't offer: anonymity, grandeur, escape. Why Iceland? Opinions differ.

Damon claims it was largely accidental, arising from discussions about new and inspiring recording locales. Andy Ross thinks it was a bolthole first visited in the wake of the 'Country House' insanity. Stephen Street is more specific. 'We were in the pub; myself, Sarah my wife and Damon discussing the *Blur* album. One idea he'd had was not to use Maison Rouge. I was delighted that they were changing studio, not producer. So we were brainstorming cities and towns. Amsterdam? Maybe. Berlin? Bowie had already done it, and U2. We decided it shouldn't be somewhere sunny. That was the wrong vibe. Jokingly, I think Sarah said Reykjavik. And we thought it might be quite a good idea. In March, Damon went and did a recce and absolutely loved it.'

Damon was convinced of the 'rightness' of Iceland. Not so Graham. 'I said, "There's no fucking way I'm going." I'd just bought a flat and just come back off a six-month tour. I didn't see the point after all that of going off somewhere else and spending twelve hours a day with each other again. It was preposterous. I couldn't believe he'd suggested it.'

A compromise was reached. Initial sessions would take place at Mayfair studios in London and then, halfway through, the results would be transferred to tape and taken to Reykjavik where Street, engineer John Smith, Damon and Alex would continue working mainly on vocals and keyboards. Another major change was that

Street had acquired a new piece of hardware – 'muso-ish to talk about but really useful' – that enabled him to sample loops and otherwise cut and paste entire sections of the band jamming.

These sessions occupied the band for the remainder of the year. There were few other media-profile activities beyond a charity football match in which Damon and Liam Gallagher were seen to symbolically bury the hatchet with a handshake for the cameras and the release in the late spring of a fourth, perfunctory single from *The Great Escape*, ironically 'Charmless Man', the song Damon sees as the barrel-bottom of his character study period.

They showed themselves for one major outdoor gig at the RDS showgrounds in Dublin in June. It was a commendable set, per-formed to enthusiastic fans under a leaden Irish sky, just hours after England put Spain out of the Euro 96 tournament on penalties. What lingered in the memory, though, were the enormous pyrotech-nics that showered glitter and confetti on the crowd as 'This Is A Low' climaxed in the gathering dusk and the two new songs performed that day, the fruits of their new processes and endeav-ours. 'Chinese Bombs' and 'Song 2' had a jaw-dropping effect on the legions who'd hitched themselves to Blur's juggernaut no earlier than *Parklife*. In place of chirpiness and chipper and winking 'how's yer father' were two blasts of aggressive and inchoate noise; the former tiny, impacted and insane, the latter maniacally gung-ho as it vacillated between spartan verses and belligerent choruses just like, well, 'Smells Like Teen Spirit' had all those years ago.

These songs were put into their splendid context when the fifth Blur album, entitled, simply, *Blur*, was released eight months later in early February 1997. The deliberately austere and neutral title, with its clear implication of 'back to basics' and Year Zero, and the sleeve – an out-of-focus, harshly lit shot of someone being rushed into or out of a hospital ward or operating theatre – made explicit the move towards something darker and odder than we had lately been used to.

The opening track, 'Beetlebum', derives its title from a comic piece on an ancient Spike Jones And His City Slickers album but the connection seems unclear. Damon has stated that the song is 'about drugs, basically', and probably has its roots in the darker moments of his relationship with Justine Frischmann. Musically, the song's antecedents would seem to be The Beatles, evident in the expansive middle eight where practically the album's only harmonies nestle, and in the music of Krautrockers Neu, which Damon and Graham had been dabbling in. Vocals were entirely added in Iceland. Stephen Street remembers the routine of 'working till nine or ten then getting pissed,' followed by the usual bracing morning walk of a mile across Reykjavik to the studio. 'I did that the morning after "Beetlebum" and I played it back and thought, This is awesome.' Note Graham Coxon's typically ungainly, irresistible guitar line and the subterranean meandering of Alex James's terrific bass part.

'Song 2' was a working title that was kept for the finished track in keeping with the unvarnished, rudimental ethos of the album. 'Done in ten minutes,' according to Graham Coxon, though Dave Rowntree asserts, 'It took half an hour to do and it was touch and go whether it would be on the album. It's difficult to do well. The sort of song that sorts the musicians from the boys.' The punkish drum track is actually played in real time on two drum kits set up facing each other by Graham and Dave. 'Two drum kits made to sound like they're recorded really cheaply which is actually very expensive,' comments Graham wryly. 'Graham's a very loose and groovy drummer,' says Dave. 'I'm very measured and precise. We spark off each other quite well.' Alex decided that the root notes in the chorus would give power and there was no need to play in the verses. The 'guide vocal' track was used practically in its entirety – 'He pretends it means something but it doesn't,' says Dave – which inadvertently added to the song's most immediate and enduring feature. Damon's 'woo hoo's were entirely ad hoc but they became a hook line heard around the world. 'Damon went woo hoo because he had nothing else prepared but it's something everyone understands,' comments Street, echoing Graham Coxon's view of the 'la la's of 'For Tomorrow.'

Damon offers 'Country Sad Ballad Man' as another example of 'automatic lyric' writing on the album. Yet it seems fairly clear that the song is partly autobiographical and partly based on the tale of briefly luminous 60s pop star PJ Proby. Damon acknowledges that the song draws in part on Proby's wilderness years in a mobile home in Northamptonshire, his 60s earnings having long gone. Whatever the lyric concerns, the music is wonderfully ramshackle and rustic while deceptively cogent. It would be no surprise if the 1998 Mercury Music Prize winners Gomez are familiar with it.

'I like listening to "Country Sad Ballad Man",' says Graham Coxon. 'It has a quality to the sound that really makes me feel good.

The real organicness of it, the fact that just the bass and the guitar are so far out of tune from each other. That makes me quite happy. That slickness sometimes can get a bit sickening, you know. Something that felt good even though it was way out of tune. It makes me feel happy.'

'M.O.R.', by contrast, is a strident homage to David Bowie and Roxy Music. Bowie's 'Boys Keep Swinging' is knowingly echoed in the vocal line and the twin guitar interlude at 2.03. The call and response tactic is, according to Damon, influenced by Roxy Music.

Of 'On Your Own' Damon later said, 'This kind of set the tone for the album. It was one of the first demos I did for this album and I was just far more aggressive in the way I put it down on tape. I was far more uncompromising in using weirder sounds, and it wasn't about anyone in particular, it was more of a personal statement. It's a bit Dylan-y, a bit of a Happy Monday groove and the guitar riff's quite typically Blur.'

'Theme From Retro', with its brooding organ chords full of unexpected turns into dark corners, owes a clear debt to Jerry Dammers' work with The Specials. Persistent rumour says that the snatches of speech at the track's close come from the bar in Reykjavik that Damon had bought part shares in but Damon is clear that it is, in fact, the doorman from an American club the group visited. 'Yeah, we taped that. This guy on the door talking about us as we went in.' Likely enough, as the accent is American and the content ('Uh-oh, what is that device right there?') seems to refer to the tape machine itself.

'You're So Great', if we ignore the comedy B-side 'Rednecks', is the recorded debut of Graham Coxon. Graham, to the relief of Damon, had given up drink days after the Dublin show of late June. 'You're So Great' is not so much a hymn of praise to alcohol as 'about states of mind: the alcohol state of mind and the caffeine state of mind, which is what I have now. I suppose I'm a bit speedier. It could be dedicated to anything – could be a bottle of Scotch, could be my mum, could be a radiator . . . It's me filling in some time on an afternoon. I wrote it quite quickly and I'd never really written a song before. I didn't have J Mascis in the mind. It was more to do with listening to *Sister Lovers* by Big Star and those cute little songs in there. How it's recorded and the way it sounds is more to do with chronic shyness. Just trying to cover up my voice and fuck it up, really.' Mortally embarrassed, Graham recorded the song while sitting beneath a table in the darkened studio. As a sworn enemy of cynicism, the song's engagingly naive and rickety feel is quite deliberate. In a poll conducted by *Blurb*, Blur's official fan magazine, this song was chosen by a wide margin as the song people would most like Blur to perform live.

'Death Of A Party' is the oldest track on the album and had originally been demoed at the time of *Modern Life is Rubbish*. When the aforementioned *Blurb* were looking for a rarity to give away, Food suggested this, causing the group to re-evaluate the song. The lyric concerns AIDS paranoia and the rise of a new puritanism. The swirling, sinister Hammond organ arrangement recalls 'Theme From Retro' and 'Ghost Town'-era Specials.

'Chinese Bombs' is a nod towards Graham's fixation with obscure American hardcore. Damon told *Select* magazine, 'I wrote that after watching a load of Bruce Lee films – the lyrics are pretty much taken straight from the dialogue. It's a bit of a grunge take-off.'

'I'm Just A Killer For Your Love' was recorded in two and a half hours at Damon's west London demo studio and intended as a potential B-side but included on the album at the last minute. Damon describes it as 'Sly And The Family Stone meets Black Sabbath'. 'Look Inside America' is the album's most conventional track although a perfectly enjoyable outing with echoes of Mott The Hoople. It is the only track that contains strings, Street and the band having broken their self-imposed rule for the good of the song. 'Musically', says Damon, 'there's some Ray Davies in there too.' The lyric explicitly concerns Blur's early, detested promotional visits to the States but, tellingly, the tone is far more rueful and ambivalent than previously: 'Got to play a second-rate chat show/A nationwide deal, so we gotta go/Jeff from the company says it'll be all right/Got an ad on KROQ. And there's an in-store tonight.'

'Strange News From Another Star', arguably *Blur*'s finest moment, existed in demo form for some time until Street realised that the spare keyboards-only track could barely be improved upon. 'So we used big chunks of that which is why it feels like there's no real time signature and then added things over the top.' Though the title is 'borrowed' from one of Herman Hesse's lesser-known novels, the song is about Iceland. 'Just the majesty of the place,' in Damon's words. 'The death star mentioned is the depression I was suffering prior to arriving in Iceland.' At the very start of the track, a snatch of Icelandic radio can be heard. At the end, Graham and Dave are double-tracked on different drums to provide the thunderous final section. The completed track – beautiful, eerie and remote – is a perfect evocation of the land it describes, and reflects Damon's ongoing admiration for mid-period Bowie.

'Moving On' is less complicated; a straightforwardish heavy-metal pastiche garnished by strange antique Moog sounds. The treated voice, almost ubiquitous on the record, is redolent of dour, indomitable northern mavericks The Fall.

Which leaves just the album's most difficult and contentious track, 'Essex Dogs'. Damon had read the lyric as a poem at the Poetry Olympics event at the Albert Hall the previous year. Street knew that Damon planned to record 'this weird track' but the prospect seemed daunting so band and producer procrastinated. 'I'd heard the demo,' says Street, 'but couldn't work out how to approach it. One day we'd been out for a bit of lunch up Primrose Hill and when we got back I said, "Come on, let's have a go at this track." We got the drum pattern together as a starting point and then Graham pretty much immediately got that motorbike revving effect. They jammed for fifteen or twenty minutes, then I asked them to leave it with me and I edited it together using the new hard disc I had. It was pretty much one take.' The lyric is a nightmare voyage back to the Colchester of Damon's youth. 'I've written about Essex a lot in a music-hall sort of way, but "Essex Dogs" is the first time I've got close to how I really feel about the place.' The tone is sour, violent and nocturnal and reminiscent of J.G. Ballard, an influence Damon happily acknowledges. Chilling and challenging, it's a fitting conclusion to an album so avowedly different from what they had done before. If it is a little self-consciously weird – certainly encoring with it on their summer '98 shows was – then perhaps that was a necessary manoeuvre. Rumour has it that Alex is playing a hand-held hoover attachment somewhere in there.

An uncredited track – a spacey, mantra duet for corrosive guitar and electronic keyboard – and then silence. With *Blur*, Britpop's quintessential metropolitan lads had performed the most wilful hand-brake turn, the most radical piece of artistic surgery since Lou Reed's *Metal Machine Music*. Or at least David Bowie's *Low*. Who knows how many Blur fans sat as the CD display returned to 14.57:01 and echoed the words of the teenage Stephen Street on hearing Bowie's *Low* for the first time: 'What the fuck was that, then?'

11 Per Ardua Ad Astra

EARLY IN THE RECORDING of Blur's eponymous, transformational fifth album, Andy Ross and Stephen Street were playing football in Regent's Park one Sunday morning, as is their weekly wont. At this stage, Ross had heard two tracks of the forthcoming record, namely 'Beetlebum' and 'Song 2'. At half-time Ross inquired innocently of the producer, 'Any singles yet?' Street was exasperated. 'Any singles?! "Beetlebum" was such a powerful, awesome track and he was asking if there were any singles yet? I thought he put his foot right in his mouth. No wonder the band didn't want him to come down to the studio any more.'

'Beetlebum' was released 20 January 1997 and went straight to the top of the UK singles chart. But let's not be too hard on Blur's oft-mocked record company man Ross. If 'Beetlebum' is a great single, it's not an obvious one given the late 90s pop milieu. Its power lies in the strung-out remorselessness of Lennon's Plastic Ono Band period rather than Sheryl Crow, The Prodigy or Steps.

'When I first heard the album,' admits Andy Ross, 'I was taken aback. We'd won Brits, we'd won two consecutive _Q_ magazine albums of the year and I thought initially it was awkward and difficult. My immediate reaction was, "Are we going to sell as many records? Where's my royalties?" Everyone's first reaction to it was that it was a departure; that's quite clear from the artwork onwards. Damon might play this down but there's no doubt this was a response to the second backlash – "let's keep our head down and make an album that sticks two fingers up and is avowedly non-commercial". Ironically, it becomes their biggest international record. Damon is extremely astute. Brilliant at anticipating. It is a departure but after a few plays there's that inherent songwriting ability and musicianship. Damon has an acting background and he's good at playing roles as a songwriter in a way other bands aren't capable of. The Beatles reinvented themselves all the time. Why shouldn't Blur?'

'It was obviously more lo-fi, more aggressive,' says Mike Smith. 'There was a great deal of excitement amongst Stephen, the band and me. I think initially Alex was having problems with it; he felt it was uncommercial, as did Andy. Damon and Graham and Stephen were very positive. Damon would always play you the most aggressively noisy things and ask, "Well, what you think?" as if testing you out. So there were some doubts. But I felt it was just as melodic as *The Great Escape*, just different.' When Alex was asked by the *NME* whether this is the record he would have chosen to make he replied, 'Well . . . I don't know how you can choose the records that you make. I'm happy just to play the bass, it's probably the easiest job in the world . . . Do I like it? Ahh, yeah, y'know, I think we've achieved things that we haven't achieved before. We had to do something radical. I don't feel the same way as Damon; he has to sing about the way he feels and I think it was a catharsis making this record for him. I think it's more Damon and Graham's record than mine. It's coming out of their headspaces. But Blur is an argument between me and Graham. It's kind of an argument that sounds nice to the ear. I didn't really notice the record that we were making. We just go in and play really hard. You go in and do it and then you go, "What on earth have we done?" '

Damon recalls that EMI had their misgivings about the new venture. 'The usual thing – "It's got no singles on it". Meanwhile, they're giving Radiohead the full marketing works. That hurt for a while because we'd done so well for them. We were trying to be really brave. But it was all made up pretty quickly.' In fact, Graham remembers being pleasantly surprised by Parlophone MD Tony Wadsworth's reaction. 'We played him "Song 2" as a bit of a test of whether he was on our wavelength. We told him this was the second single. Course, we had no idea that it would be. He sat there, grinning. "Definitely! Definitely a single." '

Manager Chris Morrison feels that far from being a dicey commercial manoeuvre, Blur's creative rethink was essential. 'If they'd put out another *Parklife/Great Escape* style album, they would have gently slid down into obscurity. They'd gone as far as they could in that direction. *Blur* reinvigorated them. They got some new audiences. They lost some but probably only the occasional record buyer.

They did themselves a lot of good. The public now realise that you don't know what they'll do next.'

'It took enormous strength of personality to do it,' says Mike Smith. 'That huge corporate machine will always want to sell more records; that's their job. Eventually everybody really got behind the project. It felt right. This is what the band should be: art-school punk rock. It was right back to their roots. Finally, with the album finished and Andy and Alex right on board, everybody was really positive but no one knew what the world would make of it.'

In much the same way that *The Great Escape*'s early eulogies were rewritten or shamefacedly glossed over, it's now fashionable to claim to have always 'got' the *Blur* album. In actual fact, the reception varied from enthusiasm to blank incomprehension. Andrew Collins in *Q* analysed correctly the album's central thrust towards scruffy, dark and quixotic and away from pristine and pin-up glossy and was warmly praising, but even he noted the absence of 'hit singles' in a review written pre-'Beetlebum''s chart entry. The *NME* claimed that this was the kind of record only a rich and successful group could afford to make, to which Graham rightly responded, 'We made a lot of unlistenable music when we were really poor.' Dave Cavanagh was with Damon and Alex on a 'bloody promo' jaunt to New York at the time and later recounted, 'As the WTN camera crew is setting up in the Virgin boardroom, the first British broadsheet reviews of the new album are coming through on the fax. They're mixed: the *Guardian* loves it, *The Times* is ambivalent and the *Independent* is hostile. "What a cunt," snarls Albarn.'

Enthusiastic, supportive or not, few were so short-sighted or detuned to their cultural radar that they could not pick up the unmistakable messages that the *Blur* album gave off. Greyhound races or pop-chart sweepstakes – all bets were off. Goodbye Phil, goodbye Lionel, goodbye little girls. It had all been fun while it lasted but, as even Dean Street's most celebrated habitué Alex James was now admitting, 'It was more interesting to go and abuse Thurston Moore in New York than hang out with Pulp in the West End.'

It's a testament to how much improved relations were between the group that directly after *Blur*'s UK release, the group set off – if not with spring in step then certainly without slouch of shoulder – for what would be effectively nine months on the road across 25 countries. Partly this was due to the energising nature of the new music and its compatibility with raucous nightly performance. But it was also down to a growing acceptance of each other. Dave Rowntree once said that Blur's relationship was like brothers in the truest sense. It wasn't sweetly affectionate or bland – indeed, often angry and awkward – but always close and loyal. Now it was becoming grown-up too, as he explains: 'The end result of all the hostility and Graham and Damon communicating by letter and the rest was that we began to accept each other as four individuals. Damon started to stand back a little. In interviews he'd often expound a particular line whether we agreed or not. Up till then he'd been very authoritative and if you disagreed you were wrong. Everybody started to get a voice. It was never actually said but the feeling was, if we're staying together then there's no party line. Everyone could do their own thing. It was the end of our adolescence.'

Late January and February saw them playing a series of intimate venues that seemed designed to present the group in more honest and intimate settings, in towns such as Liverpool, Hull, Nottingham, Cambridge and Newcastle rather than the arena gigs of the *Great Escape* tour. The ambience was very different, from the intro music of Stravinsky's 'The Swan' played on the hip, esoteric proto-synthesiser the Theremin. The set list reflected Blur's new mood of 'pleasing themselves'. The bulk of the material came from *Blur*, as yet unheard by most of the audience. Gone were 'There's No Other Way' and everything from *The Great Escape*, except a late encore of 'The Universal'. In their place came B-sides 'Inertia' and 'Sing' from their earliest days, and from *Modern Life is Rubbish*, 'Oily Water'.

Beginning in Boston on the 7th, they were to spend most of March in the US. Once their affection for the Great Satan had been positively Iranian in its warmth; now going there even seemed something like fun. *Rolling Stone* loved the album, astutely noticing that the 'scrupulous sonic contouring' and 'porcelain finishes' of the last two albums were now intriguingly cracked and soiled. Released in late March, the album entered the Billboard Hot Hundred at 89 as compared to their previous best showing at 152 for *Parklife*. The 3,000-seater New York shows sold out in a day. The success of 'Beetlebum' and the popularity of the US shows had given the group a galvanising dose of self-confidence. The two rancorous old foes, one with a population of 250 million, the other with a population of four, were nearing some kind of rapprochement. 'The negative perception of us being pro-British,' reflects Dave Rowntree, 'was that we were all very anti-American, which we weren't really. What worked to our advantage was that the way American music works is shockingly different. After *Parklife*, it looked like we'd never make it in America and shot ourselves very badly in the foot. But by the time *Blur* came round, the American market doesn't realise it's the same band. Hey, now it's head-down no-nonsense rock. One of my best friends who lives in New York didn't know "Girls And Boys" was us. So there was no baggage.'

Through most of April they toured the Low Countries (throat infections), Germany and Scandinavia before heading south to Spain (floods) and Italy, where they were now more popular than at any time previously. 'In Spain they were chased through the streets,' recalls Mike Smith. 'It was like *A Hard Day's Night*. They were as big a pop phenomenon as they'd ever been.'

That April brought another corkscrew twist in Blur's never plottable trajectory. 'Song 2', the incandescent, white-hot nugget of gonzoid metal with the 'woo-hoo' hook improvised on the hoof, was released as a single. Blur had once thought this such a lunatic strategy they had used it to taunt their corporate bosses. Far from it. Ironically, like Leeds anarchists Chumbawamba's 'Tubthumping', it was to become the bellowed anthem of beer boy and off-duty executive team players the world over. It had all the right credentials: it was loud and rebellious and catchy, it had a hook that spoke to all nations in pop's teenage Esperanto and it had the 'go for it' mood of gung-ho vigour that the corporate world still adores.

A month before the single was released, US computer hardware giants Intel released their Pentium II processor and they instantly fell upon 'Song 2' as their ad anthem. Nike followed suit. It became the theme music of the USA ice hockey team, the trailer music for the movie *Starship Troopers* and was used as a theme for the Sony Playstation game FIFA 98. Number 2 in the UK, it was Number 1 from Australia to Greenland. It all added up to 'a very nice ker-ching factor', as Alex James puts it. An estimated two million pounds' worth.

GRAHAM COXON: What a ridiculous thing that was. 'Song 2' made more of a difference financially than anything else. It could have made a hell of a lot more of a difference, actually, if we had listened to the

devil even more. The American army wanted to use it as the theme
music for video packages when they unveiled the brand new Stealth
bomber. They were offering phenomenal amounts of cash. We couldn't
agree to it, of course, but it was quite cool. So we put it on FIFA which
was OK cos the *Guardian* had said football's OK.

Blur continued a shift in the band's sales patterns across the world.
Parklife had sold 1.2 million copies here and made some inroads in
further-flung territories. *The Great Escape* sold roughly a million
here and sizeable amounts overseas. The *Blur* album dipped to sales
of half a million here but sold strongly in other territories, selling
one and a half million copies abroad. At two million and rising, it is
easily their most successful album.

While Blur criss-crossed Europe, Britain was getting used to its
first Labour government for two decades. Blur were finishing their
set at the Zurich Volkshall while the nation cheered Michael Port-
illo's hubristic demise. But the landslide victory had even more
resonance for Damon Albarn than for the average member of the
British electorate. Since early 1996, he had pledged his support to
the cross-party Rock The Vote organisation, an idea borrowed from
the US and intended to raise political awareness and involvement
among young people.

But New Labour, whose architect was Tony Blair, had more
specific designs on Albarn. According to sources close to the band,
Tony Blair's office had courted the group with increasing ardour
since he had succeeded the late John Smith as leader in 1994. Mike
Smith explains: 'They were interested in the group in a major way.
Initially it was all very exciting. New Labour people were hanging
around the band a lot. There was this guy called Darren Calliman
who was fantastically Machiavellian. We were hanging out with the
big boys, going to functions with Tony and John. Again, you got the
feeling, this is as good as it gets. They were talking about us being a
big part of the election campaign. Labour were obviously very
sussed. Blur were at that time a big part of the British resurgence.'

DAMON ALBARN: I got a couple of letters from Tony Blair's office.
This was at the height of the whole Oasis/Blur thing and winning the
Brits. Basically it said, 'If you're still this successful come the election
maybe we could do some business.' I met him a few times and felt
very uneasy about it all. Emotionally it was a very bad time for me so I
know that that's partly my fault. But I saw through him before the others

did. I had a frightening meeting with John Prescott and Tony Blair. I could have been a lot more sycophantic and gone for it, but I'm glad I didn't. I never bought into it, ever. I think it's disgraceful what's happened to student grants and I feel no connection with this new vision for Britain. So I didn't go to his bash at Number Ten. I got on the cover of the *Telegraph* for not going. I sent him a note to the House of Commons saying, 'I'm sorry, I won't be attending as I am no longer a New Labour supporter. I am now a communist. Enjoy the schmooze, comrade.' Fuck 'em all.

At the horrid triumphalist Number Ten champagne reception to which Damon refers, a parade of Britain's 'finest' such as Noel Gallagher, Zoe Ball and Chris Evans – New Labour wears its lowbrow credentials proudly – sipped Krug and cosied up to Tony while a block away in the House of Commons, the Labour government tried to impose legislation to take £10 of benefit away from single mothers. The symbolism was unforgettably sickening. Damon is at present involved with Ken Livingstone's campaign for Lord Mayor of London, which Blair and his supporters are currently and undemocratically trying to thwart.

The last leg of 1997's overseas odyssey was the most exciting. In late August, Blur played in Iceland, Knud, Greenland and the Faroe Islands, territories the average rock group doesn't know exist, let alone visit. In Reykjavik, they played the Laugaardshall, the national sports hall, and were supported by evocatively named local acts Silt and The Bloodhound Gang. It was the night after Princess Diana's fatal car crash. Rut Runarsdottir, an audience member, remarked that the group seemed stunned and sad. Not so their entourage. 'Forty-eight hours of sheer hell,' remembers Andy Ross. 'Phenomenal amounts of drinking. Most of the crew copped off on the first night. The women there are something else. They must have lost a fortune on the Greenland gigs. There's no market for pop there. Damon just got it into his head that he should play there.'

'Greenland was pretty insane,' agreed Damon afterwards. 'There were only 1,200 people there but considering there's only about 45,000 in the whole country and it's the size of Australia, that's quite a good turnout. There were loads of old men, all wrecked, and a sign saying "Leave your rifles and harpoons outside."' All the group were mesmerised by the desolate beauty of the place. 'It was a culture shock,' says Dave Rowntree. 'I'd much rather have gone to

Greenland on my own as a private individual. For me, it's totally the wrong way to see places like that. I can't have a spiritual experience if I've constantly got the tour manager phoning up, going, "Hotel lobby. Ten minutes." '

Early autumn found them back in the USA for the second time in a year and twenty more well-received shows. The *San Diego Tribune* notice was typical: 'Here's a band that Americans just aren't supposed to get and instead Blur has a sold-out crowd shouting out its lyrics and tearing at its leader's T-shirt . . . nerve, musical muscle, guts and courage.'

October saw them playing their first-ever dates in Australia. Justine Andrew's father, who lives down under, had mentioned to Alex that he had seen little publicity for the shows. The reason was there was no need for any. The eight gigs, some in 10,000-seater arenas, had sold out in three days. Alex took his mum and dad with him. While the band had been touring, two further singles from *Blur*, 'On Your Own' and 'M.O.R.', had been released, reaching 5 and 15 in the UK respectively. The videos were perforce filmed wherever the band happened to be. Hence 'On Your Own' is shot in Barcelona while the video for the latter was actually put together in Australia. The band had become obsessed with the action and stunts movie *Danger Freaks* on their tour bus and got that film's stunt choreographer Grant Page in to make the promo for 'M.O.R.'. 'It was going to be the greatest pop video ever made,' recalls Mike Smith. 'Really exciting with the band performing these daredevil motorbike stunts except they'd be played by stuntmen in prosthetic masks. Hugely expensive. Course, when the masks arrive they're terrible. They all look like the Incredible Hulk. In the end the stuntmen wore balaclavas so it was pathetically obvious it wasn't the group.' From there to Korea, Singapore and Thailand, where they played to the Thai royal family and their dysfunctional princess, who were seated on thrones, and where Damon was in a Bangkok hotel room when he was amused to receive the fax from British Gas asking to use 'The Universal' in their new TV campaign.

The world tour had seen another break with Blur's past when, during a gig in America, they lost their veteran tour manager Ifan Thomas. Generally unhappy, he got the group on stage for their gig and during the hour and a half they were playing, packed a bag and disappeared, later calling Dave Rowntree to apologise.

They returned to the UK to begin a climactic year-end arena tour beginning in Hull on the 31st and working its way wonkily south through Newcastle and Glasgow, Manchester, Sheffield, Cardiff and Birmingham to London and thence to Bournemouth and finally Brighton, eight days before Christmas. In the tired, emotional, raucous aftermath of the Brighton show, the final gig of practically a year spent on the road in 25 countries, Damon took Stephen Street to one side and told him that Blur were going to work with a new producer on their next album.

STEPHEN STREET: It was at the party in Brighton. I remember going home very depressed. I understood Blur's thinking but I can't say I wasn't hurt. I've had a good innings – five albums – but that didn't mean I wasn't bitterly disappointed. But I can understand Damon wanting to try something new. I say Damon because I think it was his idea.

Graham Coxon was unsure. 'I was very comfortable with Stephen and felt that change could be disastrous. I didn't want to repeat the Partridge disaster. I felt secure with what we'd got even though Stephen sometimes toned me down a little too often and wouldn't quite let me be as perverse as I wanted to be.'

'I think he was gutted,' confides Alex.

Gangs are great fun when you're a kid but tiresome when you develop a mind of your own. With even the youngest member of Blur, Graham, entering his 30th year, the room to be oneself and the acceptance of individual space and identity had become crucial in the band's continued existence. All four had had preoccupations, traumas, conflicts and happy diversions in the recent past that would come to have greater and greater bearing on the group's future.

Dave had now been sober for almost four years and had found ample convivial, life-affirming pleasures to take the bottle's place. He had a domestic life with a wife he was properly protective of. His long-standing fascination and expertise with computers had led him to be a pioneering net surfer and HTML designer. More latterly, he had become absorbed in computer animation and been working with MTV.

Chief among his new passions, though, was aviation. Learning to fly had been a childhood fantasy. In January 1995 he'd commenced lessons and in late February of that year, after Blur's four-award haul at the Brits, he'd bought half-shares in a plane. By the summer, the unexpected success of *Parklife* meant he could take the plunge and buy his own light aircraft. 'I thought that learning to fly would be all I could afford but then everything went mental.' In August 1995 he got his pilot's licence, with the help of instructor Tony at Elstree, and has since splashed out on a larger plane, a Cessna 310, selling his old one to Mike Smith and Alex James jointly, who have caught the flying bug. He has now moved on to advanced flight techniques such as flying aided only by instruments, essential in bad weather as an inexperienced pilot's life expectancy in cloud is three minutes.

Alex had taken to flying, by his own admission, as an alternative leisure activity from getting drunk. He had, of course, taken up the sacred torch of pop-star hedonism with alacrity and enthusiasm. He had become everyone's favourite (except possibly Graham's) louche, bibulous *bon vivant*. Even at his most grossly incorrect – informing uppity support musicians he had 'shagged their sisters' and earnest music journalists that he was a 'fucking Tory' while asking the prettier ones, 'Any chance of a shag?' – he had a charm all of his own.

He had also instigated various musical projects of his own. 'Proper Girls', a song of his attempted by his girlfriend Justine and a friend, had almost been released but met with difficulties. A social acquaintance with Stephen Duffy, the quaintly uncategorisable song-writer who'd spent over a decade living down his former chart sobriquet 'Tin Tin', led to the formation of ad hoc indie supergroup MeMeMe: Alex, Duffy and Elastica drummer Justin Welch. A minor hit ensued – Alex's likeable 'Hanging Around' in late 1996 (it would appear again on Duffy's *I Love My Friends* album two years after). Later came collaborations with Marianne Faithfull on the 'Hang It On Your Heart' single, the theme to the TV series *Born To Run* and, with Guy Pratt and Pete Thomas, two tracks for the *Mojo* film soundtrack as the Stone Cold Strollers.

Most notoriously, though, he joined forces with Keith Allen and Damien Hirst to create the post-modern Lieutenant Pigeon that is Fat Les. Their first effort, the vulgar, nightmarish, irresistible 1998 World Cup anthem 'Vindaloo', was ubiquitous that summer in every bar and playground and was only kept off the top of the singles chart by the disturbingly earnest 'Three Lions'. Their Christmas single, the wilfully crap 'Naughty Christmas', was more selective in its appeal, as Spinal Tap would say. 'You can't do pop music just for money,' observed Alex afterwards. 'Once you start doing that you just look a twat as I discovered with Fat Les this Christmas . . . Fat Les is just . . . funny. Obviously the records are shit. But you wouldn't get Radiohead making a Christmas record, would you? If I want to make stupid records with a bunch of idiots from the Groucho Club then fuck off, I will.'

Like MeMeMe, there was some initial anxiety on the part of EMI and Blur management about Alex's extra-curricular activities, feeling that it undermined the new Blur ethic. All parties now seem happy with a compromise that sees Alex involved with his own label, Turtleneck, in consort with Damien Hirst. Graham amiably sums up Fat Les as 'a private joke gone bizarrely public'.

Sans his regular diet of 'beer, wine and Jameson's', Coxon found life consisted of new highs and lows, trials and treats. 'It was essential I stopped drinking,' he acknowledges. 'When we started the *Blur* record I didn't have to tour or play in the evenings so I didn't have to stay sober. I wasn't eating either. At one point I was too weak to get off the floor in the studio. Stephen told me to go home. At this point I thought I'd better do something about it. I played sober on stage in Spain for the first time. It was really frightening. There were some tears and far too much coffee and it was really cold so it wasn't the easiest of situations. I'd always been worried about not drinking and the stage stuff; thought it might affect the vibes. Alex had been telling me for ages not to drink before playing and how it felt great but I didn't have the will not to have a few beers. It was very strange coming off stage and not partying, just having a Coke. All in all, it was pretty difficult but that's probably why I got so involved in the record. I even had my own little song on there about giving up drinking.'

The frazzled and frayed ambience of *Blur* had led many, mindful of his enthusiasms, to see it as 'Graham's album'. This is too glib and Stephen Street insists, 'It's not Graham's album. Graham's always made musical decisions. The whole band are involved on *Blur*. Alex's bass playing may be his best. It was a record done to please ourselves and those who understand us.' Graham, though, understood the received wisdom. 'It's not Graham's album but that has some truth. Damon's songs were very open and unstructured. My playing's not careful. It's a lot freer. We'd use guide guitar lines that I'd put down sloppily and had the right feel. What was the point of spending half a day ruining them? I'd learned that the pristine approach might be pasteurising any heart in the music. It was quick and free and that might have been my influence. That's maybe why it's seen as Graham's record.'

Furthermore, 'Graham's album' was to come, a bona fide solo work in the shape of the excellent *The Sky's Too High*, which arose directly from enforced sobriety. 'I quit drinking completely on my own. I'd go to the pub and have two pints of Coke then go home and drink loads of coffee and watch TV and write little tunes which became my record. It was part of my therapeutic routine like shopping or making mashed potato. It began with a song about a dead boxer I wrote for a neighbour's film. These songs started to pile up in my head and I thought I had got to get them out, get them exorcised before we started a new Blur album. Then I was advised to put them out. I'm very proud of my record. It was done very quickly because I'd recorded it in my head so many times. It was recorded in five days and mixed on Saturday.'

At the same time, Graham was approached by friends of his in the Chicago band Assembly Line People Project to produce their record. This was done in ten days – Graham obligingly footing the bill for studio time and accommodation – with John Smith at Matrix. Niamh Byrne at the Chris Morrison organisation, who'd taken over the day-to-day running of the band, suggested Graham start his own label for these projects. 'It was a scary thought because I had no idea what to do but she said she'd help me out.' Out of these ventures grew the Transcopic label on which two Assembly Line People Project singles and their album *Subdivision of Being* appeared before their split, as well as Graham's solo album, *The Sky's Too High*.

Anyone expecting a barrage of noise was to be disarmed by the charming primitivism and fetching melancholy of the first Blur solo album. 'It's mostly written completely bored at 2 a.m. when I wasn't feeling mentally very happy so they all turned out folkish.' That's not quite true but some of the record's most endearing moments are its most limpid and fragile: the fluid, gently melodic 'Where D'You Go' with its echoes of Syd Barrett, the darkly romantic 'A Day Is Far Too Long' or the desolate 'Waiting', which recalls the agonised last songs of Nick Drake. Drake himself makes an appearance: 'I wish I could bring Nick Drake back to life' in the truly wonderful 'I Wish'. Angry and cute by turn in words and music, it is a wonderfully warm portrait of its author, full of eccentric wit: 'I wish I didn't feel so flipping mad . . . I wish the rain would just leave me alone/I can't wear that stupid rain hat.' A deeply personal and cherishable thing, it was gratifying that the reaction to *The Sky's So High* was so uniformly positive and generous. Transcopic, though in abeyance, is a going concern. 'There's some really great little groups that I'm in e-mail contact with. These people do demos which sound amazing and the bad noise is the stuff that's so great and intuitive. It seems like genius to me but it's all mistakes.'

On one level, Damon's life was busy and involving. In the autumn of '97 he appeared in a Radio 3 broadcast of Joe Orton's *Up Against It* (originally written for The Beatles but never performed because Brian Epstein disapproved). Albarn took the part intended for George Harrison. He had also appeared as a gangster in Antonia Bird's *Face* and worked with Michael Nyman on music for a Noel Coward tribute album. He was finding musical inspiration in much that was new: Eno, Dub, Neu and American curiosities such as Pavement, whose leader Steven Malkmus he was briefly, ambivalently friendly with. But his personal life was in the darkest disarray. His relationship with Justine was disintegrating under sundry pressures. While they had never been rigidly monogamous, gossip mounted about infidelities on both sides, involving everyone from female Austrian VJs to Brett Anderson to the vocalist in defunct indie outfit Kingmaker.

DAMON ALBARN: It was unrealistic or naive to think we could go through the mill of that fame thing and it not throw you right off centre. But I shouldn't just blame it on celebrity. I was in the wrong relationship. My life was not right. Not in harmony. Everything stems from your emotional life and mine just wasn't working at all. It was really dysfunctional. So I was misfiring everywhere. Iceland helped. It was a very strong positive experience but the truth is it gets more fucked up and worse back at home. There'd been times over the past year, when my panic attacks had started, that I really needed support and Justine didn't provide it. Quite the opposite. She had her own problems, but she could have been a lot more helpful. I don't know how she could have done some of the things she did when you consider what I'd done for her.

Damon feels that his major contribution to Elastica's success and the help and support he offered Justine went largely unrecognised and unreciprocated from his partner. 'It was almost as if she didn't like me for some reason.' Jealousy? 'Well, you start to think so, don't you. The rest of the band never really knew what was happening. But they knew enough. I don't think it ever occurred to them that I was keeping hidden how fucked up I was. Maybe they knew. Certainly everyone's a lot happier now that I'm happier. I think they were angry for me.'

Damon acknowledges that Elastica were in a troubled state themselves. Dark rumours of heroin addiction had swirled around the group since Annie Holland had left, citing repetitive strain injury, two years earlier. 'I think it's very difficult to talk about drugs in a responsible way, however genuine your intention is,' he had said in late 1997. 'It's not discussable because it's not controllable. I have no say over anything once it's down on tape.'

> **DAMON ALBARN:** Elastica and Justine had got into a weird, bad place. There were bad things happening. Not healthy. There seemed to be darkness around all the time. I had a period there myself. If the truth be known, a lot of *13* stems from that period. I'd rented this flat for a year and I wrote a lot of lyrics there. 'Tender' dates from then. Very painful. Agonisingly slow. Getting caught up in your own misery. Misery is something you mustn't just wallow in. Great if you're running from it as fast as you can and not wallowing. I did a bit of that. But then I knew we'd reached the end. It was sad . . . and finished. I had to get away.

So, in a gloomy one-bedroomed flat in the shabby genteel immigrant enclave of Golborne Road, west London, the seeds of what would become Blur's sixth album, *13*, were sown. Here and elsewhere. Early in 1998, a Japan-only CD had been released entitled *Busting and Droning*, the results of Blur putting out to tender various tracks from the *Blur* album for remixing. Blur had traditionally been wary of remixes; as Alex famously said, 'It's like giving your dog to someone to take for a walk and them coming back with a different dog.' But in this case, they enjoyed the results arrived at by Thurston Moore, Mario Caldato, Moby and Tortoise leader John McEntire. The band's favourites, though, were those undertaken by LA-based British producer William Orbit: skewed, impressionistic reworkings of 'Death Of A Party', 'On Your Own' and 'Moving On'.

Orbit's first musical endeavour had been the acclaimed but

largely unsuccessful Torch Song in the early 1980s, a collaboration with Laurie Mayer and Grant Gilbert. Though that group foundered, he became one of the earliest breed of remixers. 'I got into that simply by having a record deal, not selling any records and the company having to improve their losses somehow.' After working with the likes of Erasure, Prince, The Human League, Belinda Carlisle, Malcolm McLaren and Seal, Orbit struck out on his own, having hits with commercial dance act Bassomatic and developing a cult following for his electro-ambient Strange Cargo series of albums. In the mid-90s he worked with Beth Orton, briefly his girlfriend, on the album *Superpinkymandy*, which pre-dated her breakthrough and is now a collector's item. But in 1998 Orbit, real name William Wainwright, became a household name, at least in households which knew their music, for his terrific, idiosyncratic production on Madonna's Grammy-winning *Ray of Light* album, widely regarded as her best work of the decade. 'William Orbit was my idea,' claims Andy Ross. 'Like when I told them "There's No Other Way" was a hit and not a B-side.'

August brought an emotional performance at the top of the bill at Glastonbury. The mind was led inexorably back to previous appearances. Their 1992 Glastonbury debut, captured on the *Star Shaped* video, culminated with Albarn coming a cropper on one of his expeditions up the rigging (as was his precarious wont) and breaking his foot ('Did you see what happened?' he yelps on film, nursing his throbbing ankle beside a backstage van). In 1994, they stopped the show by common consent. 'I remember the sun setting during "This Is A Low" – that was one of those moments. It was as perfect as I could imagine anything could get,' remembers Damon. In 1998, there were countless reminders of how expansive and adventurous the group had become, from the callow disco of 'Girls And Boys' to the splenetic hoopla of 'Song 2' and the protracted, self-absorbed weirdness of the closer 'Essex Dogs'. As well as this there was the now obligatory hideous quagmire and organisational hell. There were cases of trenchfoot and vehicles becalmed in lagoons of mud and broken ankles sustained by falling into three-feet ruts of dried sludge. Alex James finds Glastonbury inhospitable and uncivilised and has referred to organiser Michael Eavis in a stream of invective only one word of which – 'yokel' – is suitable for reprinting.

As summer, or what passed for it, ended, the group began to

prepare for work on the new record. The transition to the new producer was not without anxieties. Stephen Street had become the 'fifth Blur' in many people's eyes. And he had proved on the last record that he could willingly and enthusiastically adapt his supposedly pristine tailored style. Dave posits that, 'If we'd have parted company with Stephen before the last record it would have sent out all the wrong signals – as if Stephen were "old Blur" in some way. It sounds like one of those Dear John letters: it's not you, it's me.' But this was true. Blur simply felt that their creative strategies needed a shake-up and that a new personality behind the console – and in their artistic network – was essential.

Shortly after Damon and Graham's one-off collaboration with Silver Apples at the Meltdown Festival in July, work began in earnest on the new album. There were immediate changes in procedure. Working from the basic 'noodles and hums from Damon', as Alex terms them, the group convened daily to play together in their studio, Unit 13 of a warehouse and industrial complex in west London which eventually gave its name, or rather number, to the album (rejected titles included *Blue* and *When You're Walking Backwards to Hell, No One Can See You, Only God*). Orbit moved all his equipment into a rented house in north London, along with his 'oompa-loompas', as Alex terms them, his engineers and assistants. He then amassed hours of live tapes of the band which became the source materials for his later experimentations and modifications.

DAMON ALBARN: I had to evangelise for doing it because it's totally work as therapy in some ways. There was no order or timetable. We just did things as we pleased and at the end of the sessions William took away the tapes, comprising hours and hours of jams, grooves and ideas and got to work on them. It wasn't at all a comfortable decision. Graham was particularly unsure – against it, in fact, at first – but as soon as he got it he changed instantly. He originally felt he was being excluded but actually William was taking everything he did and storing it up but because the relationship was so new at that time William wasn't expressing what he was doing. So it appeared to be another conspiracy to Graham. It was quite a big thing for Graham to realise that there aren't big conspiracies going on. It's not him against the world. It's him and his mates against the world. Also, I've tried to get him to trust me, to see that I don't want to take over the world. I just want to do good work like him.

GRAHAM COXON: I was getting a bit worried about changing producer. Things like that fill me with trepidation and I'd spent a long time building up a bond with Stephen. I was very reticent to say goodbye to Stephen because I'm a coward, and I was proud of the last record. It took me a long time to meet William. I was quite scared to meet him. He was around at Glastonbury, I think, but he's not very pizzazzy or a social animal. Eventually I met him and I really liked him. He's very different to Streety who's more like a schoolteacher, more rigid. With William it was 'do what the hell you want'. Sometimes he'd sit and stare at the carpet for half a day or he'd be playing to himself on a sampler through headphones, unaware of anything else. Sometimes I wondered what was going on. But Madonna said a very perceptive thing about working with William. She said it was like making a film. You create individual scenes but you can't tell what the shape or the sense of it is when you're recording it. When you're filming a movie the scene means nothing but at the premiere it all makes sense. He takes hours and hours of music and rationalises it all. It's more like hearing your music like someone else would hear it. It's a revelation.

All of the group soon learned to relax into and love this new, challenging, open, mildly disorientating work pattern, even Alex, avowedly the most dedicated pop fan of the group. 'I've never really wanted to make challenging music – that's more Damon and Graham's thing. I'm happy to make bubblegum for the ears. I'm a pop junkie. I join in, that's what playing the bass is about, really. It's about joining in. But I'm very proud of it. I look at our history and I see how much we've improved over ten years and I realise how rare that is. Most bands get worse. But you have to move on. Pop music can get very reiterative. You have to keep thinking of new reasons to get up in the morning.' He found Orbit 'a very delicate creature with a very scientific mind, a very smart chap, sensitive . . . and a genius'.

Alex also enjoyed the speed and ease of the new routine. 'We'd done three or four backing tracks by the end of the first day. Three weeks at 13 doing a track a day lunchtime to 7 p.m. until we had about twenty songs from which we chose about fourteen or fifteen to carry on working on. Then two weeks at Mayfair studios to see what we had with only one dalliance of going down the pub and getting absolutely hammered. We were really flowing.'

'Five years ago,' claims Dave, 'we'd have been scared of change. You never know if you're going to lose the thing people like. It was quite daunting. But it was a lot more fun for me. Recording for me has previously been satisfying but not always fun. I had more of an influence on things rather than adding drums to a finished track. Recording's not very interesting for a drummer. I've certainly never enjoyed making records particularly. You know, it's hard to make great music looking over your shoulder thinking, Hang on, there's a xylophone part still to go on here, I don't want to get too busy with my cymbals. This was like a great outpouring of ideas. Once everyone realised that no idea was going to go wasted, everyone turned into these idea machines. Sessions became even more hectic and wild and interesting as time went on and I think you can see that on the record.'

The results are astonishing; as much an evolutionary leap on from *Blur* as *Parklife* was from *Modern Life is Rubbish*. Extremely human, raw, abstract, intuitive, even primal, but there's no doubt that these pieces, liberated from what Graham calls 'pop jail', will sometimes tax the fans who arrived with *Parklife* or even *Blur*. 'I hope it's a nice challenge though,' asserts Graham. 'I don't think it's too difficult. I think it sounds really nice, really great, and there's lots of interesting sounds on there. It's definitely a headphones record.'

'Tender', the album's opening track and first single, begins with Graham Coxon's boozy, vulnerable blues guitar, hammer-ons and pull-offs adding to the already woozy effect created by being recorded on a dictaphone as on 'Morning Blues' on *The Sky's Too High*. 'I used a Sony dictaphone on my record. William's Panasonic on "Tender". We haven't quite decided which has the better wobble.' The lead vocal alternates between Graham's mournful 'oh my baby' and Damon's luxuriant, soulful purr, arrived at after a recent immersion in Otis Redding. As well as the almost aboriginal thumping beat (achieved by banging planks of wood on the studio floor), the song's final striking feature is the exultant presence of the 40-piece London Community Gospel Choir. 'We were originally going to use strings,' says Orbit. 'But the song always had a gospelly feel to it, so we thought, you know, why not try a real gospel choir? It was bound to be a great experience even if we didn't end up using it.'

At nearly seven minutes, 'Tender' has the elongated, narcotic soulfulness of 'Hey Jude' or 'Give Peace A Chance'. Its mood is both wrecked and defiant; an epic hymn of consolation and a requiem for a dead love affair. In this it sets the mood for the album, which is rooted in the traumas of Justine Frischmann and Damon Albarn's break-up. This is just one of the reasons why Albarn thought a break with past associations (i.e. Stephen) was vital. 'He'll be forever part of what we are. I don't know how he feels but I think he's cool about it. But I really had to do it. I had to see if we could work with someone else. It was such a personal thing going on, we needed to have someone who didn't really know us. It's like you can be more open in front of someone who doesn't really know us. William was a bit of a psychiatrist through all of this. Everyone encouraged the emotional blood-letting. More, more, more. As much as you can get out, get out.'

'Tender' is one of the most self-consciously, self-evidently great records of its era. As Alex, who plays an upright bass on the track, says, 'Fortunately "Tender" was nailed early on. And that makes a really big difference when you've got an obvious fucking global Number 1; that takes the pressure off. Because there's nothing worse than feeling that you've got to come up with something, because then it doesn't happen. At all. Ever.' His abiding memory of the tune is, 'Walking into the studio in Reykjavik feeling like shit for reasons I won't go into and hearing the vocal to "Tender" and feeling better again'. Damon sees it ultimately as, 'A tribute to how important something was in my life. It's a celebration of love found and lost but not forgotten.'

'Bugman', for the first half at least, is redolent of the caustic rock thrashes that crept into the group's vocabulary on *Blur*. Again, there seems to be a hoover employed in the song's middle section. In its second half, 'Bugman' becomes a kaleidoscopic jam alive with sonic experiments and best appreciated on headphones. Alex's bass is to the fore here; funky in a vaguely squelchy way. 'Being selfish,' he admits, 'it's my favourite bit of the album.' 'Pure jamming,' enthuses Damon. 'Everyone reacting against each other. We've always mucked about like that, but it's the first time someone's come along and said, "This is as valid as the first part of the song."' As if to point up this section's avant-garde leanings, Damon trills 'Space is the place' over the outro, the title of a classic 70s recording by jazz maverick Sun Ra.

'Coffee & TV', a Graham Coxon composition, is perhaps the record's sweetest moment, echoing his contribution to the *Blur* album, 'You're So Great'. 'The first verse is completely anti-Camden.

And the second verse is about how shite England is. So the chorus is "I could be anywhere in the world in front of my television". The idea of travelling appeals far more now that I don't have to. I could actually face going on holiday now.' The title alludes to two of the staples that get Graham through his non-drinking phases.

Between this and 'Swamp Song' is one of the album's many mysterious and playful bridging fragments, in this case a muted, melancholic organ fugue.

'Swamp Song' was the last track to be included on the record and was, until, the last minute, an intended B-side. The faintly oriental timbre and scimitar-swish of the guitar line and the exotic cast to the backing vocals make one think of Led Zeppelin's 'Kashmir' played by Faust. The raggedly sexy vocal is one of Damon's best on the whole set.

'1992' is the album's first moment of real, unequivocal despair: the A minor/D/F sharp minor chord sequence is funerally sad and the lyric forlorn ('You loved my bed, you chose the other instead'). The tune's plaintiveness is etched with detail. There's a declamatory, off-key organ solo and a noise Graham describes as the 'UFO landing . . . we took one note, fed it into the desk and let it feedback and play itself, William trying to guide it like he was steering a huge ship. Grabbing the desk with a big toothy grin on his face while I was shouting at him, laughing hysterically.'

The sense of playfulness and fun that Damon Albarn has come to admire in the work of Pavement and, to use that horrible term, 'Krautrock' bands like Can is reflected on 'B.L.U.R.E.M.I'. 'It's a little light relief in what is ostensibly a dark album. Musical wit. A musical gag, a twist in the tale, a stab in the ribs. It's sort of a test of faith for EMI. It's like, do you see this as us being negative or us being positive? Make your own mind up. Look inside yourself: are you up for it or are you not up for it, because if you're up for it, let's go. And if you're not, be honest about it.' Somewhere between a new-wave ditty and a Situationist prank, it's an enjoyable romp. 'We've even got better at doing the punk rock songs,' claims Damon. Small children will enjoy the varispeeded and Vocodered vocal.

'Battle' was written on a remote Indonesian island during Damon's last holiday before his split with Justine Frischmann. 'Progressive rock' has terrifying connotations of silver capes and Tolkienish triple albums but used in its original sense of the late 60s experimentalism of Albarn *père*'s charges Soft Machine or the

Krautrock groups, it can be applied (without causing a fistfight) to 'Battle'.

Adventurous and abstract, it blends moods imperceptibly, from dreamlike to epic to enraged. Terrific drumming pushes the song along even in its most reflective phases and in common with low, resonant bass lines, even hints at dub. During the early stages of the recording, Graham was prone to agitated and depressed feelings. 'Quite a lot of it was done in intense moods. I got in a couple of bad moods and didn't talk for a whole day, just played, and that's why there are so many angry sounds like on "Battle".'

'Mellow Song' has the rustic, ramshackle vibe that the band have become expert in, although it's full of surprises and incongruities such as the under-recorded Glitterband stomp in the central section and the curious duet for feedback guitar and harpsichord. 'Mellow Song' features Dave Rowntree's favourite drumming of the album. An earlier version of what became this song appears as 'Mellow Jam' on a B-side to 'Tender'.

'Trailerpark', as 'South Park', was written for the US cartoon series of that name and was premiered at the group's Birmingham Que club Glastonbury warm-up in August '98. One of the best things here, it's a perfect blend of Blur's pop and rock instincts and their new-found experimentalism. Funky in the broken-backed manner of Beck and The Beastie Boys, it's lit from time to time by a queer almost atonal electric piano glissando. The hook – 'I lost my girl to the Rolling Stones' – is a masterstroke. Funny and off-the-wall, it masks a more serious truth if we can take it to refer to how the rock world and its lures destroyed Damon's relationship with Justine Frischmann.

'Caramel' has a similar progressive rock feel to 'Battle'. Its intro – fustian, doomy church organ and sombre, muted vocal – could even be Van Der Graaf Generator, which would seem ludicrous but for Graham Coxon's youthful enthusiasm for Peter Hamill and the presence of a Van Der Graaf pastiche, 'Es Schmecht', in the Blur back catalogue. After that things get busier and knottier briefly but still resolutely odd enough to warm the cockles of anyone who ever owned a Popul Vuh album.

'Trimm Trabb' takes its name from a particular brand of 70s 'old school' trainer from the German company Adidas; its name is German for 'air-cushioned sole'. A clanking industrial intro ushers in more lo-fi folksiness with a bilious kernel – 'All us losers on the piss gain, that's just the way it is . . . I sleep alone'. Albarn sees the song as further evidence of his subconscious equating of shoes and melancholy.

The album's penultimate track and last song proper is the most nakedly personal in Blur's repertoire, a straightforward, heartfelt statement of Albarn's emotional state in the wake of personal trauma. 'It's over. I hope you're with someone who makes you feel safe in your sleep. I won't kill myself trying to stay in your life. I got no distance left to run.'

'It upsets me, that song. It upset me singing it. Doing that vocal upset me greatly. To sing that lyric I really had to accept that that was the end of something in my life. It's amazing when you do have the guts to do that with your work, because it don't half help you.'

The simplicity of the arrangement adds to the poignancy and the country blues guitar lines are frayed and lyrical. Though one can feel great sympathy for the protagonists, there's something almost horribly fitting in the notion that one of Britain's most over-exposed and spied-upon showbiz couples should have this piteous memento of their break-up in the public domain too. It's serious and affecting but never cloying. Most listeners will agree with Chris Morrison when he says, 'Everyone knows what that phrase means . . ."no distance left to run" . . . I've been there . . . We all have.'

According to some reports, 'No Distance Left To Run' was first essayed in the same session as 'Swallows In The Heatwave' and 'Optigan 1', the album's lovely, strange closing waltz with its gently tolling bell, in Barcelona in June 1997. Alex's recollections are the most illuminating. 'It's a shame in some ways we didn't make "Optigan 1" into more of a tune. We did that after our Barcelona show in June 1997, after a big night out in Barcelona, feeling terrible and then making something beautiful and that making us feel a lot better. We demoed that and it was the first point where we realised where we were going on this album. We were meant to be doing B-sides for "M.O.R." or something. We did "Swallows In The Heatwave" the same day and said, "Fuck it, we'll put out just the one CD", and it got to Number Shit as a result.'

Back in the here and now, with *13* completed, Damon states, 'It has moments of great misery and uplift. Everyone in the band realises that it was difficult for me to do this and that made everyone much more determined to do it right.'

13 is bold and bewildering, often very beautiful and frequently stranger and more thoughtful and madder and darker than pop music usually gets in these freaky pre-millennial days where, at this very moment, Blondie, Tony Christie, Isaac Hayes and old Chic, Doctor Hook and Bees Gees songs wallow side by side in our screwy pop chart. It's hard to imagine any commentator improving on Graham Coxon's description of *13* as 'a devil worship bad trip Gong album'.

And as Alex James puts it, 'The emotional currency of the record is Damon splitting up with Justine. There's blood on the tracks.' Without being maudlin or confessional, it ranks among music's most frank exhumations of personal tragedy, echoing music as different as Peter Hamill's 'Over', Yoko Ono's 'Season Of Glass' and Herbert Howell's 'Hymnus Paradisi'. There's a lot of grief there and a well of darkness but a sense of salvation too. In Graham Coxon's only partly joky words, 'We've found the higher power, man. Music is the higher power.'

It's as if they've finally breathed out, as Dave puts it. Accepted each other as individuals, accepted they are in this for the long haul, but that they have their own lives too. The beginning of spring 1999 finds Graham, who provided the artwork for *13*, planning for exhibitions in Prague and Paris, extending his modern jazz collection and carrying on his long-overdue domestic improvements on the flat he bought from Andy Ross.

Damon has just travelled to Utah's Sundance Festival for the premiere of Antonia Bird's *Ravenous* for which he and Michael Nyman have collaborated on the music. He is also in training to climb Mount Kilimanjaro. 'Nice link there to Julian Cope and Dave Balfe,' he says, smiling. He has even mended his relationship with the old enemy and spent social time with David Balfe.

But talk of higher powers leads logically to the oddest, funniest, most presumptuously wonderful venture the group have ever been associated with. During their 1997 US tour, Dave and Alex ('the sciency ones') were mortified to learn that only fifteen people in the UK had applied to train to teach physics that year. They found themselves talking till the early hours about British science in general and specifically bemoaning the absence of a British science programme.

On their return to the UK, though, they found out that there was indeed space research going on in Britain, unfunded by government and getting by on the generosity of a consortium of industry and universities. Professor of Planetary Science at the Open University, Dr Colin Pillinger, a bearish fellow who carries a bit of Mars in his lab coat pocket, has been working on the Beagle, the 'business end' of a European Space Agency rocket, an ingenious 27kg landing device whose projected destination is Mars if the funds could be found. Since discovering this, Alex and Dave have made themselves useful in many ways, upping the project's media profile considerably, attending 'drinky dos' and schmoozing money out of industrialists. They have thrown themselves with suitably boyish zeal into this *Boy's Own* adventure. But this is no comic-book fantasy: in early 2004, the Beagle should bounce down on the red planet, gently unpack itself like a waking spider and bring back the fossilised bacteria and micro organisms that may prove the existence of life on Mars. 'Then,' says Dave evangelically, 'of the two planets we know about, we'll have found life on both. A probability of one of finding life wherever we go.'

Big, bamboozling stuff. And not the usual shop talk of chimney sweeps. More than anything they or their lessening detractors can say, Blur's involvement in a mission to Mars speaks volumes about what a funny, unfathomable, endlessly fascinating pop group they are. It says something about their own story too. As always, the Romans had a phrase for it. The RAF made it their motto.

Per Ardua Ad Astra: through adversity to the stars.

A Fine Time to Be in Blur

Epilogue

THAT'S THEIR STORY.
What happened to me was this.
In early 1991, the *NME* sent me to Hanley, one of Arnold Bennett's five towns of the Potteries, to report on a gig by a new group whose languidly distinctive single 'She's So High' had created something of a buzz about the group. As the train crawled through unlikely-sounding places like Etruria, I felt no great enthusiasm for the assignment. Music was in a slump; pop meant Jason Donovan and 'indie' meant vacantly posh ninnies making gormless, dull fluff.

Later, I'm in this tiny basement club with 50 or so other people, one of whom was David Balfe, plucking excitedly at my sleeve, exclaiming, 'Great, eh?', as Blur played like madmen, frankly. It was a set of goofy, electrifying brilliance; all Syd Barrett naiveté and punk rock rage and demented self-belief. I loved them.

Later, at the mid-price hotel that probably 'welcomed' a regional conference of photocopier salesmen, I met the group properly. There were some *Spinal Tap* shenanigans over late-night sandwich orders. One of them – I was still trying to work out who was who – behaved like a wanker. So I said so and there was an argument diffused by another, unnecessary round of drinks and I saw their true, raffish, incorrigible, likeable selves. And even then, little Japanese girls hung around discreetly like stagehands in some larger drama.

And then later still . . .

Tokyo, 1992. The Lexington Queen, a shadowy night-club beneath the pavements of the Rappongi district where pale, slender hostesses handed you bottles of home-made whisky and, in a moment of insanity, we all danced to A Flock Of Seagulls and Graham showed me the fingering to 'There's No Other Way' on a fag packet. On the journey back to the hotel, Damon wobbled atop the minibus in a terrorist balaclava, yelling through a crowd-control loudhailer, and Dave sprawled comatose across my lap, Tokyo scrolling by like an arcade game.

Later that year, I'm at a horrible, drunken lig in London to celebrate the launch of the *NME*'s *Ruby Trax* charity album for which Blur have contributed a surly version of 'Maggie May'. Even with George Best and a host of hoary indie rockers in evidence, Damon Albarn is the drunkest person here, reeling and clinging to me as he curses the state of British culture, harangues everyone in sight and tells me repeatedly of some great graffiti he has seen on the Bayswater Road proclaiming 'modern life is rubbish'. We get a taxi back to Damon's flat and he attempts to climb out of the window and on to the roof as it speeds through Kensington. We get thrown out, not unreasonably. Back at Damon's flat, we have a go on his new scooter in the street and wake all the neighbours up. Then we blunder indoors and wake Justine when Damon attempts to 'do a fry up'. There's a door-slamming row and I feel like a fool and try to curl up on the sofa without anyone noticing . . .

Hyde Park in 1994, drinking champagne and Earl Grey incongruously close to the dog toilet while they tell me excitedly about their new record, *Parklife*, and bubble over with theories about England and Englishness, and later, back at Damon's flat, Graham strums Nick Drake on an out-of-tune acoustic guitar and I notice that, pinned to the wall above his keyboard, Damon has a handkerchief showing the sea regions of the shipping forecast.

September 1994; in an upstairs bar at the Savoy Hotel where Blur have just lost the Mercury Music Prize. M People are on the dance floor celebrating. I'm trying to talk to Damon but Phil Daniels is being insufferably geezerish and attention-seeking and singing 'his Chelsea song' into our faces. He stumbles and knocks my drink over and while I wonder what to do next, he goes on to the dance floor to tell M People that 'that should've been fackin' ours'. Shovel of M People, no shrinking violet himself, tells him, in no uncertain terms, that if he doesn't shut up and make himself scarce, he may be killed. As I'm leaving, Damon dashes up to me on the staircase. He's leaving for America at 8 a.m. 'Sorry about Phil. He's all right really. He just . . . he just thinks he's in the group . . .'

Summer 1995; Bournemouth. The madness is at its height. Blur have played an uneasy but dynamic set in the town's conference centre. The hotel is under siege from fans and we look on from the safety of the bar where Alex's mum and dad look proud and bemused simultaneously. Their son and I repair to the snooker room for a frame and are immediately challenged to doubles by two hefty beer monsters. We try to demur and one says, 'Pop stars too good to play snooker with the local constabulary, eh?' We instantly, expediently change our minds and lose deliberately in about seven minutes. Much, much later I'm on a balcony at dawn and I realise that the tiny, sodden figure I see emerging from the sea below me is Alex . . .

June 1996; a field in Dublin. Seaman's save against the Spaniards has just put England through to the Euro 96 semis and we're shivering in the thin evening drizzle on the huge RDS agricultural showground more used to shire horses and tractor salesmen. The battalions of little girls turn to each other in horror, grimacing as the band thrash through 'Chinese Bombs' and 'Song 2'. En route to the after-show party, there's stout after stout in bar after bar and an ebullient 'fan' gets redder and nastier as his offers of Guinness are politely declined, until the affable Smoggy, gently but forcefully, informs him of his presumption. In the dark of the club, Leo Finlay is as mischievous as ever – the last time I saw him alive – and Sean Ryder, in a vast, daft fur coat holds court and buys me a brandy before falling acrobatically down the stairs.

December 1997. Blur have just finished the NEC show where Damon had announced the band's 'retirement' from touring. We are all drunk beyond reason and I am trying to teach Alex the chords to 'Walk On By' on the baby grand at one of those soulless, expensive out-of-town hotels; carvery and pastel livery and gym facilities. Tony the flying instructor lies generously – 'That's very good' – and Graham stands by the piano, defiantly off the wagon for the evening, berating the bassist with enraged, obscene invective. The victim sits, smiling wearily, hearing it for the umpteenth time, and moves on to some boogie-woogie.

1998. On a Virgin West Coast train on a bright November morning I get a call on my mobile as I'm headed to Bloomsbury and a business lunch with Dave. Too nice a day for interviews, apparently, and those azure skies over London mean one thing. Flying.

An hour later, we're eating cheese toasties and drinking dark ochre tea from mugs in the cafe at Elstree Aerodrome, the new 'major hang'; Dave, Alex, myself and their genial flying instructor Tony. There's an endless but crucial array of checks on the grounds and then, in a fug of the sexy, evocative stink of aviation fuel, we taxi out. We wait for our clearance from Jeffrey, the control tower's resident 'character'. 'Last week,' says Alex, 'a German asked for clearance and Jeffrey said, "No, you can't come through, you naughty German. The last time we had one of you here, we shot him down." '

A roar and a climb and we're soaring over a Subbuteo version of south-east England – toy farms, ponds, housing estates – en route to a navigational radio suppliers by an airstrip in Southend where 'Girls And Boys' hisses from a workshop tranny and the office girls shyly peep out to look at the pop stars. Then back along the Thames, over the West End and a heart-in-mouth arc over Canary Wharf. Later, with Tony by my side, I have a go myself, climbing and turning, wheeling above suburban England in the winter dusk, my head full of pilot heater check routines, non-directional beacons and yaw and pitch and Bravo Kilo Charlie Bravo . . .

Early October 1998. 11.30 a.m.. Covent Garden. Alex, who I have just woken up, is showing me round his gorgeous new flat, unshaven and in dressing gown. At the very top is a little studio space where he sifts through a pile of DATs before finding what he's after – the forthcoming single by Fat Les. It seems to consist mainly of Keith Allen lecherously saying 'You're a naughty, naughty woman' 30 or 40 times. Diplomatically, I say that 'kids will love it'. 'Oh yes,' agrees Alex. 'Kids and cunts – that's Fat Les's market.'

Christmas 98. Myself, Damon and Jamie Hewlett, creator of Tank Girl and Damon's new flatmate, are eating these queer, unimaginably salty pea-pod things in a Japanese restaurant on the Portobello Road. There is way too much food. We drive home in Damon's untidy shed of a four-wheel drive with the early mixes of Damon's work for the new movie *Ravenous* on full volume. It's wild and daring stuff, seemingly grabbed from all four corners of the globe. Jamie slopes off to buy Christmas tree lights and Damon and I sit in his flat, talking though the sombre catalogue of the recent past as the room grows darker and darker. Then he brightens up and we watch the football on his new pride and joy, a 55-inch-flat screen plasma telly. 'Did I tell you I'm going to climb Kilimanjaro?' he says, as he hunts for the remote.

Christmas 1998 again. We've just finished recording the audio interviews for the promotional discs of *13* and have ended up having an impromptu Christmas dinner in a nearby cafe. Everyone wears mobile phone headpieces at the insistence of manager Niamh, except Dave who says the talk of tumours is 'bollocks'. Everyone is taking the piss out of Alex over the Fat Les Christmas single which has failed to set the chart alight. He smokes and occasionally offers a well-enunciated obscenity.

They offer me a lift in their people-carrier to a hotel where they're going to do some Japanese press. I remind them that I'm supposed to be writing a book on them and say I'm going home. Graham calls me a puff and he and Alex pretend to beat me up like kids in playgrounds do. Apropos of nothing, I ask Dave what would make them split up. 'I dunno. If we stopped getting on, I suppose.' 'But that's happened loads,' I remind him. 'Oh, yeah.' And they all laugh as they get in the bus.

They pull away into the bright, chilly west London afternoon and disappear over the brow of the hill. As they do, I catch a glimpse of the four of them through the rear window. Happily, they appear to be arguing.

Index

Index

Index